National Geographic Learning | CENGAGE Learning

TEDTALKS

Keynote

PROFICIENT
Workbook

Jon Hird
Paul Dummett
Mike Harrison
Sandy Millin

Keynote Proficient
Workbook
Jon Hird and Paul Dummett with Mike Harrison and
Sandy Millin

Publisher: Gavin McLean

Publishing Consultant: Karen Spiller

Project Manager: Karen White

Development Editor: Ruth Goodman

Editorial Manager: Scott Newport

Head of Strategic Marketing ELT: Charlotte Ellis

Senior Content Project Manager: Nick Ventullo

Manufacturing Manager: Eyvett Davis

Cover design: Brenda Carmichael

Text design: MPS North America LLC

Compositor: MPS North America LLC

National Geographic Liaison: Leila Hishmeh

Audio: Tom Dick and Debbie Productions Ltd

Cover Photo Caption: Mark Ronson speaks at TED2014,
Session One - Liftoff! - The Next Chapter, March 17–21,
2014, Vancouver Convention Center, Vancouver, Canada.
Photo: © Ryan Lash/TED.

ISBN: 978-1-305-57835-7

National Geographic Learning
Cheriton House, North Way, Andover, Hampshire, SP10 5BE
United Kingdom

Cengage Learning is a leading provider of customized learning solutions
with employees residing in nearly 40 different countries and sales in more
than 125 countries around the world. Find your local representative at
www.cengage.com.

Cengage Learning products are represented in Canada by Nelson Education Ltd.

Visit National Geographic Learning online at **ngl.cengage.com**

Visit our corporate website at **www.cengage.com**

CREDITS

Photos

Printed in Greece by Bakis SA

Print Number: 01   Print Year: 2016

Contents

1 Creativity

1.1 Do schools kill creativity?

TEDTALKS

Sir **KEN ROBINSON** was born in Liverpool, UK, in 1950. He was educated in and around Liverpool and then studied for a BEd (Bachelor of Education) in English and drama at Bretton Hall College of Education, graduating in 1972. He then worked as a teacher and, in 1981, he completed a PhD at the University of London, researching the role of drama and theatre in education. From 1985 to 1988, he was the Director of the Arts in Schools Project, an initiative to develop arts education throughout England and Wales. He then became Professor of Education at the University of Warwick in the UK, where he is now professor emeritus.

Sir Ken works with governments, education systems, businesses and other agencies and organizations across the world, advising on the development of creativity, innovation and human resources in education and in business, an area in which he is recognized as one of the world's leading authorities. He is also recognized as one of the world's leading speakers on these topics and videos of his famous TED Talks have been seen by a record estimated 250 million people in over 150 countries. In fact, his 2006 talk *Do schools kill creativity?* became the most viewed in TED's history. He has also written a number of best-selling books, some of which have been translated into over 20 languages.

Sir Ken has received many prestigious awards and accolades. In 2011, *Fast Company Magazine* listed him as 'one of the world's elite thinkers on creativity and innovation'. He has also been named as one of *TIME/Fortune*/CNN's 'Principal Voices' and has been ranked among the Thinkers50 list of the 'world's top business thought leaders'. He has received a number of honorary degrees from UK and US universities in recognition of his work in the arts and education, the Benjamin Franklin Medal for outstanding contributions to cultural relations between the United Kingdom and the United States and has been knighted by Queen Elizabeth II for his services to the arts.

Sir Ken Robinson

CAREER PATHWAYS

1 Read the text. Answer the questions.

1 In terms of academic background, what were Sir Ken Robinson's two main fields of study?

2 What is Sir Ken Robinson a global expert in?

3 What TED Talk records did Sir Ken achieve?

4 In which areas has Sir Ken's work been recognized?

5 For what did he become 'Sir' Ken Robinson?

TED PLAYLIST

2 Other TED speakers are interested in topics similar to Sir Ken Robinson's TED Talk. Read the descriptions of four TED Talks at the top of page 5. In your opinion, which is the best title for this playlist, a, b or c?

a Celebrating the individual in learning
b Unlocking the doors to learning
c Leaving the textbook at the classroom door

3 Read the TED playlist again. Find a speaker who ...

1 realized their method of teaching was ineffective.
2 wants a switch of focus from academic to practical learning.
3 is making an appeal specifically to other teachers.
4 wants education to be adapted to individual learning styles.

▶ **Sir Ken Robinson: Bring on the learning revolution**

In this poignant, funny follow-up to his fabled 2006 talk, Sir Ken Robinson makes the case for a radical shift from standardized schools to personalized learning – creating conditions where kids' natural talents can flourish.

▶ **Ramsey Musallam: 3 rules to spark learning**

It took a life-threatening condition to jolt chemistry teacher Ramsey Musallam out of ten years of 'pseudo-teaching' to understand the true role of the educator: to cultivate curiosity. In a fun and personal talk, Musallam gives three rules to spark imagination and learning, and get students excited about how the world works.

▶ **Rita F. Pierson: Every kid needs a champion**

Rita Pierson, a teacher for 40 years, once heard a colleague say, 'They don't pay me to like the kids.' Her response: 'Kids don't learn from people they don't like.' A rousing call to educators to believe in their students and actually connect with them on a real, human, personal level.

▶ **Geoff Mulgan: Intro to the Studio School**

Some kids learn by listening; others learn by doing. Geoff Mulgan gives a succinct introduction to the *Studio School*, a new kind of school in the UK where small teams of kids learn by working on projects that are, as Mulgan puts it, 'for real'.

4 Find adjectives in the TED playlist that describe the talks as …

a inspiring   b touching   c legendary
d entertaining   e concise

5 Which talk would you most like to see? Why? Watch the talk at TED.com.

AUTHENTIC LISTENING SKILLS
Rhythm and stress

6 🎧 **1 01** You are going to hear a podcast in which a member of the *Keynote* team talks about Rita F. Pierson's TED Talk, *Every kid needs a champion*. Circle the content words in the sentence below. Then listen and underline the stressed words and syllables. Were they the same?

I've seen this talk quite a few times and I still get really emotional watching it.

7 🎧 **1 02** Now listen to the next sentence and write in the missing content words. Then underline all the stressed words.

I _____ it has _____ to do with the kind of _____ _____ – _____ even – that Rita F. Pierson _____ her students.

LISTENING

8 🎧 **1 03** Listen to the full podcast. Choose the correct words to make true sentences.

1 Paul is a teacher and *lecturer / teacher trainer*.
2 Paul admires Rita F. Pierson as a teacher because of the emphasis she puts on human *dignity / connections*.

9 🎧 **1 03** Listen again. Complete the reasons.

1 Why Paul gets emotional watching this TED Talk:
a) Rita F. Pierson's kindness to her pupils b) the _____ of her pupils c) Pierson's power as a(n) _____ .
2 Why Paul says some teachers emphasize discipline: they've failed to _____ their students.
3 Why kids underperform at school: they're born into a) _____ b) the wrong _____ .
4 Why Paul thinks the talk should be renamed: so that _____ _____ sees it.

VOCABULARY IN CONTEXT

10 Read the extracts from the podcast. Choose the correct meaning of the words in bold.

1 … they're from disadvantaged backgrounds and that sort of **tugs at the heartstrings** too.
Makes you feel: a sympathetic ☐   b upset ☐
c hurt ☐
2 I've had kids so educationally **deficient** I could have cried.
a unintelligent ☐   b lacking ☐   c uninterested ☐
3 The best teachers are the ones who seem to befriend their pupils and **win them over** …
Get someone to: a obey you ☐
b agree with you ☐   c admit they are wrong ☐
4 She put a smiley face on his paper and told him he was **on a roll**.
a not being serious ☐   b making good progress ☐
c falling behind ☐
5 Kids have to feel that you're on their side and **rooting for** them.
a supporting ☐   b working for ☐
c explaining things for ☐

1.2 What have you been up to?

GRAMMAR Definite and indefinite time

1 Read the text about creativity in the professions. Match the events or situations (1–10) with what they are expressing (a–c).

a finished event or situation in a finished time ☐ ☐ ☐ ☐ ☐

b finished event or situation in an unfinished time ☐ ☐

c event or situation that continues to the present ☐ ☐ ☐

> Creativity ¹ *has for a long time been seen* as important in a number of professions. But until recently, only a limited number of fields ² *were considered* to be primarily creatively driven: the arts, product design and marketing. Architecture is also an area which ³ *has always been* associated with creativity. By contrast, fields such as science and engineering ⁴ *have traditionally experienced* a less explicit relation to creativity. However, a number of studies in recent years ⁵ *have shown* how some of the major scientific and industrial advances of the 20th century ⁶ *came about* as a direct result of the creativity of individuals. And a 2010 study, which ⁷ *interviewed* around 1,500 company CEOs, ⁸ *showed* that the leadership trait, that today is considered to be most crucial for success, is creativity. This suggests that the world of business ⁹ *has begun* to accept that creativity is of value in a range of industries, rather than being simply the preserve of the more traditional creative industries. But this is not such a new concept. In the early part of the 20th century, many economists ¹⁰ *considered* creativity to be the key factor in economic growth.

2 Choose the correct words or phrases to complete the quotations.

> I think the human race ¹ *made/has made* a big mistake at the beginning of the industrial revolution, we ² *leaped/have leaped* for the mechanical things; people need the use of their hands to feel creative.
>
> *Andre Norton, writer*

> I think it's fair to say that personal computers ³ *became/have become* the most empowering tool we ⁴ *ever created/have ever created*. They're tools of communication, they're tools of creativity, and they can be shaped by their user.
>
> *Bill Gates, businessman and co-founder of Microsoft*

> Without this playing with fantasy, no creative work ⁵ *ever yet came/has ever yet come* to birth. The debt we owe to the play of the imagination is incalculable.
>
> *Carl Jung, psychiatrist*

I ⁶ *didn't see/haven't seen* it then, but it ⁷ *turned out/has turned out* that getting fired from Apple was the best thing that could have ever happened to me. The heaviness of being successful ⁸ *was replaced/has been replaced* by the lightness of being a beginner again, less sure about everything. It ⁹ *freed/has freed* me to enter one of the most creative periods of my life.

Steve Jobs, businessman and co-founder of Apple

3 🎧 **1 04** Read the extract from an interview with a psychologist, who is talking about creativity and the brain. Complete the interview using the correct verb form: present perfect simple, present perfect continuous, past simple or past continuous. Then listen and check your answers.

Interviewer: Is it true that to be creative you need to be right-brained?

Psychologist: This idea that right-brained people are more creative and imaginative and that left-brained equals logical and analytical ¹ _____ (be) around for a long time. But it's an oversimplification and possibly simply untrue. We ² _____ (know) since the 19ᵗʰ century that the two hemispheres of the brain function differently, but most functions in fact involve the two sides working together. Furthermore, a recent study, which ³ _____ (involve) scanning the brains of over 1,000 people, ⁴ _____ (find) no evidence for people being predominantly either right-brained or left-brained. So, even though we ⁵ _____ (talk) about this distinction for a long time, it seems we may ⁶ _____ (be) misguided all along.

Interviewer: What about the idea that the most creative people are loners and eccentric geniuses?

Psychologist: Yes, this stereotype of a highly creative person as a lonely, perhaps eccentric, artist or poet ⁷ _____ (be) around for a long time. Indeed, recent research suggests that people tend to consider work to be of higher quality and have greater value if they ⁸ _____ (be told) that the person who ⁹ _____ (produce) it was eccentric. The reality, however, is that creativity is, more often than not, a result of collaboration. For example, Thomas Edison, who is often considered as a lone genius, ¹⁰ _____ (have) a great deal of input and support from a large group of scientists and engineers. Similarly, Michelangelo, when he ¹¹ _____ (paint) the Sistine Chapel, ¹² _____ (work) in collaboration with a creative team of artists.

4 Complete the sentences using the verb given in: the present perfect simple, the present perfect continuous, the past simple and the past continuous.

1 *work*
  a She _____ on a couple of similar projects already.
  b She _____ on this project for over six months now.
  c She _____ on her new project when I last spoke to her.
  d She _____ on a similar project in her old company.

2 *finalize*
  a They _____ the schedule for a few days now.
  b I think they _____ the schedule a few days ago.
  c _____ they _____ the schedule yet?
  d They _____ the schedule this morning. I'm not sure if it's ready yet.

3 *wait*
  a I saw you earlier. You _____ for a bus outside the university.
  b We _____ and _____ , but he didn't turn up. So, we went without him.
  c We _____ only _____ for a few minutes so far. Let's give him a little longer.
  d Come on, let's go. We _____ long enough.

4 *go*
  a Sorry I couldn't stop for a chat. I _____ to my creative writing class.
  b I _____ to my creative writing class last night.
  c I _____ to creative writing classes for about a year now.
  d I _____ to my creative writing class only once this term.

LANGUAGE FOCUS Expressions with statistics

5 Complete the sentences. Use the words in the box.

almost	significant	small	vast
good	relatively	sizeable	tiny

1 Only a _____ handful of startups go on to become successful businesses.
2 The _____ majority of people, around 90%, are right-handed.
3 Research suggests that the effect of environmental factors on children's creativity is _____ negligible.
4 A _____ number of people with dyslexia work in creative fields such as graphic design.
5 Only a _____ fraction of new patents go on to become successfully commercial products.

6 In many countries, a _____ proportion of students leave school with no qualifications.
7 _____ few people consider themselves to be creative.
8 A _____ deal of research suggests that creativity can be as valuable as intelligence in terms of employability.

6 Find and correct the mistakes in each sentence.

1 Globally, about one of eight males have some form of colour blindness, whereas only about one from 200 women is colour blind.
2 About one in each sixteen Americans plays a musical instrument.
3 In most of countries, over 99 per cents of all students graduating in medicine find jobs or enter further study within six months of graduating.
4 Geography is the worst degree for gaining employment in a number countries, with only around three out from every ten graduates in subject-related employment six months after graduating.
5 Research suggests that only one from four employees believe they are allowed to fulfil their creative potential at work.
6 According to a study, about four in of every ten people consider themselves to be in some way artistic.

DICTATION

7 🎧 **1 05** Listen to someone talking about the Italian architect Renzo Piano. Complete the sentences.

Renzo Piano is an Italian architect and engineer, born in Genoa in 1937, who is known for his ground-breaking and creative designs. He [1] _____ . In 2006, *TIME Magazine* [2] _____ in the world and as the tenth most influential person in the Arts and Entertainment category. In 2013, [3] _____ in the Italian Senate.
Over his career, Piano [4] _____ , including Louis Kahn, Richard Rogers and Gianfranco Franchini. With Franchini he [5] _____ Centre Georges Pompidou in Paris, which [6] _____ 'turned the architecture world upside down'.
Since 1981, Piano [7] _____ Renzo Piano Building Workshop and, since 2004, he [8] _____ for the Renzo Piano Foundation. This [9] _____ to promote the architectural profession through education.
Recently, a number of Piano's [10] _____ _____ . These include the Shard in London, at the time Europe's tallest skyscraper, and The New York Times Building in Manhattan.

1.3 How talent thrives

READING

1 Read the first paragraph of the text. What kind of text is it?

a an academic essay ☐
b a text book extract ☐
c a book review ☐

2 Read the whole text. Which is the best summary?

a An account of how certain working practices tend to be associated with certain fields of creativity. ☐
b A description and analysis of how different people prefer different working practices. ☐
c An explanation of how changes in working practice can negatively affect the creative process. ☐

3 Read the text again and answer the questions.

1 Which of the paragraphs (1–4) has each purpose (a–d)?
a Summarizes what the book gives the reader. ☐
b Describes the broad concept of the book. ☐
c Gives examples of working practices. ☐
d Explains the origins of the book. ☐

2 What is Mason Currey's main source of information?
a The individuals themselves and their associates.
b The work of other writers and academics.
c A combination of the above.

3 Which of the people mentioned in the text:
a had a strict quota of work to be done each day?
b worked in short bursts?
c had a novel way of refocussing the mind?

Working habits of creative minds

When aspiring to complete a particular project or task, we may look to the example set by former greats for inspiration about how best to organize our time and optimize creativity and productivity. This is exactly what author Mason Currey did and, after discovering that great minds don't think so alike after all, he set about writing a book on the subject. *Daily Rituals: How artists work* describes the habits and routines of some of history's most creative minds, breaking their days down into where and when they ate, slept, attended work, exercised and dedicated time to their crafts.

Based on each individual's letters, diaries and interviews, and drawing on some secondary sources, the book summarizes and analyzes the daily rituals of over 160 world famous novelists, poets, musicians, playwrights, painters, philosophers, scientists and mathematicians. The poet W. H. Auden, for example, who once said that 'routine is a sign of ambition', set himself an exacting timetable, in which eating, drinking, writing, shopping, and even doing crossword puzzles, were all timed to the minute. The writer Thomas Wolfe only wrote standing up in his kitchen, using the top of the refrigerator as a desk. Novelist Anthony Trollope forced himself to write 3,000 words (250 words every fifteen minutes for three hours) every morning before going off to his job at the postal service, which he kept for 33 years during the writing of more than two dozen books. In contrast, novelist and poet Gertrude Stein could never sustain writing for more than half an hour at a time. The choreographer George Balanchine did his ironing while working, while Igor Stravinsky had to be absolutely sure he was out of earshot in order to compose. Additionally, when suffering from creative block, he stood on his head to 'clear the brain'. Charles Darwin started the day by doing exercise.

Charles Dickens did several hours' exercise in the afternoon. And while the writer Mary Flannery O'Connor worked only in the morning, Franz Kafka generally only wrote at night, often until dawn, and then slept for most of the afternoon.

Bizarrely, Currey's own book was a product of procrastination while trying to write a story for an architecture magazine. As he did everything but write the article – reading *The New York Times* online, tidying his desk, making endless cups of coffee – he decided to search the Internet for information about how other writers managed to focus. Finding the results highly entertaining, he started to collect them. These soon became a blog, and later evolved into the book.

By writing about the mundane details of artists' daily schedules, Currey initially hoped to shine new light on their personalities and careers. But what the reader gains insight into is how grand creative visions are often the product of efforts made in small daily increments and how working habits themselves strongly influence the end product. *Daily Rituals* is a fascinating book about the raw mechanics of genius and eccentricities of the personalities behind it.

4 What initial event led to the publication of the book?

   a Currey was looking for ideas to help him concentrate on his work more.

   b Currey wanted to find out how to efficiently combine work and leisure.

   c Currey felt being entertained would help him and others work better.

5 What was Currey's original aim for the book?

   a To write a novel based on the entertaining personalities he had researched.

   b To relate an individual's working practice to their character and personality.

   c To show how creativity and working practices are dependent on each other.

4 Complete definitions (a–f) with words or phrases from the text.

   a _____ = separating into parts (paragraph 1)

   b _____ = using something that is available to you (paragraph 2)

   c _____ = needing a lot of effort and care (paragraph 2)

   d _____ = the act of delaying something that you should do (paragraph 3)

   e _____ = not interesting or exciting (paragraph 4)

   f _____ = a small section or part of something (paragraph 4)

VOCABULARY Creativity collocations

5 Complete the sentences with a word from each box.

broke	build	came	came	devoted
express	follow	had	take	

angle	convention	experience	freely	hobby
idea	inspiration	path	work	

1 The creative arts, be it painting, music, dance or writing, allow you to _express_ yourself _freely_ with few constraints.

2 Chester Greenwood always claimed that the idea for the earmuff, which he invented in 1873 at the age of 15, came to him after he _____ a flash of _____ while ice skating.

3 People had been using the wheel on its side to make pottery for hundreds of years before someone _____ up with the _____ of putting it upright and using it for transport.

4 Talking about his debut album *In The Lonely Hour*, singer Sam Smith said he wanted to write an album about love that _____ from a different _____ .

5 Studies suggest that if you really want to stay sharp in old age you need to _____ up a new _____ to boost your memory.

6 After the death of her husband Pierre in a road accident in 1906, Marie Curie _____ herself to her _____ on radioactivity.

7 Romanticist landscape artists such as Constable _____ with _____ to change the way we see the world.

8 Most creative geniuses first _____ on the _____ of others before they _____ their own _____ and start to create a niche of their own.

WORD FOCUS create

6 Complete the words with the correct endings.

1 It is thought that the Ancient Greeks are responsible for the **creat**_____ of the first true alphabet.

2 Brazilian footballer Pelé is widely regarded as one of the most **creat**_____ players of all time.

3 Tim Berners-Lee is best known as the **creat**_____ of the World Wide Web.

4 **Creat**_____ is increasingly recognized as an essential higher-order skill for learning.

5 Studies indicate that teachers who teach **creat**_____ and enthusiastically tend to be more popular with their students.

6 The temple, one of the oldest in Asia, is a truly impressive **creat**_____ .

7 A recent online trend is to make short films **recreat**_____ famous movie scenes.

8 **Creat**_____ is the belief that the universe and life originated from acts of divine creation. Those who believe in this are known as **creat**_____ .

7 Complete the sentences. Use the words in the box.

demonstrate	force	foster	highly
impression	stifling	streak	thinking

1 For a student to get high marks, he or she needs to clearly _____ creativity and originality in academic thinking and writing, whatever the discipline.

2 Creative _____ requires a very different set of skills to critical thinking.

3 Most of us have a creative _____ hiding somewhere inside us, be it for music, art, dancing, writing poetry or just having a vivid imagination.

4 Steven Spielberg was for many years the biggest creative _____ in the world of cinema.

5 Because of her flamboyant style, the singer tended to create an _____ wherever she went.

6 Research suggests that _____ creative children often require more individualized attention at school.

7 Many would say that having too much objective assessment and testing in schools is _____ creativity or even inhibiting it completely.

8 The course aims to encourage and _____ creativity in a number of ways, from course design to lesson planning.

1.4 It's not really my thing

DESCRIBING LIKES AND DISLIKES

1 🎧 **1 06** Listen to two people talking about likes and dislikes. Tick (✓) what they like and cross (✗) what they don't like.

Conversation 1:

  1 films in general ☐

  2 psychological thrillers ☐

  3 more lightweight films ☐

Conversation 2:

  4 rugby ☐

  5 football ☐

  6 live sport ☐

Conversation 3:

  7 Van Gogh ☐

  8 contemporary art ☐

  9 Turner ☐

2 🎧 **1 06** Complete the sentences. Then listen and check your answers.

  1 Well, yeah, **I'm not that** _____ films to be honest. **It's** _____ **really my** _____ .

  2 I _____ **like** a good psychological thriller, though ... But **I'm** _____ **so** _____ **on** the more lightweight stuff.

  3 What sports **are you** _____ ?

  4 **I'm** _____ **huge** rugby _____ . My favourite sport by a mile. **I'm** _____ **really** _____ football. It's OK, but **I can** _____ it or _____ it.

  5 **I'm** _____ **big** _____ of Van Gogh.

  6 I _____ **really get** _____ **about** much contemporary art, to be honest. **It just doesn't** _____ **to me** at all.

DESCRIBING TALENTS AND ABILITIES

3 🎧 **1 07** Listen to four people talking about what they are good at and not good at. Tick (✓) what they are good at and cross (✗) what they are not good at.

  1 playing the piano ☐   singing ☐

  2 teaching ☐   administrative tasks ☐

  3 making tea ☐   cooking ☐

  4 shopping ☐   saving money ☐

4 🎧 **1 07** Put the words into the correct order to make sentences. Then listen again and check your answers.

  1 Well, I play the piano, so I guess *quite / one / at / I'm / thing / that's / good* _____

  2 *great / I'm / singing / not / at* _____

  3 *I'm / a / teaching / think / I / quite / at / natural* _____

  4 *a / not / when it comes to / most definitely / I'm / natural* all the admin side of it. _____

  5 *my / can't / a cup of tea / I / to / make / life / save* _____

  6 *a / I / for / talent / do / cooking / have* _____

  7 *it / I'm / at / saving / hopeless / pretty* _____

  8 *born / I'm / a / spendaholic* _____

5 Use the words to write full sentences.

  1 I / not / fan / rock music

  _____

  2 Football / OK / but / I / take / leave

  _____

  3 I / can't / excited / modern art / just / not / appeal

  _____

  4 Anna / natural / when / comes / learning languages

  _____

  5 I / cook / save / life

  _____

  6 He / born / leader

  _____

PRONUNCIATION
Emphasis and de-emphasis

6 🎧 **1 08** Underline the words you think will be stressed. Then listen and check your answers.

1 I do like watching a good film.
2 I really want to learn the piano one day.
3 The lecture was quite good, but I thought it was a bit slow in places.
4 Modern art's really not my thing, I'm afraid.
5 I quite like modern art, actually. Especially earlier modern art.
6 Sam does tell a good story.
7 I did enjoy that film last night.
8 I know it's quite expensive, but I really do think it's worth it.

WRITING SKILL Nominalization

7 Complete the sentences so the meaning is similar. Use a noun and any other words necessary.

1 We intend to submit the proposal later this week.
Our _____ to submit the proposal later this week.
2 It has been decided that we will extend the trial period by a further two weeks.
The _____ to extend the trial period by a further two weeks.
3 It is vital that departments communicate clearly and openly with each other at all times.
_____ departments is vital at all times.
4 Satisfaction levels have increased significantly since the new system was implemented.
There _____ satisfaction levels since _____ the new system.
5 Not many people responded to the survey and a number of people complained about its length.
There _____ to the survey and _____ about its length.
6 We need to further consult about distributing the new product.
We need _____ about _____ the new product.

8 Rewrite the sentences using noun phrases in place of the phrases or clauses in bold. Make any other changes necessary.

1 **When it was published, it** caused a sensation.
Its publication caused a sensation.
2 **If you don't get sufficient sleep it** can affect your concentration.
_____
_____
3 **They have changed a number of things in** the proposal.
_____
_____

4 **Technology is advancing alarmingly**.
_____
5 I think **what the marketing department is proposing** is too technical and **unnecessarily complicates things**.
_____
_____
6 Thanks for your email. I'm just about to go away on a work trip, but I'll have a think about **what you suggest** and get back to you **when I get back** in a couple of weeks.
_____
_____
_____
_____

9 Rewrite the short progress report using nouns in place of the words in bold. Make any other changes necessary.

Online marketing: A progress report

We **attempted** on two separate occasions to market the product online, but neither **succeeded** very well. In hindsight, the way we **developed** the two sites was not based on any kind of comprehensive e-commerce strategy. We didn't think enough about the way we **designed** them and the way they **functioned**. In addition, we didn't properly **implement** how to **process** credit card transactions and the way we **fulfilled** orders was inefficient. Looking forward, we have been **consulting** with a specialist e-commerce firm and we are currently **discussing** with the board about additional financial and human resources **being available**.

There were two separate attempts to market the product online, but neither was very successful. In hindsight, ...

_____
_____
_____
_____
_____
_____
_____
_____
_____
_____

Presentation 1 | TALKING ABOUT TALENT

YOUR IDEA

1 Read what each person says about discovering their talent and answer the questions a–f.

1 **Joel:** I have a very analytical mind. I was good at school, doing well in subjects like maths and science. That's not very cool, though, is it? Being good with numbers has served me well in my career – I'm an accountant – but I never thought it could lead to anything very exciting. Then I read something about how mathematical patterns and classical music might be related. I did a lot of reading around the subject and decided I wanted to learn a musical instrument to find out if there really was a link between maths and music. I took up violin classes at a local music school and just loved it. It hasn't always been easy and it takes me a long time to pick up different tunes. My teacher is great though, and she's always pushing me to do better. In fact she entered me for a talent show.

2 **Tammy:** When I was younger, I didn't take part in school sports activities. I was excluded from most activities for health and safety reasons – being in my wheelchair, I could watch and cheer on my classmates, but I couldn't get involved. I didn't think that you could be an athlete and be in a wheelchair. That all changed when I went to see a wheelchair marathon. I was so interested that I bugged my parents to find out how I could train to be like the marathon competitors. I ended up going to a try-out at a local sports club and raced for the first time in an upright chair. Luckily my time was good enough to join the team and since then I've trained and raced in a proper racing wheelchair. I'm looking forward to my next track meet – I've got a great chance of winning a medal.

3 **Claudia:** I think I was quite misunderstood as a child. My mum always told me that I seemed to have unlimited energy – I'd never sit still and always fidgeted. I think the teachers at school agreed, and there was some talk of taking me to see a doctor. Not all of them though, thankfully. One of my teachers, Mrs Giles, suggested something different to my parents. She was really passionate about dance and theatre and gave my mum and dad the idea of taking me along to dance classes. To be honest, I've never really looked back – now I run my own dance school and our students compete all over the world. I sometimes wonder what would have happened if Mrs Giles hadn't been there to give me the push I needed. I might never have discovered that I had a real knack for dancing.

a Who wasn't fully involved in sporting activities at school? _____

b Who experienced difficulty at school? _____

c Who did well academically at school? _____

d Who received encouragement from a teacher? (2 people) _____ _____

e Who is confident they will succeed because of their talent? _____

f Who sometimes thinks about what their life would have been like without their talent? _____

2 Write notes about a talent you have or would like to have.

3 Answer the following questions about your talent or a talent you would like to have.

If you have a talent …

1 How did you discover your talent? How do you think you could develop it?

_____

2 Who helped you develop your talent? Who could help you?

_____

3 What opportunities does having this talent give you?

_____

If you would like to have a talent …

1 How do you think you could develop this talent?

_____

2 Who could help you develop this talent?

_____

3 What opportunities would having this talent give you?

_____

4 Practise describing your talent out loud. Remember to practise using humour in your presentation, but remember …

- its purpose is to relax people.
- it should illustrate the point you are making and not distract from it.
- it should not offend any group or individual.
- it helps if the humour is based on an anecdote about you or your experience, which others can easily relate to.
- it's essential to test any jokes on friends or colleagues before your presentation.

ORGANIZING YOUR PRESENTATION

5 Match the five steps of a presentation (1–5) with the examples of useful language (a–e).

1 Introduce yourself and your topic ☐
2 Say what talent you're talking about ☐
3 Say who or what helped you develop this talent ☐
4 Say what opportunities this talent would give you ☐
5 Finish ☐

a I left my office job and I've opened my own art gallery to showcase my and my friends' work.

b Hello everyone. Welcome to my presentation today. I'm going to talk about a talent I am lucky to have.

c I'm very fortunate to have had the support of my partner while I attended evening classes.

d I wasn't very artistic as a child, but I've been able to develop my skills as a painter.

e That brings us to the end of my presentation. If you have any questions, please feel free to ask them.

YOUR PRESENTATION

6 Read the useful language on the left and make notes for your presentation.

1 Introduce yourself and your topic Hello everyone. Welcome … The purpose of the presentation is to …	
2 Say what talent you're talking about I've been able to … Something I'm good at is … Something I'd like to do is …	
3 Say who or what helped you develop this talent … has/have been so helpful to me. I couldn't have done this without … I would need … to help me … They could help me by …	
4 Say what opportunities this talent would give you Now I've … I'd be able to …	
5 Finish That brings us to the end of … If you have any questions, please …	

7 Film yourself giving your presentation or practise in front of a mirror.
Give yourself marks out of ten for …

- using humour in your presentation. ☐/10
- acting naturally as you talk. ☐/10
- following the five steps in Exercise 6. ☐/10
- using correct grammar. ☐/10

2 Hopes and fears

2.1 Why I live in mortal dread of public speaking

TEDTALKS

Australian singer/songwriter, **MEGAN WASHINGTON**, was born in Papua New Guinea in 1986 and lived there until she was ten years old, when the family moved to Brisbane, Australia. During her teenage years she developed a love of music and, after finishing school, studied for a Bachelor of Music degree at the Queensland University of Technology and then studied jazz voice at the Queensland Conservatorium of Music. Early in her career, she played jazz piano with a number of acts and, before going solo, founded a band called *Washington*. Her style has evolved from jazz via blues and roots to indie pop and alternative rock, and today she sings and plays piano and guitar. On her Facebook page, she describes herself as a chanteuse.

Washington has won a number of awards, including Australia's 'Best Female Artist' and 'Breakthrough Artist', following the release of her platinum-selling debut album in 2010. She has since released a number of other best-selling albums, including *Insomnia* and *There There*. Washington tends to sing about issues such as heartbreak, insecurity and rage, and the lyrics to her songs have been described as having a beautiful and confessional tone.

Since her breakthrough solo album, which reached number three in the Australian charts, she has attracted the attention of a wider audience by appearing on a number of Australian TV music shows. A number of her songs have also appeared on other kinds of high-profile TV shows.

Washington developed a stutter early in her life, but avoided sharing this publicly until her talk at the TEDxSydney event in 2014. She explained that while it can hamper her during conversations, it tends to disappear when she sings. This has helped her to develop a number of strategies for coping with her speech impediment, which include avoiding certain letter combinations where possible and by 'singing' the things she has to say rather than speaking them.

Megan Washington

CAREER PATHWAYS

1 Read the text. Are these statements true (T) or false (F)?

1 The first group she played with was called *Washington*. ☐
2 Washington's voice has been described as beautiful. ☐
3 She first came to fame when she appeared on TV. ☐
4 The public didn't know about her stutter until her 2014 TED Talk. ☐
5 Singing has helped Washington to cope with her stutter. ☐

TED PLAYLIST

2 Other TED speakers are interested in topics similar to Megan Washington's TED Talk. Read the descriptions of four TED Talks at the top of page 15. In your opinion, which is the best title for this playlist, a, b or c?

a Music is a medicine
b There's a song inside all of us
c The power of music

3 Read the TED playlist again. Find a speaker who ...

1 re-found their voice.
2 told their story through music.
3 overcame a physical setback.
4 uses music to help others.

▶ **Robert Gupta: Between music and medicine**

When Robert Gupta was caught between a career as a doctor and as a violinist, he realized his place was in the middle. He tells a moving story of society's marginalized and the power of music therapy, which can succeed where conventional medicine fails.

▶ **The Lady Lifers: A moving song from women in prison for life**

The ten women prisoners in this chorus share a moving song about their experiences: their hopes, regrets and fears. 'I'm not an angel,' sings one, 'but I'm not the devil.' Filmed inside Muncy State Prison, it's a rare and poignant look inside the world of people imprisoned with no hope of parole.

▶ **Sting: How I started writing songs again**

Sting's early life was dominated by a shipyard – and he dreamed of escaping its industrial drudgery. But after a nasty bout of writer's block that stretched on for years, Sting found inspiration in the stories of the shipyard workers from his youth. In a lyrical, confessional talk, Sting treats us to songs from his musical based on this theme.

▶ **Charity Tillemann-Dick: Singing after a double lung transplant**

You'll never sing again, said her doctor. But in a story from the very edge of medical possibility, operatic soprano Charity Tillemann-Dick tells a double story of survival – of her body, from a double lung transplant, and of her spirit, fuelled by an unwavering will to sing.

4 Find words in the TED playlist that mean the same as the words and phrases a–d.

   a traditional   **c** unpleasant
   b emotional   **d** strong and determined

5 Which talk would you most like to see? Why? Watch the talk at TED.com.

AUTHENTIC LISTENING SKILLS
Listening to songs

6 🎧 1 09 You are going to hear a podcast in which a member of the *Keynote* team talks about Robert Gupta's TED Talk, *Between music and medicine*. Look at the lyrics in the song extract that the podcaster plays at the end. Complete the lines. Then listen and check your answers.

> I see the sun in your smile
> Watching it rise in your _____
> See the dusty road ahead
> Stretching out for miles and miles
> Sick and tired of skipping the _____
> Dodging the holes in the road
> I need a helping hand
> To help me shoulder this _____
> Do, do you, well, wouldn't you
> Do the same in my _____ ?
> I wouldn't do, just couldn't _____
> Another mile without you
> Another mile without you

LISTENING

7 🎧 1 10 Listen to the full podcast. Answer the questions.

   1 Who does Robert Gupta aim his music therapy at?
   2 In what way does Mike Harrison think that Gupta's presentation is different to a lecture?

8 🎧 1 10 Listen again. Complete the facts using one word in each space.

   1 Robert Gupta's profession is _____ ; his hobby is playing the _____ .
   2 Gupta uses music to give _____ to people in distress.
   3 Mike Harrison has tried using music in his _____ .
   4 Mike Harrison is not really a _____ , but he believes in the _____ of music.

VOCABULARY IN CONTEXT

9 Read the extracts from the podcast. Choose the correct meaning of the words in bold.

   1 I was interested to watch this TED Talk exploring how medicine **intersects with** another creative pursuit.
      a connects with ☐   **b** changes ☐
      c enhances ☐

   2 ... about music is about its potential to help people in really **dire** circumstances.
      a frightening ☐   **b** unusual ☐   **c** desperate ☐

   3 Gupta shows us how music can give society's most **marginalized** some sort of hope.
      Treated as: **a** unteachable ☐   **b** disregarded ☐
      c unintelligent ☐

   4 I think it's sad that most of the time we **take** music and other sounds **for granted**.
      a neglect ☐   **b** undervalue ☐   **c** ignore ☐

   5 .... particularly when it can be so effective at **articulating** our emotions.
      a stimulating ☐   **b** expressing ☐   **c** mirroring ☐

2.2 Optimist or pessimist?

GRAMMAR Future forms

1 Read the sentences below. Do the phrases in bold refer to present (P), general (G) or future (F) time?

1 Give him a call. His meeting **will have finished**. ☐
2 **I'll watch** a couple of hours TV before bed most evenings. ☐
3 I'm a bit busy now. **I'll call** you back. ☐
4 We**'re about to leave**. Are you ready? ☐
5 They've been driving all day. They**'ll be** exhausted. ☐
6 Get a move on! The taxi **will be waiting**. ☐
7 The exhibition **starts** on Friday. ☐
8 He **will insist** on singing that awful song. ☐

2 Choose the best words or phrases to complete the news article.

New population growth forecast

A recent analysis shows that the Earth's population ¹*will continue / will be continuing* to rise from around 7bn today and ²*will be reaching / will have reached* 11bn by 2100. This means that by the end of the century, the world population ³*is likely to be / is likely to have been* between 50% and 75% larger than today and ⁴*is still going to grow / will still be growing*.

The study overturns the long-standing theory that the global population ⁵*is peaking / is going to peak* in around 2050 at about 9bn people and then possibly even decline. Experts now believe that population growth should return to the top of the international agenda. James Oliver, of the international think tank Population Awareness who ⁶ *hold / are holding* a conference in London next month, said 'This new projected population growth, unless it ⁷ *is slowed / will be slowed*, ⁸ *is going to cause / is going to have caused* all kinds of challenges.' He went on to say that if we ⁹ *don't take / won't take* action very soon, in 50 or so years, we ¹⁰ *are very likely facing / will very likely be facing* a number of issues which are all linked to rapid population growth, such as insufficient healthcare, increasing poverty and rising social unrest and crime.

3 Complete the news items using the correct future form of the verbs in italics.

> not / be able   may / double   likely / have

1 By the end of the decade, demographers say China _____ a surplus of around 25 million men who, because of China's gender imbalance, _____ to find a wife. It is thought that by the middle of the century, this figure _____ .

> live   continue

2 If the current rate of increasing longevity _____ , it is likely that some people born today _____ to be 130.

> focus   meet

3 The United Nations Expert Group on Population Change _____ in New York next month to discuss 'changing population trends and development'. The meeting _____ particularly on fertility issues.

> prove   only / be   soon / be able
> may / eventually / follow

4 Medical scientists predict that we _____ to regrow damaged body parts. At first it _____ possible to regrow fingers and toes, but if this _____ successful, the regeneration of whole limbs and even internal organs _____ .

> travel   start

5 It is predicted that by the end of the century, humans _____ to colonize Mars and it is possible that we _____ between the two planets on a regular basis.

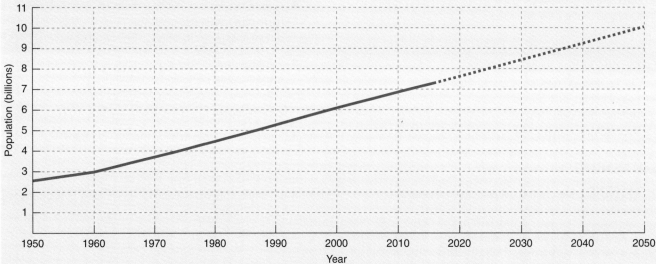

4 🎧 **1 11** Complete the dialogues with the correct future form of the verbs in the box. Then listen and check your answers.

be	call back	do	finish	have
have	make	say	start	tell

1 A: Have you booked the meeting room yet?
B: I'm just about _____ it.

2 A: I can't speak. I'm in a meeting right now.
B: OK, I _____ later this afternoon.

3 A: Did you get an invite to Jenny's do next week?
B: Oh, she _____ a party, is she?

4 A: See you at six, then.
B: Well, as long as the traffic _____ OK.

5 A: Term _____ on the 15th, right?
B: The 22nd, I think.

6 A: Where are they? The gate's about to close.
B: Yep, doesn't look like they _____ it, does it?

7 A: I'll pop round at 7.30ish.
B: We _____ dinner then. Can you make it nearer nine? We _____ eating by then.

8 A: _____ you _____ anything to him?
B: Yep, I _____ him exactly what I think!

LANGUAGE FOCUS Expressions of certainty

5 Put the words in the correct order to make sentences.

1 all / will reach / likelihood, / the population / in / by the year 2100 / eleven million

_____

2 to / a cure / we / sooner or later / bound / find / 're / for cancer

_____

3 well / may / one day / very / a third world war / happen

_____

4 colonize / foregone / a / that / it's / we'll / conclusion / one day / Mars

_____

5 likely / is / remain / the / for a long time / to / the US / world's / economy / biggest

_____

6 certain that / it's / means / by / on another planet / no / there / is / life

_____

6 Rewrite the sentences using the word or words given so the meaning is the same.

1 I'm sure she'll know what to do.   *bound*

_____

2 It's very possible that they won't agree.   *no means*

_____

3 It's possible it was my fault.   *may well*

_____

4 I'm pretty sure it won't be here.   *highly unlikely*

_____

5 I suspect we'll never hear from them again.   *likelihood*

_____

7 Complete the responses.

1 A: Do you think we'll get there in time?
B: Unless the traffic improves, it's _____ unlikely.

2 A: How many people do you think will turn up?
B: No idea. _____ anyone's _____ .

3 A: Do you think we've done the right thing?
B: I think it _____ well turn _____ to be a bad move, actually.

4 A: How come you're so sure about it?
B: Oh, it's a _____ conclusion.

5 A: Are they going to be there?
B: I think so, but it's _____ no means _____ .

DICTATION

8 🎧 **1 12** Listen to part of a lecture about population growth in China. Complete the sentences.

China has one of the lowest birth rates in the world. At about 1.26 children per female, it is currently less than half of the world's average and below the fertility replacement rate of 2.2, which a country needs to maintain its current population. This means that if
[1]_____ , China's population [2]_____ .
It has been suggested that by the end of the century, China's population [3]_____
30 per cent. And if this prediction [4]_____
_____ , then China
[5]_____ demographic crises in the world. The sharply declining birth rate means that by 2050, between a quarter and a third of China's population [6]_____
age. They, of course, [7]_____
_____ to the economy while at the same time government expenditure on the elderly [8]_____ .

READING

1 Look at the five opening sentences of the blog and say which one(s) you think give:

a advice ☐ ☐ ☐

b a word of caution ☐

c a definition ☐

2 Read the whole text. Find examples of types of adversity that people face in paragraphs 1–5.

1 _poverty, lack of education and discrimination, illness, personal loss_

2 _____

3 _____
_____

4 _____
_____

5 _____
_____

3 Read the text again. Choose the best option to complete the sentences.

1 It's _illogical / natural_ to feel depressed in the face of adversity.

2 Not getting a promotion at work _is / isn't_ an example of facing adversity.

3 Negative events _generally have / don't necessarily have_ a negative effect.

4 Dealing with adversity _makes us better able / doesn't actually help us_ to deal with it when it arises again.

5 We can _specifically relate to / generally learn from_ the stories of others who have triumphed over adversity.

6 Talking about your problems always helps to _find solutions / relieve the tension_.

7 Facing adversity has a positive outcome for a _majority / minority_ of people.

8 Many people _are overwhelmed / simply give up_ in the face of adversity.

Five things you should know about adversity

1 Adversity is not just an occasional setback. It usually refers to a chronic situation or condition that seriously hampers your ability to achieve your ambitions or to find security and happiness. Adversity may come from your social situation – poverty or lack of education or discrimination – or it may come in the form of a personal tragedy, like illness or loss of a loved one. In fact, most of us face adversity at some point in our lives and will, quite understandably, feel depressed and hopeless as a result. The first thing to do is not to allow a series of seemingly minor setbacks (not getting a promotion at work, a big repair bill on your car, etc.) to snowball into a feeling that you're facing overwhelming adversity.

2 What doesn't kill you, makes you stronger. Scientific studies have shown that those who have experienced adversity in their lives are better equipped to deal with fresh difficulties or challenges when they arise. That is not to say that negative events don't have negative effects; simply that if we're able to work our way through traumas and setbacks, we come out the other side more resilient. One study showed that among people who suffered serious back pain, those who had experience of some other adversity in life were more mobile and better able to cope than those who had no such experience.

3 Stories can inspire. The pages of magazines – business magazines in particular – are full of stories of people who have triumphed over adversity. Richard Branson, CEO of Virgin Group, has struggled with dyslexia all his life. Jim Carrey, the comic actor, was the son of an unemployed musician and dropped out of school at 15 to support the rest of his family. The film _The Theory of Everything_ celebrates the life of the famous physicist Stephen Hawking who has survived motor neurone disease against all the odds. All these stories serve as a useful metaphor for our own struggles against adversity, whatever they might be.

4 A problem shared is a problem halved. As I said, we all face adversity at some point in our lives so you can almost always find a sympathetic ear in a friend or colleague. Talking about your financial problems, for example, will automatically make you feel less burdened; you might even feel able to share a joke about it. Additionally, as you talk through what's happened and what you're feeling, solutions that had half-formed in your mind, but not yet been articulated, may begin to appear.

5 Adversity can be crushing too. For every one person that has achieved success in the face of adversity there are nine people who feel crushed by it. Recognize that there are situations – notably chronic poverty and social discrimination – that many people cannot escape from, however valiantly they try. So it's incumbent on all of us either to give a helping hand directly to such groups in society or to encourage our governments to do so.

4 Choose the correct word to complete the definitions.

1 **hampers** your ability to = makes it more *difficult / impossible* for you to ...
2 allow [something] to **snowball** = to allow something to become *bigger / smaller*.
3 we become more **resilient** = we become more able to *ignore / resist* shocks or stresses
4 survived against **all the odds** = survived in spite of a *high / low* probability of not surviving
5 talking will make you feel less **burdened** = talking will lift a *weight / pain* from your shoulders
6 not yet been **articulated** = not yet been *explained / expressed* clearly
7 **chronic** poverty = being poor for a *short / long* period of time
8 it's **incumbent** on all of us to = it is our *choice / duty* to ...

5 🎧 **1 13** Listen to someone talking about adversity in their life. Which of the points about adversity in the article do they talk about?

6 🎧 **1 13** Listen again and answer the questions.

1 What was the main adversity the speaker faced in their life?
2 What was the main adversity J.K. Rowling faced?
3 Where did J.K. Rowling usually do her writing?
4 What was the lesson the speaker took from J.K. Rowling's life?

VOCABULARY Idioms: hopes and fears

7 Complete the idioms in the extracts with the correct words.

1 Some people feel they are facing adversity when their expectations are not met. They [1]p_____ their hopes on getting something – like a new job or a flat they have been looking for – and then their hopes are [2]d_____ when they don't get it. But that isn't really adversity. It's just an ordinary setback. Real adversity is about facing conditions which are extremely tough and not [3]g_____ up hope.

2 Did you see the story of the girl who stood up to other girls who were bullying her at school? I was really moved by it. She had been getting bullied for three years and had thought several times about going to the head of the school, but she got [4]c_____ feet. Then one day she [5]p_____ up the courage to speak about it in a school assembly – in front of all the teachers and pupils. At first she was a bundle of [6]n_____ , but once she got started she spoke very articulately and with real passion. At the end everyone got to their feet and applauded her.

3 Her parents were very poor and she was sent away at sixteen to earn money in a laundry in the city. I think that's what made her the person she is. She set up her own laundry company at 23 – it was a complete [7]l_____ in the dark – and made a success of it. Now the sky's the [8]l_____ for her.

WORD FOCUS Courage, guts and bravery

8 Choose the correct word to complete these expressions about bravery and courage.

1 It *needs / takes* **guts** to stand up and disagree with a course of action you think is wrong when everyone else is in favour of it.
2 She took a risk investing all her savings in her new venture, but it turned out to be a huge success. **Fortune** *assists / favours* **the brave**.
3 He was very disappointed not to be chosen for the team, but he **put a** *brave / courageous* **face on** it.
4 The ruling party lost the election by 45% to 55%. They **put** *on / up* **a brave fight**, but people wanted a change.
5 The best advice my father ever gave me was 'Lead your own life, in spite of what others may say or think and **have the courage of your** *convictions / beliefs*'.
6 You'll get soaked if you cycle to work now. I admire the fact that you're prepared to *brave / gut* **the elements**, but why don't you just take the car instead?
7 She **took her courage in both** *arms / hands* and jumped into the cold water.
8 Only Dan would *have / feel* **the guts to** speak to the boss like that.

9 Complete these sentences with the correct form of the expressions in Exercise 8.

1 The open-air concert turned out to be on one of the wettest weekends on record, but still, over 10,000 people _____ to come and see their heroes play.
2 Our manager says that he is going to support us and argue against the new working contract. I just hope he _____ .
3 You shouldn't be disheartened. You _____ , but you just came up against someone who was exceptionally talented.
4 _____ to admit that you've been wrong all along.
5 It's no good carrying on and _____ . If you're feeling that stressed, you've got to do something about it or you'll end up having a breakdown.
6 I admit it: I'm a coward. I don't _____ to confront her about it.

2.4 Worst-case scenario

GIVING AND JUSTIFYING ADVICE

1 🎧 **1 14** Listen to a university tutor talking about plagiarism. According to the tutor, are these statements true (T) or false (F)?

1 The university routinely checks submitted work for evidence of plagiarism. ☐

2 It is OK to use open-source websites such as Wikipedia. ☐

3 Plagiarism may result in a student being thrown out of the university. ☐

4 Using synonyms and changing the word order is the best way to avoid plagiarism. ☐

5 Your tutors will help you to understand what is and isn't plagiarism. ☐

2 🎧 **1 14** Complete the extracts from Exercise 1. Then listen again and check your answers.

1 You need to be _____ that the university routinely checks submitted work for evidence of plagiarism.

2 And on that subject, we strongly _____ _____ using open-source websites such as Wikipedia that have unverifiable content.

3 In the _____ _____ plagiarism, you will be given a formal warning and have to rewrite your essay.

4 To avoid plagiarism, the _____ _____ is to become familiar with the principles of good academic practice as soon as you start your university studies.

5 That _____, you _____ more quickly develop an awareness of the requirements ...

6 ... although it is _____ _____ thoroughly check them through before you submit your work.

7 _____ simply using a few synonyms and changing the word order. The _____ are that you will be caught out.

8 Following his or her advice will _____ that your work is plagiarism-free.

3 Complete the responses using the words in brackets.

1 A: I just don't know what to do about it.
   B: I'd _____ (time / think) it through if I were you. _____ (talk / someone / also / good idea).

2 A: Work's really starting to get me down.
   B: Maybe it's time _____ (consider / look) something else?

3 A: This hotel is in a better location, but this one has better facilities.
   B: I'd _____ (opt / location / facilities) every time.

4 A: I just can't help wondering if he's OK.
   B: _____ , (own / peace / mind) why don't you give him a call?

5 A: Do you think I should ask for a meeting with them?
   B: I think for now _____ (best thing / say) nothing. _____ (way / not) pre-empt anything. I think things will probably sort themselves out.

6 A: What should I do about my new boss?
   B: Well, I _____ (advise / against / do) anything too rash and _____ (avoid / be) too confrontational. _____ (the chances) he's also a little uneasy about things.

PRONUNCIATION Consonant clusters

4 🎧 **1** **15** The following words contain combinations (or clusters) of consonants that can be difficult to pronounce. Underline the consonant clusters and practise saying the words. Listen and check and then practise again.

1	sixth	**11**	hundredth
2	through	**12**	filmed
3	spring	**13**	health
4	asked	**14**	crisps
5	clothes	**15**	helpful
6	length	**16**	splendid
7	months	**17**	explained
8	depth	**18**	instincts
9	twelfth	**19**	facts
10	breathes	**20**	rejects

WRITING SKILL Future in the past

5 Complete the sentences with *was/were going to* and the words in the box.

originally/get	originally/hold	not/say
just/stay	tell	

1 We _____ for a few hours, but we ended up spending the whole weekend there.

2 I _____ anything to him, but I just felt it wasn't fair to keep him in the dark any longer.

3 I think they _____ married in June. I'm not sure why they changed it.

4 I'm really sorry you heard it from someone else. I _____ you myself, honestly.

5 They _____ the conference in Liverpool, but they went for Birmingham instead.

6 Put the words in order to complete the sentences.

1 _____ *she / as though / looked / was / she / going / something, / say / to* but she turned and walked out of the room.

2 _____ *to / tomorrow, / going / were / the two leaders / meet* but the meeting has been postponed.

3 _____ *Jones / yesterday, / originally / going / discharged / was / be / to* but doctors decided to keep him in for further observations.

4 _____ *wasn't / rain, / to / it / supposed* but the heavens opened and we got absolutely soaked.

5 _____ *resume / play / due / to / three, / was / at* but at quarter to it started raining again.

6 _____ *to / it / a working lunch, / was / meant / be* but we didn't get much work done at all.

7 _____ *would / I / was / us, / he / waiting / sure / for / be* but he must've got the times confused.

8 _____ *were / nine o'clock, / we / at / to / supposed / meet* but he didn't turn up.

7 Rewrite the sentences using the word given so the meaning is similar.

1 We had planned to leave at about six, but we were still there at seven. *going*
We _____

2 They didn't arrive on Tuesday as was scheduled. *supposed*
They _____

3 I expected them to leave early, but they stayed until the early hours. *would*
I _____

4 We hadn't planned to take a taxi, but it was raining. *going*
We _____

5 They said the flight would take off at 5.30, but it was delayed again until seven o'clock. *due*
The flight _____

6 We hadn't anticipated it taking so long. *would*
We _____

8 Complete the review from a travel forum using the words in the box.

due/move	going/have to/make	going/improve
originally/going/stay	supposed/meet	would/take
would/not/recognize		

Where do I begin? First, someone from the hotel ¹_____ us at the airport, but after waiting over an hour, it became clear we ²_____ our own way there. As the airport was pretty well deserted, it took us another 30 minutes to find a taxi that ³_____ us to the hotel. When we finally got to the hotel, it was terrible, nothing like its website and nothing at all like some of the reviews we'd read. The whole place was dark and tired and in general need of repair. The owner kept telling us how he ⁴_____ things and that we ⁵_____ the place if we came back in a few months. He insisted that no-one else had ever complained – yeah, right. Our room looked like it hadn't had a proper clean for weeks. We ⁶_____ for three nights, but, after the first night, we couldn't stand it anymore. We ⁷_____ up the coast a few miles and change hotels anyway, so we rang them and they had a room available that night.

Writing 1 | AN ARTICLE

IDEAS

You will read an article written to answer the question below.

> A business magazine is running a series of articles on attitudes to work and leisure time. The magazine has invited readers to send in articles briefly describing their work-life balance. The article should explain the importance of maintaining an appropriate work-life balance and consider what companies can do to help their employees achieve this.

Write your article in **280–320 words** in an appropriate style.

1 In the question, underline the three topics which need to be covered in the article. What points could be included in each topic?

MODEL

2 Read the article. Which topic is dealt with in each paragraph? Are any of your ideas included?

A new lease of life

[1] Exhausted, depressed and coming down with a cold, I opened the door to my office and sat down at my desk. It was 8 a.m. and I'd already been up for three hours. Looking at the list of things that I needed to get through in the next twelve hours, I realized that if I didn't change something soon, I ran the risk of burning out and having to give up a career that I had dreamed of for years.

[2] My own experience illustrates why our current obsession with working as much as possible is unsustainable. It has been proved time and time again that employees who maintain a healthy work-life balance contribute much more to their companies than those who only live to work. Their stress levels are lower, they take fewer sick days and they are able to complete tasks more efficiently.

[3] Taking this into account, the way companies encourage employees to use their time at work is an important way to change their mindsets. This can be done by following the example of businesses that provide recreation areas in their offices. Not only does this allow their staff to switch off from the stresses of work, but it also gives them the chance to build stronger relationships. Another idea is to encourage staff to leave the office at break times or earlier in the evening to spend time enjoying the natural world.

[4] The decision I made that day was one of the hardest of my life: moving from the prestigious city law firm I'd been lucky to get a job at to a local one, closer to home and demanding much shorter working hours. Only by doing this did my quality of life drastically improve. I'm happier, healthier and have more of a social life than ever before. It's a choice I would make again in a heartbeat.

3 Read the article. Say which section (1–4) each of the following statements (a–d) matches.

a Businesses have a responsibility to encourage staff to use their time wisely.

b The author felt overwhelmed by all of the work they had to do, despite being in the career they wanted.

c By changing jobs, the author has seen huge positive changes in their life.

d It's healthier to have a good work-life balance than to work too much.

USEFUL LANGUAGE

4 Match the phrases (1–3) with three alternative ways of saying the same thing (a–i).

1 The author **realized** they needed a different job.
☐ ☐ ☐

2 Having a good work-life balance **is important to** stay healthy. ☐ ☐ ☐

3 Helping employees to reduce stress levels **can be done by** providing recreation areas at work. ☐ ☐ ☐

a The author **came to realize** a new job was necessary.

b **It suddenly occurred to** the author **that** they should change their job.

c **The essence of** being healthy **lies in** having an appropriate work-life balance.

d **A possible route to** reducing employees' stress levels **would be to** give them places to relax at work.

e **One way to approach** the reduction of employees' stress levels **is to** provide places to relax at work.

f **It dawned on** the author **that** it was time for a new job.

g **A key ingredient of** staying healthy **is** balancing work and relaxation.

h **A possible course of action for** helping employees to reduce stress levels **is to** give them somewhere to relax at work.

i Balancing your work and home lives **is vital to** remain healthy.

5 These sentences are taken from the article in Exercise 2. Rewrite the sentences using a–i. Each sentence can be rewritten in three different ways. Try to do it without looking at Exercise 4.

1 I realized that if I didn't change something soon, I ran the risk of burning out.

I came to realize that if I didn't change something soon, I ran the risk of burning out.

2 The way companies encourage employees to use their time at work is an important way to change their mindsets.

_____

_____

3 This can be done by following the example of businesses that provide recreation areas in their offices.

_____

_____

6 A stylistic device often used in articles is the 'rule of three'. This involves repeating a similar grammatical structure three times in the same section of the article. Sometimes a sound is also repeated to add to the effect. Find three examples of the rule of three in the model in Exercise 2.

Note: If one of the three points is longer than the others, it is usually the last of the three, e.g.

My job was too challenging, too stressful and taking up far too much of my time.

7 Match one phrase from each column to create five more 'threes' which could be used in an article about work-life balance.

over-worked, under-paid and under-valued

over-worked	encouraging job shares	or simply lunch at a local restaurant
by organizing a night out	more creative	and under-valued
by allowing flexi-time	under-paid	and breathing their jobs
having been awake since six	sleeping	and not likely to get home until seven
they are more productive	a weekend away	and their imaginations are given free rein
living	at my desk since eight	or letting staff leave early on Fridays

PLANNING

You will answer the following question.

> A technology magazine is inviting readers to contribute to a series of articles about our changing relationship with technology. You decide to submit an article about how one piece of technology has affected your life. You should briefly describe why the technology is important to you, explain what people would have done before this technology existed and assess whether these changes are positive or negative.

Write your article in **280–320 words** in an appropriate style.

8 Plan your article. Write notes to answer these questions. Don't write full sentences yet.

1 Which piece of technology will you write about?
2 Why is it important to you?
3 What did people do/use before this technology existed?
4 Has this technology had a positive or a negative effect on society?

WRITING

9 Write an article to reply to the question in Exercise 8. In your article you should:

- include a title and introduction which will attract the reader's attention and encourage them to read on
- describe how one piece of technology has affected your life
- explain what people did/used before this technology existed
- evaluate whether any changes in society have been positive or negative

Write **280–320 words**.

ANALYSIS

10 Check your article. Answer the questions.

Content: Does the article describe your personal experience? Is this contrasted to life before this technology existed? Are the effects of this technology on society clearly evaluated? Is it 280 to 320 words long?

Communicative achievement: Does the title attract the reader's attention? Is the article interesting to read?

Organization: Is the article logically organized? Are the links between paragraphs and ideas clear?

Language: Does it use correct grammar and vocabulary? Is there a good range of structures and stylistic devices, such as the 'rule of three'?

3 Perception

3.1 The 4 ways sound affects us

TEDTALKS

JULIAN TREASURE was born in London, UK. He was educated at the 600-year-old St Paul's School, one of the UK's original public schools, then at the University of Cambridge, where he studied economics. After university, he worked in advertising and then in magazine publishing. He started TPD Publishing in 1988, which produced magazines for brands like Apple, Lexus and Microsoft and which went on to become one of the UK's leading contract magazine publishing companies. Treasure sold the company in 2001, but stayed on working there for a further two years. Around this time, he also held a number of senior posts in various publishing associations and agencies and, in 2002, he received a Professional Publishers Association Award for services to the UK magazine publishing industry.

In 2003, Treasure had a change of direction, leaving TPD to pursue his passion for sound. As a drummer and musician – his band, *The Transmitters*, once played on live TV to an audience of 18 million – he had for a long time been interested in the noise of modern life, and in particular how businesses and other organizations were using sound in their work. As he researched this, he discovered that most sound in business environments was having a negative effect on people and he realized there was an opportunity for businesses to improve their results by becoming more sound-conscious. As a result, he started The Sound Agency, which advises organizations on all aspects of sound. Examples of this include the use of ambient sound to reduce crime in urban areas and the creation of in-store soundscapes that increase both sales and customer satisfaction. The company's motto is 'Good sound is good business'. Treasure has also written the best-selling book *Sound Business*, which was published in 2007.

Treasure is a sought-after international speaker and has given a number of TED Talks on various aspects of sound and communication.

Julian Treasure

CAREER PATHWAYS

1 Read the text. Answer the questions.

1 What three main areas does Treasure have a background in?
2 What particular successes in publishing did Treasure have?
3 What led to Treasure's interest in 'the noise of modern life'?
4 What prompted Treasure to start The Sound Agency?
5 How has The Sound Agency helped with (i) crime and (ii) customer behaviour?

TED PLAYLIST

2 Other TED speakers are interested in topics similar to Julian Treasure's TED Talk. Read the descriptions of four TED Talks at the top of page 25. In your opinion, which is the best title for this playlist, a, b or c?

a The importance of sound in our lives
b Designing for all the senses
c Raising awareness of our senses

3 Read the TED playlist again. Find a speaker who ...

1 wants to create calmer environments.
2 is primarily interested in enhancing our sensory experiences.
3 is interested in the relationship between senses and feelings.

4 Find words or phrases in the TED playlist that mean the same as the words and phrases (a–e).

a slowly diminishing   b attack   c range   d pay attention to
e practical

5 Which talk would you most like to see? Why? Watch the talk at TED.com.

▶ **Julian Treasure: Shh! Sound health in 8 steps**

Julian Treasure says our increasingly noisy world is gnawing away at our mental health – even costing lives. He lays out an eight-step plan to soften this sonic assault (starting with those cheap earbuds) and restore our relationship with sound.

▶ **Jinsop Lee: Design for all 5 senses**

Good design looks great, yes – but why shouldn't it also feel great, smell great and sound great? Designer Jinsop Lee shares his theory of five-sense design, with a handy graph and a few examples. His hope: to inspire you to notice great multisensory experiences.

▶ **Mira Calix: Sound and sentiment**

What does happiness sound like? What about misery? Mira Calix explores the emotional qualities embedded in music and noise, and shares a sound-based spectrum of human sentiments that emerged from her recent work.

▶ **Julian Treasure: Why architects need to use their ears**

Because of poor acoustics, students in classrooms miss 50 per cent of what their teachers say and patients in hospitals have trouble sleeping because they continually feel stressed. Julian Treasure sounds a call to action for designers to heed the 'invisible architecture' of sound.

AUTHENTIC LISTENING SKILLS
Understanding fast speech

6 🎧 1 16 You are going to hear a podcast in which a member of the *Keynote* team talks about Mira Calix's TED Talk, *Sound and sentiment*. Tick (✓) the things (1–4) she will talk about. Then listen to the opening sentences and check your answers.

1 the speaker's background ☐
2 whether the talk was enjoyable ☐
3 what she knows about the subject already ☐
4 what the talk is about ☐

7 🎧 1 16 Listen to the extract again. What other details does she give about 1–4 in Exercise 6?

LISTENING

8 🎧 1 17 Listen to the full podcast. Which words in italics are not true?

According to the podcaster, Mira Calix has very *fixed* ideas about the effects of *music* on our *emotions*.

9 🎧 1 17 Listen again. Complete the summary.

Mira Calix worked on a project to transform an old railway 1_____ into a walkway for 2_____ .

As people walk along, light and music 3_____ are switched on. The music makes people think of a particular 4_____ . It reminded the speaker of when she was in 5_____ , listening to a Fado 6_____ and she could really feel the emotion in the music. The message is often that the feelings that music provokes are beyond 7_____ .

VOCABULARY IN CONTEXT

10 Read these sentences from the podcast. Tick (✓) the correct meaning of the words in bold.

1 Actually, I **put that badly**. It's not her intention to change their perceptions, but to …
  a expressed that negatively ☐
  b expressed that unkindly ☐
  c expressed that wrong ☐

2 As people pass along the tunnel, they **trigger** light and music installations …
  a are faced with ☐
  b cause to function ☐
  c are surprised by ☐

3 She just tries to **coax** a certain *kind* of emotion out of her audience.
  a gently persuade ☐
  b strongly provoke ☐
  c quickly generate ☐

4 *Fado* is a deeply **melancholic** genre of music.
  a sad ☐
  b serious ☐
  c confusing ☐

5 … it's about a **yearning** for things or people lost or things that have disappeared into the past.
  a longing ☐
  b search ☐
  c sadness ☐

3.2 Judging by appearances

GRAMMAR Stative and dynamic verbs

1 Read the article giving advice about how to create a good first impression. Are the verbs in bold stative (S) or dynamic (D)?

Whether at work or in your social life, first encounters [1] **matter**. You usually [2] **have** just a few seconds to make that all-important first impression, so it's important to get it right from the word go. Much of what you [3] **need** to do to make a good first impression is common sense, but here we [4] **provide** you with a few basic tips.

Be punctual: Whether they [5] **believe** you or not, a person you [6] **are meeting** for the first time [7] **has** no interest in your excuse for being late.

Be well-presented: Your appearance [8] **matters**. You [9] **are meeting** someone who [10] **does not know** you, and how you [11] **look** will have a lasting first impression. So, whatever image you [12] **are wanting** to present, make sure that's precisely what you present.

Be relaxed: If you [13] **are feeling** nervous, this can make the other person feel uncomfortable. If you [14] **are** calm and relaxed, the other person will [15] **feel** the same.

Be yourself: To make a good first impression you [16] **do need** [17] **to fit** in to a certain extent. But do not go out of your comfort zone in trying to give the right impression. Be true to yourself and the other person [18] **will see** that.

Be focussed: The person you [19] **are meeting** will [20] **be expecting** you to be focussed and attentive, so be just that. And he or she [21] **deserves** your undivided attention, so [22] **resist** reaching for your mobile phone.

1 ☐	5 ☐	9 ☐	13 ☐	17 ☐	21 ☐
2 ☐	6 ☐	10 ☐	14 ☐	18 ☐	22 ☐
3 ☐	7 ☐	11 ☐	15 ☐	19 ☐	
4 ☐	8 ☐	12 ☐	16 ☐	20 ☐	

2 Choose the correct words and phrases to complete the texts. More than one answer may sometimes be possible.

1 Do first impressions last? Well, it *depends / is depending* what you *mean / are meaning* by that. I *think / 'm thinking* it's the last impression of a first meeting that's important. It *seems / 's seeming* to me that it's the impression you leave someone with that really *counts / is counting*.

2 You *think / 're thinking* of going to Budapest? Well, my first impression was that it was quite like Prague, if you've ever been there. It sort of *looks / 's looking* quite similar, the old bridge and the view of the castle and church on the hill in front of you with the centre behind you. But after a while you *realize / 're realizing* that it's quite different. I *think / 'm thinking* people *seem / are seeming* to *prefer / be preferring* one or the other, and I *guess / 'm guessing* that might *depend / be depending* on which one you *see / are seeing* first.

3 Their apartment *is / is being* just amazing. Really nicely done, very tasteful and *must've cost / been costing* a fortune. Mind you, I think they *own / are owning* two or three flats that they *rent / 're renting* out so they can't be short of a few quid. Anyway, it's all very modern and minimalist, and you really *get / are getting* that 'wow factor' when you walk in.

3 🎧 **1 18** Complete the dialogues using the correct verb form: simple or continuous. Then listen and check your answers.

1 A: _____ (you / know) those people over there?
B: No, they _____ (not / look) familiar. But then again, I _____ (not / know) many people here, anyway. As you _____ (know), I _____ (not / work) here long.
A: No, I _____ (not / recognize) them either. I _____ (not / think) they _____ (work) here. Well, I _____ (not / see) them here before, at least.

2 A: Ah, David, I _____ (mean) to talk to you. I _____ (trust) you _____ (settle) in well in your new role.
B: Yes, thanks. Everything _____ (seem) to _____ (go) fine. I _____ (really / enjoy) the challenge, actually.
A: That's good to hear. And how _____ (you / get on) with everyone in the department? _____ (you / work) with any of them before?
B: No, I haven't, actually. But everyone _____ (seem) really nice, very welcoming.
A: Well, it _____ (sound) like everything _____ (go) fine. OK, I _____ (leave) you to it. And _____ (not / forget) my door _____ (be) always open if you _____ (need) anything.

3 A: _____ (you / know) who this bag
_____ (belong) to?
B: It _____ (look) like Tamara's.
A: Yes, I _____ (think) you might be right.
I _____ (imagine) she _____ (come
back) for it. I _____ (not / suppose) she
_____ (get) very far without it.

4 Complete these quotations about first impressions using the correct form of the verbs in the boxes. Then circle the stative verbs.

be	have	not/get

1 The strangest part about being famous _____
you _____ to give first impressions anymore.
Everyone already _____ an impression of you
before you meet them.
Kristen Stewart, actor

matter	say	size

2 First impressions _____ . Experts _____
we _____ up new people in somewhere
between 30 seconds and two minutes.
Elliott Abrams, diplomat

not/always/appreciate	come from	not/know	mean

3 We _____ where our first impressions
_____ or precisely what they _____ ,
so we _____ their fragility.
Malcolm Gladwell, journalist and author

LANGUAGE FOCUS Emphatic structures

5 Rewrite the sentences using the words given.

1 What impressed me was their attention to detail. *it*
It was their attention to detail that impressed me.

2 I don't understand how on earth this was allowed to happen. *what*
_____

3 I enjoyed that meal. *did*
_____

4 What worries me is not knowing the dangers. *it*
_____

5 I want to know where he got all his information from. *thing*
_____

6 It wasn't what he said, but the timing of it that surprised me. *what*
_____

6 Complete the responses with words or phrases to make them more emphatic.

1 A: The new marketing manager seems pretty good, don't you think?
B: Yes, his energy and drive struck me.
Yes, what _____ .

2 A: How's work?
B: Work's fine. But I'm not so keen on the commuting.
Work's fine. But it _____ .

3 A: There just seem to be more and more talent shows on TV these days.
B: Yeah. I can't understand why they are so popular.
Yeah. The thing _____ .

4 A: What a great place, hey?
B: Yes, I really like that you can get everywhere on foot.
Yes, what _____ .

5 A: Well, what did you think?
B: What really impressed me was their enthusiasm for the project.
Their _____ .

DICTATION

7 🎧 **1** **19** Listen to some advice about having a job interview. Complete the sentences.

1 _____
to start as you mean to go on. First, your interviewers will start to form an impression as soon as they see you, so
2 _____
you get your appearance right. 3 _____
your body language, eye contact, smile and handshake, so make sure they are all positive. 4 _____
can make all the difference; be as positive as you can and show interest in the interviewers' questions.
5 _____
to show that you want the job because it is a positive career move, not because you're not happy in your current or previous job. 6 _____
sets the tone for the interview and a positive attitude makes an invaluable first impression. Research suggests that
7 _____
determines whether or not they will be considered for the job.

READING

1 Look at the title of the article. What do you think the following colours, used in branding and web design, convey to the viewer or customer?

   a red   **b** black   **c** green   **d** blue   **e** orange

2 Read the whole text. How does the article describe the symbolism of each colour in Exercise 1? Did they match your ideas?

3 Read the text again. Choose the best way to complete the statements.

  1 The effect each colour has varies from person to person because …

    a colour has both natural and social/cultural associations.

    b when it comes to colour, people's individual tastes are different.

    c symbolism is related to different natural environments.

Colour in branding

Colour psychology is the study of how colours affect moods and behaviour. It is founded on the principle that each colour carries a different meaning for us: either an association with nature, such as the calming effect of the blue in the sky, or an association with social or cultural habits, like the happy yellow of the smiley face. This cultural aspect means that the same colour can have different significance for different people. White, for example, is a symbol of purity and cleanliness in western society, whereas in eastern culture, it more often has associations with unhappiness or mourning.

For marketers and advertisers, whose job is to get us to make the right associations (primarily through visual stimuli), appropriate use of colour has enormous significance, as colours convey emotions far more quickly and powerfully than words ever can. On average, people form an impression of a brand within 90 seconds and the most influential factor (70%) in that is colour.

While an agreed palette of colours and meanings exists – blue for calm and stability (e.g. Barclays Bank), red for passion and excitement (e.g. Ferrari), green for health and nature (e.g. Whole Foods Market), orange for friendliness and fun (e.g. Harley Davidson), and black for elegance and power (e.g. Chanel) – colour symbolism also has to do with context. Each colour has a whole host of cultural, linguistic, historical and political associations. In English-speaking countries, blue is associated with the cold and with sadness ('feeling blue'); in the United States blue is for the Democratic party, but in Britain is for the Conservative party. Colours are also subject to local changes in fashion – an avocado green bathroom suite was a must-have in British homes in the 1970s.

As cultures become closer through globalization and the Internet, companies can no longer be so certain about the associations that colours will provoke. Increasingly, they have to test their colour choices through market research and customer feedback. When Yahoo used its traditional logo purple as a background colour for its new weather app, the reaction (not to the app but the colour) was surprisingly negative – so much so that for a while they reverted to a blue background.

There is a tendency in web branding to opt for safety, using softer colours – blues, greens, greys, subtle shades of white – which convey simplicity and modernity and are unlikely to offend. The problem is that such colours are also unlikely to prompt action. Hubspot conducted an experiment to see if a button asking users to 'Get started now' would be more effective with a green or red background. They expected that the more friendly green and its association with 'go' (rather than red with its associations with warnings and 'stop') would yield higher action rates. In fact the eye-catching red gave 21% better results. Our emotional connection with colour is strong, but not entirely predictable. There is security in following traditional symbolism, but, as with other aspects of business, with colour it pays to experiment – with a little homework, of course.

2 It's very important to marketers and advertisers that people …

   a form a quick judgement about the meaning of a brand.

   b pay more attention to colour in brand design than to a verbal message.

   c interpret the brand's message correctly when they first see it.

3 The symbolism of each colour …

   a depends on many factors.

   b is more or less fixed.

   c is changing all the time.

4 The article implies that an avocado green suite in a bathroom …

   a is no longer fashionable in Britain.

   b was an unattractive colour.

   c was an unpopular choice of colour at the time.

5 Yahoo's new weather app is given as an example of …

   a how unpredictable the effects of a particular colour choice can be.

   b how companies are not prepared to admit they have made a mistake with colour choice.

   c how important it is not to ignore obvious colour associations such as blue with weather.

6 The author believes that experimenting with colour …

   a is a dangerous game for a company.

   b is the only way forward for companies.

   c is good for companies provided they test their ideas.

4 Complete the definitions with words from the text.

1 _____ = feeling or showing sorrow for the loss of a person

2 _____ = things which provoke a physical, mental or emotional reaction

3 _____ = a great number

4 _____ = returned to a previous state or condition

5 _____ = degrees of colour

6 _____ = attracting attention

VOCABULARY Feelings and emotions

5 Match the words (1–9) with their meanings (a–i).

1 off-putting		**a** soothing
2 stirring		**b** energizing
3 tempting		**c** distracting
4 disconcerting		**d** reassuring
5 infuriating		**e** compelling
6 relaxing		**f** rousing
7 stimulating		**g** enticing
8 comforting		**h** unsettling
9 irresistible		**i** maddening

WORD FOCUS *sense*

6 Add the correct word ending from the box to the word being defined.

-ation	-eless	-ibility	-ible	-itive
-itivity	-itize	-or	-ory	-uous

1 sens_____ adj. able to make or based on good judgements based on reason and experience

2 sens_____ adj. 1 aware of and able to understand something or someone's feelings, 2 easily offended or upset

3 sens_____ noun 1 the ability to understand something or someone's feelings, 2 easily offended

4 sens_____ adj. connected with your physical senses, e.g. sight

5 sens_____ noun a device that reacts to a stimulus such as light

6 sens_____ adj. giving pleasure to your senses

7 sens_____ adj. 1 having no meaning or purpose, 2 not using good judgement

8 sens_____ noun the ability to experience and understand deep feelings, especially in art and literature

9 sens_____ verb make someone more aware of something, negative is *de-*

10 sens_____ noun 1 a feeling when something affects your body, 2 a general feeling that is difficult to explain

7 Complete the sentences with the words (1–10) from Exercise 6.

1 The outside light has a _____ which is triggered by movement.

2 It wasn't very _____ to book the hotel without checking out the reviews first, was it?

3 Be careful what you say. He can be very _____ to criticism.

4 The eyes, ears and tongue are examples of an animal's _____ organs.

5 You need to show a bit more _____ towards people at times. What you said was quite hurtful.

6 I had a sort of _____ of falling, like in a dream, even though I was standing perfectly still.

7 The musical _____ of Stravinsky was influenced by jazz.

8 The demonstration was marred by what the police described as unprovoked and _____ violence.

9 Research suggests that, because of the Internet, people are becoming more _____ to seeing acts of violence.

10 I find some of Debussy's music to be very _____ .

3.4 Contrary to popular belief

DESCRIBING BELIEFS AND FACTS

1 🎧 **1 20** Listen to four short talk extracts. Are these statements true (T) or false (F)?

1 A computer monitor screen should ideally be 50–60 cm away from the eyes. ☐

2 We should ideally drink eight glasses of water a day. ☐

3 Einstein was good at maths and science as a child. ☐

4 Sherlock Holmes often used the phrase 'Elementary, my dear Watson'. ☐

2 🎧 **1 20** Complete the extracts. Then listen again and check your answers.

1 In the work place, the c_____ wisdom is that your computer monitor should be about 50–60 cm away. In a_____ fact, the best distance is as far away as possible while you are still able to read what's on the screen. The 50–60 cm recommendation is probably too near and could be damaging to the eyes over time.

2 S_____, we should be drinking eight glasses of water a day. But, in r_____, the amount we need depends on a number of factors ... It s_____ that this figure was thought up basically as part of an awareness-raising campaign ...

3 It has often been said that Albert Einstein failed mathematics at school. But this, however, is not the c_____. On the f_____ of it, Einstein was actually very good at maths as a child. He did, however, ap_____ fail the entrance exam into polytechnic school ... and he al_____ scored highly in the mathematics and science sections.

4 The popular b_____ is that Sherlock Holmes used to use the phrase 'Elementary, my dear Watson' ... The t_____ is, however, that the character never actually said those words ... The words 'my dear Watson' and 'elementary' did both appear a few lines apart in ... *The Crooked Man*, but they never in f_____ appeared together as in the famous misquote.

3 Put the words in the correct order to complete the sentences.

1 _____

think / you / that / would aging is the biggest cause of hearing loss. But _____
fact / actual / in the majority of cases of hearing loss are due to prolonged listening to excessive noise.

2 _____

of / face / the / on / it, the film was a success, but apparently it hardly made any money at all.

3 Ostensibly, the minister resigned.

_____

matter / but / the / of / truth / the is that he was forced out. And _____
lies / the / surface / behind a rather intricate trail of evidence against him.

4 _____

is / belief / popular / the that career success is due primarily to hard work, belief and perseverance.

_____

truth, / however, / is / the that the biggest factor is luck.

_____

that / seems / it being in the right place at the right time can be the difference between success and failure.

5 In terms of financial investment, _____

the / wisdom / is / conventional that wide diversification is best. _____
case / but / not / always / that's / the. In reality, too much diversification can result in a trade-off between diversification and returns.

6 _____

the / of / outward / gives / he / appearance someone who is confident and in control. _____

_____

told / if / be / truth, however, he's not like that at all. In fact, he's rather shy and insecure.

PRONUNCIATION Stress in contrasts

4 🎧 **1 21** Read the sentences. Underline the word in the second sentences you think will be stressed. Then listen and check your answers.

1 In terms of light, mixing red and green makes yellow. But with paint it makes a sort of brown colour.

2 They say you can see the Great Wall of China from the moon. But, in fact, you can't.

3 Contrary to popular belief, Thomas Edison didn't invent the light bulb. He did, however, patent and improve an existing design.

4 Bats are not blind. All bat species have eyes and can see and, in fact, some have excellent vision.

5 Humans have more than the five commonly cited senses of sight, smell, taste, touch and hearing. Among other things, humans can sense balance, acceleration, pain and relative temperature.

6 Chameleons do not change colour to match their background. But they do change colour to communicate and as a response to mood, temperature and light conditions.

WRITING SKILL Describing different perspectives

5 Read the sentences. Correct the mistakes.

1 In term of communication and collaboration, an open-plan workspace may have positive results. However, research suggests that it may have an adverse effect when comes to concentration and productivity.

2 From point of view for office equipment, heating and electricity costs, an open-plan workspace can benefit economically a business.

3 The chairless office has a number of benefits for the employee, notably when coming to reported physical well-being.

4 Financial speaking, family-run businesses tend to have long-term rather than short-term goals.

5 From purely business perspective, the aim is simply to maximize the value of the organization.

6 Statistical, there are more billionaires in London than in any other city in the world, with over 80 claiming the city to be their home.

6 Complete the sentences using a word formed from the adjectives in brackets. Make any other changes necessary.

1 _____ perspective, it is likely that coins were first used as an expression of gratitude. (historic)

2 In _____ , the software delivers excellent performance. (flexible)

3 _____ , laser eye surgery is a relatively simple procedure. (technical)

4 _____ speaking, isn't using a tablet preferable to buying books? (environmental)

5 The film is _____ inaccurate in a number of instances. (factual)

6 _____ perspective, there needs to be a number of modifications to the device. (safe)

7 Complete the text using the words in the box.

| commercially | historically | socially | in terms |
| of engineering | from a social science perspective |
| from a business point of view |

¹ _____ , autonomous robots have been largely used for tasks requiring very little interaction with humans. Today, however, robotics is concerned more and more with the development of ² _____ interactive robots. And one of the main driving forces for this is the use of robots in the workplace. ³ _____ , there is an ever-increasing range of applications for robots that interact with humans, especially in the tourism and hospitality sector. In the US, one hotel has introduced a robot bellhop that accompanies guests to their rooms. Robotic tour guides are being developed that not only direct people around cities, but which respond to questions about the places being visited. Robot waiting staff have been used in restaurants for some time and a US hardware store is currently experimenting with a robot that welcomes customers and accompanies them to the correct aisle. ⁴ _____ , this makes sense. The novelty factor seems, at least for now, to be generating income while, in the long run, companies will benefit from reduced staffing overheads. Business and commerce aside, building robots that can interact with humans is benefitting us in a number of other ways. ⁵ _____ , we are learning a lot about ourselves from the process of building and programming socially intelligent robots. And ⁶ _____ , mimicking human movement, speech and expression is driving biomechanics technology forward at an unprecedented rate.

Presentation 2 | MY PIECE OF ADVICE

YOUR IDEA

1 Read three different pieces of advice. Match each piece of advice with a topic (a–c).

1 Pawel: It's not very exciting. Boring as managing your money might seem, there is no doubt that it is very important. But where do you begin? Some people find saving to be a real challenge. They might worry about not having enough cash for day-to-day purchases if they've committed to saving money. Sometimes it is better to set an overall saving goal. To stop yourself worrying about the money you have to set aside every month, it can help to have a target to focus on. The first target might just be to make sure you have a back-up fund in case of emergencies. But after that you can start saving for bigger things – a new computer, a car, maybe even a house? See, saving can be exciting! ☐

2 Simone: I'm sure I'm not the only person who has trouble when packing for a trip. I go away quite often for business and, as you can imagine, I always struggle with the weight limits that airlines have for passenger luggage. So here are my tips for business travellers. Try just taking hand luggage if you can. This might limit what you can take, but you'll be surprised how much you can fit into a carry-on case. Now, I recommend making a list of exactly what you need to take – just the bare essentials that you cannot do without. This makes it much easier to get organized and pack sensibly. Ever since I started making a packing list I've always managed to fit my things into a smaller suitcase. It makes my journeys abroad much more stress-free, and I'm sure it will for you too. ☐

3 Gastón: I used to get called terrible nicknames by my friends. They were only joking, but I knew the reason why – I'd turn up late again and again whenever we met up for a get-together. I knew I had to do something about this, so I took action. Whenever we planned an activity, I would save the date and time in my smartphone calendar. I'd also set reminders a week and a day before the actual event. It might not be for everyone, but if you're having trouble like this then I really recommend taking advantage of technology in this way. Now that my phone keeps track of my appointments, I never have to worry about being late again! ☐

a Timekeeping
b Finances
c Travelling

2 Write notes about a piece of advice you could give.

_____

_____

_____

_____

3 Organize the information from your notes. Write sentences on these areas.

1 The main focus of my advice _____

_____

2 Who this advice is aimed at _____

_____

3 How this advice could help someone do something

_____

_____

4 Practise your presentation out loud. Focus on the structure of your presentation. Try to …

- begin strong – think about how you will really grab the audience's attention and hold it.
- create a need to listen – explain why you're talking about this topic and why it's important to the audience.
- end powerfully – summarize your main message and emphasize your emotional attachment to it.

ORGANIZING YOUR PRESENTATION

5 Match the five steps of the presentation with the examples of useful language (a–e).

1 Introduce yourself and say why you're talking about this topic ☐
2 Set the scene and give your main piece of advice ☐
3 Explain the effects of this advice ☐
4 Summarize the main points from your presentation ☐
5 Thank the audience for listening ☐

a So, to sum up what I've said, you can solve this problem very simply. Just a small change can improve your shopping experience immensely.

b This practical tip should help you avoid hurting your hands when you have to carry a lot of shopping home. You do have to make an investment in buying the plastic ring, but you can use it time and time again.

c Thank you for your attention! We have a bit of time left. If you have any questions, I'll do my best to answer them.

d Hello. My name's Patricia, and I'm here today to offer you a piece of advice.

e Have you ever had trouble carrying your shopping home? All those bags can get pretty heavy. Well, the solution is to buy a special ring-shaped piece of plastic. Just loop all the bag handles onto the piece of plastic and you'll be able to carry them all easily.

YOUR PRESENTATION

6 Read the useful language on the left and make notes for your presentation.

1 Introduce yourself and say why you're talking about this topic What's one piece of advice that you always give? Well, I'm here today to suggest … This talk will …	
2 Give your main piece of advice Have you ever … ? The solution is … You can solve this by …	
3 Explain the effects of this advice This practical tip … You do have to … It should help you …	
4 Summarize the main points from your presentation My conclusion is that … So, to sum up what I've said, … Going over the main points again …	
5 Thank the audience for listening Thank you for … We have … If you have any questions, I'll …	

7 Film yourself giving your presentation or practise in front of a mirror. Give yourself marks out of ten for …

- using relaxed body language. ☐ /10
- including relevant stories about yourself or people you know. ☐ /10
- following the five steps in Exercise 6. ☐ /10
- using correct grammar. ☐ /10

4 Human interaction

4.1 Your body language shapes who you are

TEDTALKS

AMY CUDDY was born in 1972 and grew up in the small town of Robesonia in Pennsylvania, USA. She was a classically trained ballet dancer and, through high school and as an undergraduate at the University of Colorado, she continued to take her dancing seriously. While a student, she also worked as a roller-skating waitress at a local diner.

When she was in her second year of her university studies, Cuddy was involved in a road accident and suffered severe head trauma. She was told it was likely that she would not fully recover and that she might not be able to finish her undergraduate degree. Her IQ fell by about 30 points. Cuddy had to take time off from her studies and had to 'relearn how to learn'. She worked hard and 'studied circles around everyone'. After two years, her IQ had returned and she could dance again. By the time she returned to university, because of her experiences and her understanding of how the brain functions, she had developed a deep interest in social psychology.

Cuddy completed her studies and graduated from the University of Colorado in 1998. She then began a job as a research assistant at the University of Massachusetts. She completed an MA in social psychology and earned her PhD in the same subject from Princeton in 2005. Cuddy then held the position of Assistant Professor of Psychology at Rutgers University and Assistant Professor at the Kellogg School of Management at Northwestern University before joining the Business Administration faculty at Harvard Business School in 2008, where she teaches courses in negotiation and power and influence. Cuddy's main areas of research are the psychology of power, stereotyping and discrimination. She also specializes in nonverbal communication and how body posture can be empowering, known as 'power posing.' She believes this interest in nonverbal communication stems from her time as a ballet dancer.

Amy Cuddy

CAREER PATHWAYS

1 Read the text. Answer the questions.

1 Where does Cuddy's interest in social psychology stem from?
2 From how many universities did Cuddy obtain an academic qualification?
3 Which phrase in paragraph 2 means she studied harder than her fellow students?
4 How do you think Cuddy's current professional interests are related to her road accident experience?
5 How has Cuddy's interest in ballet influenced her career?

TED PLAYLIST

2 Other TED speakers are interested in topics similar to Amy Cuddy's TED Talk. Read the descriptions of four TED Talks at the top of page 35. In your opinion, which is the best title for this playlist, a, b or c?

a Problems of self-image
b Posture and gesture
c Body and mind

3 Read the TED playlist again. Find a speaker who ...

1 wants to help people deal with physical issues.
2 can give us more confidence in our abilities.
3 is interested in the effects of body language.

▶ **Ron Gutman: The hidden power of smiling**

Ron Gutman reviews a raft of studies about smiling, and reveals some surprising results. Did you know your smile can be a predictor of how long you'll live and has a measurable effect on your well-being? Flex a few facial muscles as you learn more about this contagious behaviour.

▶ **Meaghan Ramsey: Why thinking you're ugly is bad for you**

About 10,000 people a month Google the phrase, 'Am I ugly?' Meaghan Ramsey of the Dove Self-Esteem Project has a feeling many of them are young girls. In a deeply unsettling talk, she walks us through the surprising impacts of low body and image confidence, and then shares the key things we can do to disrupt this reality.

▶ **Emily Balcetis: Why some people find exercise harder than others**

Why do some people struggle more than others to keep off the pounds? Social psychologist Emily Balcetis shows research that addresses one of the many factors: vision – the fact that we all view the world differently. In an informative talk, she offers a surprisingly simple solution to overcome these differences.

▶ **Carol Dweck: The power of believing that you can improve**

Carol Dweck researches 'growth mindset' – the idea that we can grow our brain's capacity to learn and to solve problems. In this talk, she describes two ways to think about a problem that's slightly too hard for you to solve. A great introduction to this influential field.

4 Find verbs or phrasal verbs in the TED playlist that mean the same as the words and phrases (a–e).

   a avoid   **b** expand   **c** bend
   d explain step by step   **e** prevent from continuing

5 Which talk would you most like to see? Why? Watch the talk at TED.com.

AUTHENTIC LISTENING SKILLS
Linking: assimilation and reduction

6 🎧 **1 22** You are going to hear a podcast in which a member of the *Keynote* team talks about Emily Balcetis's TED Talk, *Why some people find exercise harder than others*. Listen to this extract from the talk and mark how the sounds in the words in bold are assimilated or reduced.

   ... the **suggestion being** that we **ought to adopt what** the speaker calls an 'eye on the prize' strategy …

7 🎧 **1 23** Listen to the sentence and underline the sounds that are assimilated and reduced.

   I have to say, I'm also kind of curious about what other similar strategies could be developed …

LISTENING

8 🎧 **1 24** Listen to the full podcast. Are these sentences true (T) or false (F)?

   1 According to the podcaster, the purpose of ☐
      Balcetis's research was to show how exercise could change your perception of the world.

   2 Nick is someone who has always liked ☐
      to exercise and go to the gym.

9 🎧 **1 24** Listen again. Answer the questions.

   1 According to the podcaster, what did the unmotivated participants in the experiment feel about the finish line?
   2 Compared to the unmotivated participants, how did the motivated participants exercise?
   3 How could the 'eye on the prize' strategy be transferable?
   4 Why did Nick find the research in the talk compelling?
   5 How did Nick use the 'eye on the prize' strategy in his own life?

VOCABULARY IN CONTEXT

10 Read the extracts from the podcast. Choose the correct meaning of the words in bold.

   1 I watched Emily Balcetis's talk about how perception is ultimately **subjective**.
      a unpredictable ☐   **b** imaginary ☐
      c personal ☐
   2 I am a person who **sets great store by** fitness and a healthy lifestyle.
      a values highly ☐   **b** makes a lot of time for ☐
      c invests a lot of money in ☐
   3 … who lack the **requisite** willpower to see such a programme through.
      a strong ☐   **b** personal ☐   **c** necessary ☐
   4 I'm also curious about what other similar strategies could be developed and **deployed** …
      a made use of ☐   **b** refined ☐
      c promoted ☐
   5 **Incremental** improvements to my levels of strength have been 'prizes' unto themselves, …
      a poor ☐   **b** minor ☐   **c** small increasing ☐

4.2 How we communicate

GRAMMAR Past forms

1 Complete the extracts using the correct past form of the verbs in the boxes.

have	limit	make	measure	weigh

1 The first telephone call from a hand-held mobile phone _____ in 1973. Until then, mobile telephony _____ to phones installed in cars. The phone used for this call, produced by Motorola, _____ approximately 2 kg, _____ 23 × 13 cm and _____ a talk time of 30 minutes.

account	communicate	mark	propose
rise	will/become	work	

2 In the late 1980s, computer scientist Sir Tim Berners-Lee, who _____ for CERN (The European Organization for Nuclear Research) at the time, first _____ what _____ the World Wide Web. This _____ the beginning of the modern Internet as we know it today and it had immediate impact on global communication. In 1993, it _____ for 1% of all telecommunicated information, which _____ to 51% by 2000 and, by 2007, more than 97% of all information passing through telecommunications networks _____ by the Internet.

be	not/be	can/produce	can/also/produce
develop	discover	invent	require
seek	start	use	

3 People _____ a range of paper-like materials such as papyrus and parchment for a long time before paper _____ in ancient China around 2,200 years ago. However, these original materials _____ expensive, in limited supply or _____ extensive preparation, so an alternative _____ . People soon _____ that paper made from wood _____ easily, cheaply and in almost any location. And, after large scale manufacturing techniques _____ , it _____ in much larger quantities. Nevertheless, it _____ for another 1,000 years or so that papermaking and manufacturing _____ in Europe.

2 Choose the correct words or phrases to complete the text.

People [1] *had rhythmically beat / had been rhythmically beating* objects for a long time before then, but it [2] *wasn't / hadn't been* until around 7,000 years ago that an animal skin [3] *was first stretched / was first being stretched* over a hollow object. But the drum [4] *was / would be* for much more than simply creating music. Drums [5] *were / used to be* initially a means of communication, particularly over distance. In fact, the drum is possibly the world's first mass communication device. And historically, one of the main uses of the drum [6] *was / would be* military. Around 3,000 years ago, Chinese soldiers [7] *used / had used* drums to set a marching pace, and different rhythms or patterns [8] *would be giving / would give* orders or announcements. Different tempos [9] *were also to be used / would also be used* to influence the soldiers' mood and morale. In other parts of the world, Aztec armies [10] *were known to have used / had been known to use* drums to send orders and signals to warriors and ancient Sanskrit writings from India describe tribes charging into battle to the beat of the war drum. During the English Civil War, junior officers [11] *were carrying / would carry* drums and [12] *use / were using* them to relay commands over the noise of battle. Different regiments [13] *were having / would have* unique drum patterns that only they [14] *used to recognize / would recognize*. By the end of the 19th century the role of drums in the battlefield [15] *had all but ended / would all but end* and their use [16] *had become / would have become* limited to the parade ground and in marching bands.

3 🎧 1 25 Complete the dialogues with the past forms of the words in brackets. Then listen and check your answers.

1 A: It was great to see you last night.
   B: You too. It was great to catch up. And it's a shame we [1] _____ (have to) leave so soon. I wish we [2] _____ (could / stay) a little longer.

2 A: I really struggled with that last assignment.
   B: I didn't realize. You [3] _____ (should / say) something. I [4] _____ (would / be) happy to help.
   A: Thanks, anyway, but it's all done now. But if I [5] _____ (know) it would be difficult, I [6] _____ (might / well / choose) a different topic.

3 A: I was late for work again this morning. My phone alarm didn't work, again.
   B: You [7] _____ (should / tell) me. I [8] _____ (could / give) you a lift.

4 A: Where is he?
   B: Not here, that's for sure. He [9] _____ (might / not / get) the message.
   A: But he was here earlier.
   B: Well, he [10] _____ (might / not / pay) attention. You know what he's like.

4 Rewrite the sentences using the verbs in italics so the meaning is similar.

1 It's possible that the Internet wasn't working earlier. *might*

_____

2 It was a really bad move to phone him. I regret it now. *should*

_____

3 I couldn't get hold of them. I think I might have the wrong number. *able*

_____

4 My grandparents would often call me for a long chat at weekends. *used*

_____

5 I never used to want to go to bed as a child. *would*

_____

6 Sarah wasn't in the office yesterday so it's impossible that you spoke to her. *can't*

_____

7 Maybe you told me, but I can't remember to be honest. *could*

_____

8 He constantly used to be on his phone, whether it was WhatsApp or Facebook or whatever. *would*

_____

GRAMMAR Inversion with adverbial phrases

5 Complete the news extracts with the words in the box.

Hardly	Never before	No sooner	Not until
Only by	Only when	So	Such

1 _____ unexpected was the announcement that even the minister's own colleagues were taken by surprise.

2 _____ he arrived at the conference centre, did the minister realize the extent of ill-feeling he had generated.

3 _____ was the second edition of the book on sale than the third and fourth were being planned.

4 _____ was the hectic pace of the game, it came as no surprise when Miller quickly netted his second.

5 _____ both sides agree to and hold an unconditional ceasefire, will talks be possible.

6 _____ had the dust begun to settle on the expenses accusations when he was implicated in the cash-for-questions scandal.

7 _____ being united will they have any chance of defeating the government.

8 _____ , at all the meetings that I have attended, have I seen such enormous attendances as I have seen during this campaign.

6 Rewrite the sentences using inversion with adverbial phrases so the meaning is the same.

1 They opened the exam paper and immediately began to panic.
   No sooner had they opened the exam paper when they immediately began to panic.

2 The central bank would consider the move only if the economy suddenly got much stronger.

_____

3 You cannot leave the exam room unescorted under any circumstances.

_____

4 He didn't feel nervous until he stood at the podium ready to speak.

_____

5 I was not only leaving a special place, but also my family and friends.

_____

6 He finally left the stage after he had fully soaked up the rapturous applause.

_____

DICTATION

7 🎧 **1 | 26** Listen to someone talking about the origins of Google. Complete the text.

Google started out in 1995 as a research project by two PhD students at Stanford University, Larry Page and Sergey Brin. Page [1] _____ as his research topic and, among his ideas, was [2] _____ on the World Wide Web. His supervisor encouraged him to follow this idea, [3] _____ . Page [4] _____ , but he decided to team up with Sergey Brin, whom Page [5] _____ .

The pair soon developed a prototype search engine, which used the Stanford website and had the domain name google.stanford.edu. [6] _____ , but the pair saw the commercial potential and the domain google.com was registered on September 15, 1997. By the end of 1998, Google [7] _____ . The general feeling in the industry was that [8] _____ , but it was also considered to be more user-friendly, simpler, faster and more technologically innovative.

READING

1 Look at the definitions of the two words in the title. What do you think the article is going to be about?

Edwardian = relating to a period of British history from 1901 to 1914

Twitter = an online social networking service where users send and read short messages (140 characters maximum)

2 Read the article and match the headings (1–6) with the paragraphs (A–E).

1 Meteoric rise ☐
2 Nothing new ☐
3 Secret messages ☐
4 A passing fashion ☐
5 Snail mail ☐
6 A practical tool ☐

Edwardian **Twitter**

A

Instant messaging is seen very much as a phenomenon of 21st-century communications, but in fact the practice dates back over 100 years to what is known as the 'Golden Age' of the postcard between 1902 and 1914. According to Dr Julia Gillen of Lancaster University in the UK, postcards were 'something like the Twitter of the Edwardian Age'.

B

These days we associate postcards with holidays and view them as a rather slow, even redundant, way of communicating. In fact, it's not uncommon these days for a postcard to arrive after the sender has returned home. But in the early part of last century, the postal service was much more frequent and efficient. In some towns in Edwardian Britain, there were as many as six deliveries a day. This meant people could send a message on a postcard and be confident of receiving a reply the same day.

C

We also think of texting and tweeting as something of a communications revolution, but the postcard craze was similarly rapid and ground-breaking. The first known printed picture postcard was produced in France in 1870, but the postcard as we know it today – with a picture on

the front and a divided space on the back, one half for the message and the other for the address – did not appear in Britain until 1902. Over the next eight years, a staggering six billion cards were sent.

D

The reasons for the postcard's popularity were much the same as those for instant messaging today – it's a quick, cheap and effective way of transmitting a simple message. This can be seen in the type of messages that people sent each other in Edwardian times. 'Please meet me off the train tomorrow at 2pm' or 'George will come and fetch the peelings and bring you a bit of pork, so don't get any meat.' One obvious difference is that they were not private, since the postman, or anyone else who chanced to see the card before the receiver, could read it. But the Edwardians had a neat solution for this too.

E

By putting the stamp in a particular position on the card and at a particular angle, the sender could signify certain meanings. According to the Philatelic Database, a stamp placed in the top centre of the card meant 'Yes', a bottom centre meant 'no'; upside down in the top left-hand corner meant 'I love you'; at a right-angle in line with the surname meant 'I long to see you'; and upright on the right edge of the postcard meant 'Write back immediately'. Such codes were adopted in other countries too, but interestingly, the signification of stamp position was not universal.

F

Following the Great War of 1914–18, there was a shortage of labour and the number of postmen, who had comprised three-quarters of the Civil Service workforce before the war, declined dramatically. This, and the spread of the telephone, saw the end of the use of postcards for 'instant messaging'.

3 Read the article again. Are these sentences true (T), false (F) or unknown (U)?

1 The Edwardian era is known as the Golden Age of the postcard because it was the period when the Post Office made the most profit out of postcards. ☐

2 The writer suggests that the picture postcard is no longer a good way of communicating because modern day postal services are too inefficient. ☐

3 In the Edwardian era communication by postcard could be as quick as communication by text message is today. ☐

4 The author is clearly impressed with how quickly and widely the use of postcards grew in the period between 1902 and 1910. ☐

5 The format that is used in postcards today was established in 1870. ☐

6 The example content of Edwardian messages in the article and the use of a stamp code suggest postcards were the main way of transmitting romantic messages. ☐

7 The writer suggests that international communication using stamp codes may not have worked so well. ☐

8 The main reason for the interruption in the postcard craze was the invention of the telephone. ☐

4 🎧 1 27 Listen to a researcher talking about Edwardian postcards. Tick (✓) the reasons people at the time criticized them.

1 Offensive pictures on the cards ☐
2 Informal writing style ☐
3 Bad spelling and punctuation ☐
4 Lazy form of communication ☐
5 No legal control over what was written ☐
6 Communication was too open / not private ☐

5 🎧 1 27 Listen again. What two parallels does the speaker make with today's communication?

VOCABULARY Body language

6 Complete the extracts with the correct form of the verbs in the box.

clench	drum	fold	raise	roll
scowl	shake	shrug	tap	yawn

1 'Can I just ask a question?' he said, tentatively _____ his hand.

2 'I totally disagree,' she said firmly, _____ her head.

3 Stella stood there with her arms _____ and a disapproving look on her face.

4 He _____ his fists in a mixture of frustration and anger.

5 'OK, so what do we do now?' she asked, _____ her fingers on the desk.

6 'Don't _____ your eyes at me in that manner,' she told him.

7 'Well, I've no idea what to do,' he said, _____ his shoulders.

8 He _____ his feet nervously as he waited for his name to be called.

9 'Go away!' she _____ at him, 'and don't come back.'

10 'You've been _____ all morning. Try to get a good night's sleep before class tomorrow,' she said.

WORDBUILDING Negative prefixes with adjectives

7 Complete the words with a negative prefix (e.g. in-, dis-).

1 _____affected, _____escorted, _____ending, _____intentional

2 _____efficient, _____accessible, _____frequent, _____exact

3 _____legal, _____literate, _____legible (words beginning with *l*)

4 _____probable, _____balanced, _____mature (words beginning with *p*, *b* and *m*)

5 _____replaceable, _____rational, _____regular (words beginning with *r*)

6 _____honest, _____approving, _____allowed, _____advantageous

7 _____stop, _____alcoholic, _____verbal, _____violent

8 Rewrite the sentences using adjectives with the correct negative prefix.

1 These figures are not accurate.

2 What you're saying is not logical.

3 It's not advisable to do that.

4 Your explanation is not adequate.

5 He made a few comments that weren't tasteful.

6 They're often not obedient.

7 It's a nice idea, but not practical.

8 That is not proper behaviour.

9 The disease isn't usually curable.

4.4 Is that what you meant?

SAYING THE RIGHT THING

1 🎧 **1** **28** Listen to seven short dialogues. Match them with the topics (a–g).

a Receiving a thank you gift ☐
b Arranging a meeting ☐
c Offering someone a lift ☐
d Inviting someone for a drink ☐
e Getting someone a coffee ☐
f Offering to help someone ☐
g Asking for time off work ☐

2 🎧 **1** **28** Complete the extracts from the dialogues in Exercise 1. Listen again and check your answers.

Conversation 1

1 B_____ n_____ . There's a problem with the RBC deal.
2 I'm n_____ a_____ Friday. Thursday s_____ me though.
3 I'd rather we meet i_____ p_____ .
4 Oh, b_____ t_____ w_____, I said I'd tell Julia when we were meeting.
5 I can g_____ her a r_____ if you like.

Conversation 2

6 Can I g_____ you a h_____ with that?
7 Not a_____ a_____ . Don't m_____ it.

Conversation 3

8 Can I h_____ a q_____ w_____ ?
9 S_____ to h_____ that.

Conversation 4

10 I can g_____ you a l_____ to the station if you like.
11 I don't want to p_____ you o_____ .
12 I can d_____ you o_____ on my w_____ .

Conversation 5

13 Can I g_____ you a_____ ?

Conversation 6

14 Oh, really, you s_____ h_____ .

Conversation 7

15 OK, n_____ m_____ . A_____ t_____ .
16 And s_____ hi f_____ me.

3 Rewrite the responses by replacing the words and phrases in bold with words and phrases from Exercise 2.

1 A: Can I see Tamara Bartosz?
   B: I'm afraid she's **busy** at the moment.
   _____

2 A: I'll call you about it later in the week.
   B: I think we should discuss it **face to face**.
   _____

3 A: Shall we say 6.30?
   B: Yep, 6.30 **is good for** me.
   _____

4 A: Are you going to the shop?
   B: Yes. **Would you like** something?
   _____

5 A: You wanted to see me?
   B: Yes, can I **talk to you briefly**?
   _____

6 A: This is to say thanks for a lovely evening last night.
   B: Ah, **it really wasn't necessary for you to get me something**.
   _____

7 A: I've got so much to do.
   B: Let me **help you** with some of it.
   _____

8 A: Do you think I'll get to the station in ten minutes?
   B: I can **take you in my car if you like**.
   _____

   A: Are you sure? I really don't want to **cause you any extra effort**.
   _____

PRONUNCIATION Appropriate intonation

4 🎧 **1** **29** Listen to the dialogues. Does the intonation rise (↑), fall (↓) or stay the same (-)?

1 A: Bad news, I'm afraid. I didn't get the job.
   B: Oh, I'm sorry to hear that.

2 A: Hi, Richard.
   B: Ah, Lucas. Can I have a quick word?

3 A: This is for you. To say thank you.
   B: That's very kind of you, but you really shouldn't have.

4 A: Let me give you a lift.
   B: Are you sure? I really don't want to put you out.

5 A: See you tomorrow.
   B: Yeah, bye. Oh, by the way, I'll be a little late in tomorrow.

6 A: Can I give you a hand with anything?
   B: That's good of you to offer, but I'm fine, thanks.

7 A: Thanks again for all your help.
   B: Not at all. Don't mention it.

8 A: That seat's taken, actually.
   B: Oh sorry. I didn't realize.

WRITING SKILL Checking for errors

5 Read the sentences and correct the mistakes.

1 Thank you for taking a time to consider our proposal.
2 Thank you for agreeing meet with us on Friday, but I really don't want to put out you.
3 I think it's important that you and Susan meet in the person as soon as possible.
4 We feel that the proposed relocation is unpractical and could in fact be unadvantageous.
5 He has fully admitted that his conduct was unproper.
6 I am sorry hear that the arrangements was not to your satisfaction.
7 I had quick word with Julian and he has agreed go ahead with the proposal.
8 Only when we have the full facts we can begin to assess the situation.

6 Read the letter. Correct 20 mistakes in the email.

TO:	FROM:
SUBJECT:	

Dear Alison,

I am writing to request your approval for attend the London Business Conference, which being held from 15–17 January next year. Conference theme is Risk Management and is aimed to industry stakeholders as forum for discuss the current state of risk management in private equity. Of particularly interest to us, is a focus to co-investments versus fund investments. As well as main conference talks, there is a number of workshops.

You may to recall that Samantha Mitchell had attended the conference last year and she found extremely relevant and useful. I believe she was presenting some of the key issues to the senior management team, which I think you might attended. This is something that I am of course prepared to do.

I have included an approximate breakdown of the costs to attend below:

- Conference Registration: £300.00

- Travel, accommodation and meals: £350.00

If you would like to find more about conference, their website is Londonbusiness.org.

Thank you in advance for take a time to consider this and I look very much forward hearing from you.

Best wishes,

Tom

7 Put the sentences in the correct order to complete the email.

a Marta Masini had joined Waterwells Books January last year and since then she is reliable, effective and valuable member in sales team. ☐
b Below is my reference for Ms Marta Masini. ☐
c I believe that Marta is going to be valuable addition to some organization that she may to join. While we regret the decision of Marta for moving on, I would recommend her without to hesitate. ☐
d Yours faithful, Carmen Napoli ☐
e Please be in touch if should you require the further information. ☐
f Dear Sir or Madam, 1
g She was consistently showing that both she able work independently and as part of team. Her communication skill is excellent and she very well is liked with her colleagues and has always good rapport with customers and other clients. ☐
h Marta is professional and efficient in approach to her work and having sound knowledge and understanding both the book-selling business and wider retail industry. ☐

8 Reread the email in Exercise 7 and correct the mistakes. Then write the complete email.

TO:	FROM:
SUBJECT:	

Writing 2 | AN ESSAY

IDEAS

You will read an essay responding to the two sources below.

Source 1

> If your job requires you to do a lot of travelling, meeting people from all over the world, you need to make a good impression. To do this, it's important to consider the culture you're trying to do business in. One example would be to greet people in a culturally appropriate way, such as a *namaste* in India.
>
> However, sometimes there is a risk of offending people by inadvertently using greetings incorrectly, for example by not bowing low enough to a senior Japanese businessman.

Source 2

> A lot of cultural differences are not immediately obvious. For instance, research has shown that requirements for personal space vary from culture to culture. This means that for North Americans 1.2m is a necessary range of personal space, but for South Americans it can be much smaller.
>
> It is a shame that these kinds of cultural differences are often not taught to those involved in global business, despite the fact that being aware of other cultures can make business run more smoothly.

Write your essay in **240–280 words** in an appropriate style.

1 In the essay you need to address the four points covered in the sources. List them in the order they appear in the sources.

a _____
b _____
c _____
d _____

MODEL

2 Read the essay. Match the four sections with a description (a–d) from Exercise 1.

1 ☐   2 ☐   3 ☐   4 ☐

'Culture' is a term that can be challenging to define. For many, it is the 'high culture' of art or literature, but for those in business, it is the subtle differences in the ways people act that differ from one social group to another.

[1] One example is the handshake: a strong handshake from an English supplier may be considered overly dominant by a Filipino customer. However, unless these differences are explicitly pointed out, it can be incredibly difficult to know what to research when you begin doing business abroad.

[2] In order to reduce the potential difficulties caused by a lack of cultural awareness, it is vital that business people who work with those from other cultural backgrounds are taught about these variations in social interaction. [3] This will reduce the likelihood of committing a faux pas. For example, an executive attending a business dinner in China should know that the dishes in the centre of the table are for everyone to share throughout the meal, and they should not pile food onto their plate before they begin, as you might in many Western countries. Such a mistake made during a negotiation could change people's impressions, and therefore influence prices they are willing to pay, to give just one example.

[4] People will obviously understand you are a foreigner and cannot be expected to be familiar with all of the nuances of their culture. Nevertheless, attempting to increase awareness of the norms of the culture you are doing business in shows a level of respect which reflects well on your company.

I believe that learning more about other cultures can only be a benefit to international business, and will ease the job of negotiators around the world.

3 Correct the following statements.

1 'Culture' is defined as the art or literature of a group of people.
2 Filipino people prefer a strong handshake.
3 In China, you should take all of the food that you want to eat at the start of the meal.
4 If you make a cultural mistake during negotiations, it doesn't matter.
5 Many people expect you to understand their culture completely if you're doing business with them.

USEFUL LANGUAGE

4 Find words in the model essay which match the definitions.

1 small and not easily noticed (adjective)
2 too; very (adverb)
3 clearly or directly, so it is easy to understand (adverb)
4 an action or mistake that is embarrassing because it is socially incorrect (phrase)
5 very small differences that are not usually very obvious (noun)
6 behaviours that are usual or expected within a culture (noun)

5 Add prepositions to complete the paragraph.

When historians look ¹_____ on the beginning of the 21ˢᵗ century, they are bound ²_____ mention the role of technology and how it has revolutionized our lives. ³_____ name just one example, virtual reality headsets now allow us to immerse ourselves ⁴_____ completely different surroundings. As this technology gets cheaper, it will become accessible ⁵_____ more and more people, and the desire ⁶_____ films and games that exploit these headsets will increase. Of course, there is also the question ⁷_____ how to deal ⁸_____ the downsides of such technology, like the motion sickness some people experience on wearing a VR headset, but it is only a matter ⁹_____ time before solutions are found to these problems.

6 These words (1–5) could be used in the essay in Exercise 8. Match them with their definitions (a–e).

1 beneficial ☐
2 instant ☐
3 frankly ☐
4 patently ☐
5 creativity ☐

a without doubt
b happening immediately
c being able to think of something new or imaginative
d with a helpful or useful effect which improves a situation
e said in an honest or direct way, but which people might not like

7 Use the words (1–5) from Exercise 6 and those below (a–e) to create collocations.

a unrealistic
b blossoms
c gratification
d true
e change

PLANNING

You will respond to the following two sources.

Source 1

The advent of the smartphone has led to a world of people constantly looking down to check what's happening on social media or to play mindless games, instead of engaging with the world around them. This is particularly true of young people who have grown up with mobile phones. Whether it's at home with the family or in the middle of a business meeting, attention is constantly divided and nobody seems to focus on one thing at a time any more.

Source 2

It's now possible for everyone to have the whole world in their pockets. No longer do you have to agonize for days over an elusive piece of information; you can simply pull out your phone and 'ask the Internet'. Communication and trade are easier than ever before, with products from around the world at the tips of your fingers and a huge range of options for communicating with the outside world.

Write your essay in **240–280 words** in an appropriate style.

8 Plan your essay. Identify the four key points from the sources. Write notes to decide how you will respond to them. Don't write full sentences yet.

WRITING

9 Write an essay to respond to the sources in Exercise 8. In your essay you should:
- refer to all four of the key points you have identified
- make your own opinion on the topic clear in the conclusion
- use a neutral or formal style

Write **240–280 words**.

ANALYSIS

10 Check your essay. Answer the questions.
- **Content:** Does the essay respond to all four points in the sources? Is it 240 to 280 words long?
- **Communicative achievement:** Is it written in a neutral or formal style? Is it clear to the reader what your opinion on the topic is?
- **Organization:** Is the essay logically organized? Does it use appropriate linking devices?
- **Language:** Does it use correct grammar and vocabulary? Is a good range of structures used?

5 Economic resources

5.1 The magic washing machine

TEDTALKS

HANS ROSLING was born in Uppsala, Sweden, in 1948. He studied statistics and medicine at Uppsala University, and then public health at St. John's Medical College, Bangalore, India. He became a licensed physician in 1976 and, from 1979 to 1981, he worked as a Medical Officer in Mozambique. In 1981, Rosling encountered an outbreak of a paralytic disease called konzo. He then spent two decades studying outbreaks of this disease in remote rural areas across Africa. His work in this area earned him an honorary PhD from Uppsala University. Among a number of other roles and achievements, Rosling has been health adviser to the WHO, UNICEF and a number of aid agencies and was one of the initiators of Médecins Sans Frontières in Sweden. He has co-authored a textbook on global health and has presented and appeared in a number of television programmes. Rosling is currently professor of global health at the Karolinska Institute in Stockholm.

Having always had a deep interest in the use of statistics, in 2005 Rosling co-founded the Gapminder Foundation together with his son and daughter-in-law. Gapminder developed the Trendalyzer software that converts statistics into moving, interactive graphics. Rosling's lectures using Gapminder graphics gained a global reputation for their creativity and originality and have won numerous awards. In 2007, Google acquired the Trendalyzer software.

Rosling has received a number of awards, including 'Speaker of the Year' from the Swedish Event Academy, one of *TIME Magazine's* '100 most influential people' and, in 2012, he was named 'International Swede of the Year'. He has also received honorary degrees from universities in Sweden, Norway and the UK and is a member of the Swedish Academy of Sciences.

Hans Rosling

CAREER PATHWAYS

1 Read the text. Are these statements true (T) or false (F)?

1 Rosling has qualifications from academic institutions in Sweden, India, Mozambique, Norway and the UK. ☐
2 Rosling discovered a new disease called konzo. ☐
3 Rosling was one of the founders of the global organization Médecins Sans Frontières. ☐
4 Today, Rosling's main field is the presentation and interpretation of statistics. ☐
5 Rosling is known for his presentation techniques. ☐

TED PLAYLIST

2 Other TED speakers are interested in topics similar to Hans Rosling's TED Talk. Read the descriptions of four TED Talks at the top of page 45. In your opinion, which is the best title for this playlist, a, b or c?

a Celebrating innovation
b Affordable, practical technology
c Technology without resources

3 Read the TED playlist again. Find a speaker who ...

1 talks about improvising with old technology to make new technological solutions.
2 advocates a democratic approach to technological innovation.
3 made a technological solution for a domestic problem.
4 questions our assumptions about the universal benefits of technology.

4 Read the TED playlist again. Find five compound adjectives.

▶ **Richard Turere: My invention that made peace with the lions**

In the Maasai community where Richard Turere lives with his family, cattle are all-important. But lion attacks were growing more frequent. In this short, inspiring talk, the young inventor shares the solar-powered solution he designed to safely scare the lions away.

▶ **Jon Gosier: The problem with 'trickle-down techonomics'**

Hooray for technology! It makes everything better for everyone! Right? Well, no. When a new technology, like ebooks or health trackers, is only available to some people, it has unintended consequences for all of us. Jon Gosier explains how 'the real innovation is in finding ways to include everyone'.

▶ **William Kamkwamba: How I built a windmill**

When he was just 14 years old, Malawian inventor William Kamkwamba built his family an electricity-generating windmill from spare parts, working from rough plans he found in a library book.

▶ **Vinay Venkatraman: Technology crafts for the digitally underserved**

Two thirds of the world may not have access to the latest smartphone, but local electronic shops are adept at fixing older tech using low-cost parts. Vinay Venkatraman explains his work in 'technology crafts', for example, how a mobile phone, a lunchbox and a flashlight can become a digital projector for a village school.

5 Which talk would you most like to see? Why? Watch the talk at TED.com.

AUTHENTIC LISTENING SKILLS
Prediction

6 🎧 **1 30** You are going to hear a podcast in which a member of the *Keynote* team talks about Richard Turere's TED Talk, *My invention that made peace with the lions*. Listen to the first part. What did the podcaster notice about the speaker before watching the talk?

LISTENING

7 🎧 **1 31** Listen to the full podcast. Choose the correct words or phrases to make true sentences.

1 According to the podcaster, Richard Turere describes how he arrived at an answer to his problem *purely by chance / by trying out different solutions.*

2 Ruth likes the message of the talk because it's about *not giving up / not being satisfied with less.*

8 🎧 **1 31** Listen again. Choose the correct option to complete the sentences. Sometimes both answers are possible.

1 At a young age Richard Turere was given the task of managing his father's *farm / animals.*

2 Ruth can relate to *being given big responsibilities as a child / being determined in the face of a challenge.*

3 Ruth wonders if Richard is so mature because he wants to *win his family's respect / take care of his family.*

4 She also wonders if he is so resourceful because *resources are limited / his family trained him to be resourceful.*

VOCABULARY IN CONTEXT

9 Read the extracts from the podcast. Choose the correct meaning of the words in bold.

1 He was then faced with a major issue and **set about** trying to work out a way to resolve it.
   a worked tirelessly ☐
   b decided on positively ☐
   c started determinedly ☐

2 What's nice about his talk is how he **takes us through** his process of trial and error.
   a demonstrates to us ☐
   b explains to us ☐
   c doesn't boast to us about ☐

3 .... rather than giving up and **becoming down** about a difficult situation.
   a becoming frustrated ☐
   b becoming depressed ☐
   c feeling overwhelmed ☐

4 Was he motivated by not wanting to **let** his father and the rest of his family **down**?
   a disappoint ☐
   b seem superior to ☐
   c do the same job as ☐

5 Is that a result of always having only limited resources to **fall back on**?
   a rely on ☐
   b spend money on ☐
   c improvise with ☐

5.2 Energy-hungry world

GRAMMAR Passive forms

1 Read the extracts and decide if the verb in bold would be better in the passive voice. If it would, rewrite the extract.

1 In 1954, the Obninsk Nuclear Power Plant in the USSR was the world's first nuclear power plant to produce electricity for a power grid. It **generated** around five megawatts of power.

_____

_____

2 Piezoelectricity is the electrical charge produced in certain materials (such as crystals and ceramics) when someone or something **applies** physical pressure.

_____

_____

3 The United States is the world's second largest energy consumer. It **obtains** the majority of this energy (around 68%) from fossil fuels.

_____

_____

4 The existence of the greenhouse effect was first proposed in 1824. However, we didn't **use** the term 'greenhouse' in this way until the beginning of the 1900s.

_____

_____

2 Rewrite the sentences using the passive. Include the agent if it is needed.

1 Nuclear power currently delivers around 12% of the world's electricity demand.
Around 12% of the world's electricity demand is currently delivered by nuclear power.

2 World energy consumption is the total energy that humans use. Authorities and agencies usually calculate and measure it per year.

_____

_____

_____

3 More than 80 countries are currently using wind power. In 2013, wind generated almost 3% of the world's total electricity.

_____

_____

4 Humans have used solar energy since ancient times and today experts predict that, by the middle of the century, solar power could provide a third of all global energy. This would consequently reduce CO_2 emissions to 'very low levels'.

_____

_____

_____

_____

5 They expect to complete construction of the new nuclear power plant by 2025. The government insists that the plant will generate enough energy to power six million homes.

_____

_____

_____

_____

6 People generally agree that energy independence and security is one of today's key political issues and one which we need to address urgently.

_____

_____

_____

3 Complete the news extracts using the passive infinitive or passive -ing form of the verb.

1 The forum gave a clear message that the current global guidelines on carbon emissions need _____ (reassess).

2 A number of MPs said they were angry _____ (not/inform) of the apparent U-turn before it was announced by the Prime Minister on Monday.

3 The majority of local residents are angry at _____ (not/consult) on the matter.

4 Thousands of doctors gathered outside parliament yesterday to protest against _____ (force) to work at weekends. A new law is _____ (introduce) which means all junior doctors are likely to have to work at least one weekend per month.

5 _____ (find) guilty, Ford will return to court _____ (sentence) on Friday.

6 _____ (beat) for the sixth game in a row was enough for chairman Tony Evans and Conway can expect _____ (sack) when the two meet tomorrow.

4 Complete the text using the passive form of the verbs in the box.

be	develop	embed	generate (×2)
~~introduce~~	place	test	

In 2010, in Toulouse, France, a pilot scheme [1] *was introduced* to power street lights using energy [2] _____ by the feet of pedestrians passing by. A number of pressure-sensitive modules, [3] _____ with electricity-producing microsensors, [4] _____ under sections of pavement in the city centre. The idea of using human footsteps to generate electricity in this way had been around for a long time, but this was the first time that such a scheme was able [5] _____ on the street. Until then, the modules were unsuitable for street use as, according to the designers, Dutch company SDC, they needed [6] _____ 'virtually jumped on' for enough power to [7] _____ . However, a model [8] _____ on which you could walk normally and still produce enough energy to power nearby lights.

5 Rewrite the sentences in two ways using passive structures.

1 They offered compensation to everyone.
Everyone was offered compensation.
Compensation was offered to everyone.

2 They gave the award to Professor Helen Stephenson for her work on climate change.
_____
_____

3 The prosecution lawyer showed the court CCTV footage of the incident.
_____
_____

4 I guess someone sent me the email by mistake.
_____
_____

5 In total, people gave the charity over a million dollars.
_____
_____

GRAMMAR Nominalization in passive sentences

6 Match the words in the box with *make*, *reach* or *give*.

agreement	an allowance	an announcement
an answer	an assessment	~~an attempt~~
a complaint	a compromise (×2)	a conclusion
consideration (to)	a decision (×2)	information
an order	preference (to)	priority (to)
progress	thought (to)	

1 make   *an attempt* / _____ / _____ / _____ / _____ / _____ / _____

2 reach   _____ / _____ / _____ / _____

3 give   _____ / _____ / _____ / _____ / _____ / _____ / _____

7 Rewrite the sentences using nominalization. Use phrases from Exercise 6 with the verb in the correct passive form.

1 It looks like they didn't think about the design very much. It doesn't look like *much thought was given to the design*.

2 They didn't allow for any delays in the development process.
No _____

3 We have duly considered everything in making this decision.
Due _____

4 A number of people complained about the service.
A number of _____

5 I'm pleased to say that we have agreed on most aspects of the deal.
I'm pleased to say that _____

6 It is clear that we need to prioritize renewable energy sources.
It is clear that _____

7 Initial reports suggest that the parties seem to have compromised regarding CO_2 emission quotas.
Initial reports suggest _____

8 We progressed significantly regarding trade in ozone-depleting substances.
Significant _____

DICTATION

8 🎧 1 32 Listen to an extract from a student presentation about biofuels. Complete the text.

It is thought by many of today's leading scientists that biofuel is one solution to our future energy needs. Biofuel involves chemical energy [1] _____ such as wood, crops, animal and even human waste. The organic matter [2] _____ thermally, chemically or biochemically into energy-containing substances which are able to be stored in either solid, liquid or gas form, depending on [3] _____ . An example of biochemical conversion is the use of bacteria to break down organic matter, which [4] _____ , which in turn can be used as a fuel. Among a number of potential uses as a fuel, hydrogen [5] _____ as a means of powering or propelling vehicles and other modes of transport. A number of hydrogen-powered cars [6] _____ .

5.3 Land or all

READING

1 Look at the title of the article. What do you think is meant by a 'resilient city'?

2 Read the article and choose the statement (a–c) that best describes what a resilient city is.
  a A large city that is completely independent of national government control
  b A city that coordinates with other cities to find solutions to everyday urban issues
  c A city that plans its own responses to long-term and short-term urban problems

3 Read the article again and answer the questions.
  1 What is the size of Chennai in India?
  2 What is the population of Australia?
  3 How is the identity of individual cities changing?
  4 What type of extraordinary negative events do cities face?
  5 What kind of problems do national government initiatives seem less good at tackling?
  6 What is Bristol's traditional approach to life?
  7 What was the focus of Bristol's 'resilient cities' first meetings?
  8 What used to be the focus of such meetings about Bristol's problems?
  9 What specific issue did the meeting in Bristol highlight?
  10 What is the main advantage of the resilient city approach?

Resilient cities

Urbanization is the great trend of the late 20th and early 21st centuries. Half the world's population now live in cities and there are already 35 mega-cities in existence (cities with over 10 million inhabitants), the latest to join the list being Chennai in India. Some of these, like Greater Tokyo with 37 million and Shanghai with 25 million, have populations larger than the whole of Australia. While the economic importance of these urban hubs has been discussed for some time, the question of cities' independence and their power to determine other aspects of policy – education, transport, security and environmental protection – has moved up the agenda more slowly. But the more that globalization diminishes the significance of international borders for trade and migration, the stronger the identity of individual cities and the loyalty shown by inhabitants to them become. Ask a Londoner or New Yorker where they come from and they are far more likely to answer London or New York City than the UK or the USA.

Alongside this growth in the importance of cities has come a movement called '100 Resilient Cities', pioneered by the Rockefeller Foundation. 100RC is dedicated to helping cities become more capable of withstanding 'the physical, social and economic challenges that are a growing part of the 21st century.' This means not only preparing them for one-off 'shocks', such as flooding, earthquakes and epidemics, but also bolstering them against daily stresses such as unemployment, urban poverty, crime, road congestion, inefficient public transport and shortages of food or water. Evidence has shown that inter and intra-city networks set up to tackle the latter type of problem are much more effective at combatting them than national government initiatives.

Bristol in the UK, a city with a history of trying to do things differently, is one of the cities in the 100RC network committed to developing a resilience plan. Early meetings brought together local government representatives from different departments (transport, emergency services, public health, education, social care, etc.) and infrastructure-related businesses (e.g. water companies, road builders) to look more closely at the city's needs and to see how these could be addressed. The delegates were asked to think about worst-case scenarios for their particular area of concern. But, far from creating an atmosphere of doom and gloom, the meetings generated a lot of positivity, because there was a general feeling that they were taking matters into their own hands, rather than just complaining about inadequate national government policies and budgets as they had done previously.

One issue that came to light in Bristol was inequality of life expectancy. Bristol is a wealthy city, but delegates discovered that the poorest in the community were living eight to nine years less than the richest. Righting this injustice of wealth inequality has now become a target for the city's governors as part of their new 'social resilience' plan. This measure illustrates very well the real benefit of resilient city planning: it focusses minds on key issues and then looks at long-term, rather than short-term solutions for them.

4 Complete the definitions of the words from the article.

1 hub (paragraph 1)
the _____ of a region or activity

2 agenda (paragraph 1)
a list of points to be discussed at a _____

3 diminishes (paragraph 1)
makes _____

4 one-off (paragraph 2)
happening only _____

5 bolstering (paragraph 2)
making them _____

6 doom and gloom (paragraph 3)
a general feeling of _____

7 came to light (paragraph 4)
became _____

VOCABULARY Economics

5 Complete the headlines. Use the words in the box.

bankrupt	boom	debts	employees
interest	meet	operations	recession
recovery	unemployment		

1 Chancellor to cut _____ rates

2 Twenty firms a day going _____

3 Japan comes out of _____ , but growth still disappoints

4 One in five unable to make ends _____

5 Weak exports stifling economic _____

6 _____ rising at fastest rate for a generation

7 Most students don't ever pay off _____

8 Gaming industry enjoying _____ thanks to new 4D technology

9 American firm TRF to expand _____ into Europe

10 New government incentives for firms to take on more _____

WORD FOCUS *land*

6 Complete the sentences. Use the words and phrases in the box.

dry land	landlocked	landmark
landslide	live off the land	plot of land
strip of land	wasteland	

1 Bolivia and Paraguay are the only _____ countries in South America. All the others have a coastline.

2 The Eiffel Tower is probably the most famous _____ in Paris.

3 The first person to row the Pacific Ocean solo was Peter Bird of Britain. Bird set off from San Francisco, California, and reached _____ in Australia 294 days later.

4 They've bought a _____ and are going to build a house on it.

5 An isthmus is a narrow _____ that connects two larger landmasses, such as the Isthmus of Panama that joins Central and South America.

6 Many people are giving up their urban lives to return to nature and _____ .

7 The area round Chernobyl has been a _____ ever since the nuclear disaster in 1986.

8 The main natural causes of a _____ are excessive water caused by prolonged rainfall, vibrations caused by earthquakes, wave or river erosion and volcanic eruptions.

7 Match the words (1–3) with their definitions (a–c).

1 landscape
2 landmark
3 landslide

a an event that marks an important stage in something
b getting many more votes than an opponent in an election
c the features or current conditions of something

8 Complete the sentences with *landscape, landmark* or *landslide*.

1 The political _____ of Europe has changed enormously in the last 30 years.

2 After a _____ ruling by the European Court of Justice, hundreds of thousands of people could now demand to be paid for travelling to and from work.

3 The Middle East has a rich and varied cultural _____ .

4 Ronald Reagan's _____ victory, beating Walter Mondale by 525 to 13 in 1984, is the biggest margin ever in a US presidential election.

5 Elvis Presley's first hit single *That's All Right* is a _____ in the history of pop music.

5.4 I can well believe that

EXPRESSING BELIEF AND DISBELIEF

1 🎧 **1 33** Listen to eight extracts from discussions about the environment. For each, does the second person express belief/agree (✓) or express disbelief/disagree (✗)?

1 ☐ 2 ☐ 3 ☐ 4 ☐ 5 ☐ 6 ☐ 7 ☐ 8 ☐

2 🎧 **1 33** Complete the responses to the extracts in Exercise 1. Listen again and check your answers.

1 I can well b_____ that.
2 I'd take that with a p_____ of salt .... I'd be surprised if that was the _____ .
3 That doesn't s_____ me at all.
4 I very much d_____ that.
5 That's just an o_____ wives' tale. I don't think there's any t_____ in that.
6 I suspect that's t_____ .
7 That's a common m_____ , actually ...
8 Well, that's what they'd have you b_____ , isn't it?
9 Yeah, I think they've got that _____ on.

3 Complete the responses using the words in brackets.

1 A: Apparently there's a 50/50 chance an asteroid's going to hit the Earth in 2020.
   B: _____ (pinch/salt)
2 A: They say that if all the cows in a field are lying down, then it's going to rain.
   B: _____ (wives')
3 A: They reckon that if you turn your TV off at the mains rather than leaving it on standby, then you can save about £20 a year in electricity.
   B: _____ (suspect/true)
4 A: Don't goldfish have a memory of just a few seconds?
   B: _____ (common/misconception)
5 A: They reckon there'll be no petrol or diesel in about five years.
   B: _____ (surprised/case)
6 A: Last year was the hottest year on record.
   B: _____ (well/believe)
      _____ (surprise/at all)
7 A: I heard the melting icecaps are going to cause huge tsunamis in the next few years.
   B: _____ (much/doubt)
      I think _____ (nonsense/honest)
8 A: I saw this ad that says that turning vegetarian before you're 30 can add on average five years onto your life.
   B: _____ (have/believe)
      _____ (some/reservations/that)

PRONUNCIATION Silent letters

4 🎧 **1 34** Underline the silent letter in the word in bold. Then listen and check your answers.

1 Many students take years to pay off their **debts**.
2 Can I have a **receipt**, please?
3 I **doubt** they'll reach an agreement today.
4 He was a **colonel** in the army.
5 Can I have an **aisle** seat, please?
6 We need a more **subtle** approach.
7 Can you pass me the **scissors**?
8 Would you like a **biscuit**?
9 My sister's an **architect**.
10 He was found **guilty** of all charges.

WRITING SKILL Using passive reporting verbs

5 Underline five examples of passive reporting structures in the text. Write them in the table.

It + passive reporting verb + *that* clause	Subject + passive reporting verb + *to*
1 _____	3 _____
2 _____	4 _____
	5 _____

Deforestation, the clearing of wooded or forested areas for human gain, is believed to have begun around half a million years ago. It is thought to have started with the simple cutting down of a few trees, but was soon followed by the use of fire to clear larger areas of land. Today, about 30% of the world's land remains covered with woodland or forests, with tropical rainforests accounting for about 7%, but at the current rate of destruction, it is predicted that the rainforests of the world could be completely destroyed in less than 100 years. Forests are cut down for many reasons, but the biggest driver of deforestation is agriculture, with forested areas being cleared to provide land for planting crops or grazing livestock. Logging operations are thought to be the second biggest cause of deforestation, with urban sprawl being another. The most dramatic impact of deforestation is habitat loss. 70% of Earth's land animals and plants live in forests and it is estimated that around 50% of all land-dwelling species live in tropical forests.

6 Rewrite the conversation extracts in two different ways using the two passive reporting structures. Use the verb in bold.

1 Experts **believe** that global carbon emissions are decreasing.
It is believed that global carbon emissions are decreasing.
Global carbon emissions are believed to be decreasing.

2 They **think** that ten thousand people took part in the anti-fracking demonstration.
_____
_____

3 Everyone **expects** the minister to resign within the next 24 hours.
_____
_____

4 The authorities **fear** that thousands have been left homeless after the hurricane.
_____
_____

5 They **say** that a picture is worth a thousand words.
_____
_____

6 Unnamed sources have **alleged** that bribes had been offered.
_____
_____

7 Complete the news extracts with passive reporting structures using the verbs in brackets.

1 Big freeze continues
As the freezing temperatures continue, _____ (recommend) homeowners keep their central heating on during the night. The current cold snap _____ (think/be) the longest period of sub-zero temperatures for over 40 years.

2 Thousands homeless
The damage caused by yesterday's explosion at the Bilsborough power plant _____ (believe/be) much worse than expected. _____ (now/fear) over 30 nearby buildings, including several homes, have been totally or partially destroyed.

3 Tennis in crisis
The tennis world is in crisis after _____ (report) that at least five major tournaments in the last year have been fixed. _____ (claim) a number of as yet unnamed players were paid tens of thousands of dollars to deliberately lose games. The ITF _____ (expect/release) a statement tomorrow.

4 Lion escapes
A lion has escaped from Belmount Zoo. The animal _____ (say/be) highly dangerous and people have been warned to be vigilant. The lion _____ (think/escape) while it was being moved to a temporary enclosure.

8 Expand the notes and write the paragraph from a news article. Use passive reporting structures for the verbs in bold.
estimated / global energy consumption / increase by around 50% by 2050.
thought / half / growth / come from China and India. Moment / China and India consume about 21% / world energy / but / **expected** / 31% / middle of the century.
Also / **calculated** / China / use around 60% more energy than the US by 2050.
Fossil fuels will still be the dominant energy source and will account for around 70% of world energy use in 2050.
Over the same period / **predicted** / renewable energy / increase globally / about 3% per year.
Despite this / energy-related carbon-dioxide emissions / **expected** / continue / rise / and / 30–40% higher in 2050 than at present.

_____
_____
_____
_____
_____
_____
_____
_____
_____
_____
_____
_____
_____
_____
_____
_____
_____

YOUR IDEA

1 Read about three changes in people's lives. Match them with the summaries (a–c)

1 **Pablo:** It might seem unbelievable nowadays, but we didn't have a dishwasher at home up until last year. My partner and I had an unwritten rule – we took turns cooking meals, and whoever didn't do the cooking would do the washing up. And it worked quite well and I thought that washing the dishes, pots and pans was actually quite therapeutic. But one morning, my other half came home and said five words: 'I've just bought a dishwasher.' It was only when we had the thing installed that I realized just how much time I spent doing the dishes. We've both got so much spare time now that we've been able to do those things we always wanted to: I learned how to knit, which I've wanted to do ever since I was younger, but just never had the time before. ☐

2 **Valérie:** I always used to take public transport to get around. I'm a teacher and travelling to work I often thought that getting stuck in traffic jams was such a waste of time – I couldn't understand why anyone would want to put themselves in that position. That's why I was apprehensive when I was given driving lessons as a birthday present. It was difficult to get over, but now I can't imagine not driving. I love my car – I also realized that it meant I could leave my school job and set myself up as a private language teacher. Being able to drive to clients meant that I could set up a teaching company and work for myself. ☐

3 **Chao-Xing:** Coming from China, it can be strange when you first travel abroad. Coming from a place where you can generally understand what people are talking about wherever you are, to somewhere like Europe, where there are so many different languages, has been a challenge. Not only that, but the traditions are completely distinct from my own. I don't regret it, however. Since I moved to Madrid, I've learned Spanish and have even taken up flamenco classes. It hasn't all been plain sailing – there was some confusion about my name, because it sounds a bit like a word they use in Spanish to say 'bye'! ☐

a The change in my life allowed me to gain new skills, even though there were problems to begin with.

b I have a lot more freedom because of this change in my life – I was even able to start my own business.

c Making this change saves me so much time that I'm able to pursue new hobbies.

2 Write notes about changes you have made in your life, or the things you would like to change. Think of several ideas so you can choose the best one.

3 Choose one thing from your list. Answer these questions about it.

1 What is your change and what area of your life does it relate to?
2 How does/would this change affect your life?
3 What could you or people in your family do as a result of making this change?

4 Practise your presentation out loud. Focus on the structure of your presentation and the journey you take your audience on. You could do this by …

- establishing your idea right at the beginning and then unpacking it step by step.
- creating the need for an answer to a question or problem and then lead the listener to the answer nearer the end of the presentation.
- presenting certain benefits of your idea and revealing further or greater benefits later in the presentation.

ORGANIZING YOUR PRESENTATION

5 Match the five steps of a presentation with examples of useful language (a–e).

1 Greet the audience and introduce yourself ☐
2 Outline your change and what area of your life it relates to ☐
3 Describe how this change has affected or would affect your life ☐
4 Add a final point about your change ☐
5 Thank the audience and finish the presentation ☐

a We bought a bigger car and this has made it much easier for us to travel around.
b A big thank you for listening to me today. Are there any questions?
c Not only has it helped us with this, but my husband is now also able to act as a driver for the fans of the local football team.
d Making this change has meant that we are able to take a lot more of our children's things when we go on holiday.
e Welcome everyone. My name is Alice. In this talk I will tell you about a change I made.

6 Read the useful language on the left and make notes for your presentation.

1 Greet the audience and introduce yourself Hello … Today I would like … In this talk …	
2 Outline your change and what area of your life it relates to The change … which … I/We … and this …	
3 Describe how this change has affected or would affect your life This has meant … Now I/we can … This would mean … Then I/we could … As a result …	
4 Add a final point about your change Not only … What is more …	
5 Thank the audience and finish the presentation Finally, I'd like to thank you all … Are there … ? Do you have … ?	

7 Film yourself giving your presentation or practise in front of a mirror. Give yourself marks out of ten for …

- structuring your talk and taking the audience on a journey. ☐ /10
- following the tips in Exercise 4. ☐ /10
- following the five steps in Exercise 6. ☐ /10
- using correct grammar. ☐ /10

6 Practical design

6.1 Magical houses, made of bamboo

TEDTALKS

ELORA HARDY was born in Bali, Indonesia, and spent her childhood there. Her father is the Canadian-born jewellery designer John Hardy, who had first visited Bali in the mid-1970s and set up his business there in 1975. Hardy thus grew up surrounded by art and creativity, and spent a lot of her time with local village craftsmen, where she learned skills such as carving, painting and batik. When she was 14, Hardy left Bali to finish her schooling and to go to university in the United States. She first attended a boarding school for the arts in California and then studied fine arts at Tufts University near Boston. After completing her degree she then 'talked herself into' a job creating fabric prints for fashion designer Donna Karan in New York and spent five years there from 2005 to 2010.

In 2010, Hardy left the fashion world to return to Bali. Inspired by the design and bamboo construction of the award-winning Green School, a Balinese academy, that her father and step-mother had recently opened, she founded her own company and design brand Ibuku. Ibuku is a team of architects, designers, craftsmen and builders, many of them local Balinesians, that use locally-sourced bamboo and other sustainable natural materials to create homes and other buildings. Ibuku also designs and produces the furniture inside the buildings, much of which is bespoke. Hardy says that a large part of her motivation and inspiration in setting up Ibuku was being able to reconnect with the culture and landscape that she grew up in. At the same time, she says that she wanted to support local Balinese artisans and craftsmen in continuing their traditions alongside more contemporary and international designers and architects.

Following critical acclaim for their initial building projects, which include houses, bridges, auditoriums and even a car park, the Ibuku team have established themselves among the world leaders in bamboo design and construction. In 2013, Hardy was featured as an Architectural Digest Innovator.

Elora Hardy

CAREER PATHWAYS

1 Read the text. Answer the questions.

   1 What aspects of her childhood would you say influenced Hardy's career?
   2 Which phrase in paragraph 1 means she persuaded someone to give her a job?
   3 Which word in the text means 'made to order' or 'made to a specific requested design'?
   4 In what way could it be said that Hardy is following in her father's footsteps?
   5 What key aspects of her work contributed to her being featured as an Architectural Innovator?

TED PLAYLIST

2 Other TED speakers are interested in topics similar to Elora Hardy's TED Talk. Read the descriptions of four TED Talks at the top of page 55. In your opinion, which is the best title for this playlist, a, b or c?
   a The common mistakes of architects
   b Architectural forms from nature
   c Beyond traditional building materials

3 Read the TED playlist again. Find a speaker who ...

   1 uses building material sourced from trees and plants.
   2 is designing buildings for city living.
   3 is working in a difficult environment.

▶ **Michael Green: Why we should build wooden skyscrapers**

Building a skyscraper? Forget about steel and concrete, says architect Michael Green, and build it out of … wood. As he details in this intriguing talk, it's not only possible to build secure wooden structures up to 30 storeys tall, it's necessary.

▶ **Magnus Larsson: Turning dunes into architecture**

Architecture student Magnus Larsson details his bold plan to transform the harsh Sahara desert using bacteria and a surprising construction material: the sand itself.

▶ **Mitchell Joachim: Don't build your home, grow it!**

TED Fellow and urban designer Mitchell Joachim presents his vision for sustainable, organic architecture: eco-friendly abodes grown from plants and – wait for it – meat.

▶ **Shigeru Ban: Emergency shelters made from paper**

Architect Shigeru Ban began experimenting with sustainable building materials, such as cardboard tubes, long before sustainability was a buzzword. His remarkable structures are often used as temporary housing in disaster-struck regions, but often the buildings remain a beloved part of the landscape long after they have served their intended purpose.

4 Find the words in the TED playlist that mean the same as a–d.

a unpleasant **b** homes **c** safe **d** amazing

5 Which talk would you most like to see? Why? Watch the talk at TED.com.

AUTHENTIC LISTENING SKILLS
Word boundaries

6 🎧 1 35 You are going to hear a podcast in which a member of the *Keynote* team talks about Michael Green's TED Talk, *Why we should build wooden skyscrapers*. Listen to the sentence and mark the words that are merged.

My first reaction to this talk was not at all sceptical. I just thought – what a fantastic idea!

7 🎧 1 36 Listen and complete the next sentence with the merged words.

But _____ began _____ _____ deforestation and about how safe a wooden skyscraper _____ during an earthquake.

LISTENING

8 🎧 1 37 Listen to the full podcast. Answer the questions.

1 What two concerns did Karen have after seeing the title of the talk?

2 What reasons does Karen give for liking wood as a building material?

3 What two concerns did Karen have at the end of the talk?

9 🎧 1 37 Listen again. Are these statements true (T), false (F) or unknown (U)?

1 Karen implies that skyscrapers are not very pleasant buildings to live in. ☐

2 Karen travels a long way to her yoga class because she likes the wooden building. ☐

3 She exchanged her plastic office furniture for some wooden IKEA furniture. ☐

4 She claims not to understand the economics of growing trees for timber. ☐

5 She implies Michael Green has not thought through the noise implications of using wood on a large scale. ☐

VOCABULARY IN CONTEXT

10 Read the extracts from the podcast. Choose the correct meaning of the words in bold.

1 … So I was pleased when the speaker addressed and **alleviated** both these fears in his talk.
 a understand ☐ **b** controlled ☐ **c** eased ☐

2 … what he says about people **hugging** the wooden columns in his buildings.
 a touching ☐ **b** embracing ☐ **c** loving ☐

3 … how much this has improved my work space – mentally and in a **tactile** way.
 Relating to **a** productivity ☐ **b** emotion ☐
 c sense of touch ☐

4 the size needed to mass-produce the timber **panels** he talks about.
 a flat sections ☐ **b** long supports ☐
 c thick covering ☐

5 makes other loud and sudden **unsettling** noises as the wood expands and contracts.
 a disturbing ☐ **b** breaking ☐
 c confusing ☐

6.2 Get someone else to do it

GRAMMAR Causatives

1 Look at the pictures and complete the sentences using the causative and the words in the box.

deliver	fit	redecorate	sand	service

1 They _____ at the moment.

2 They _____ yesterday.

3 They _____ tomorrow.

4 They _____ recently.

5 They _____ last week.

2 Choose the correct words or phrases to complete the sentences.

1 The boxes are quite heavy. I'll get someone *help/to help* us with them.

2 You didn't see me? I think you need to get your eyes *testing/tested*.

3 She's not here at the moment, but I'll get her *call/to call* you back later this afternoon.

4 How on earth did you get them *agree/to agree* to that? I thought they were adamant about it.

5 Did you manage to get the iron *working/work*?

6 We had someone *give/giving* us an estimate for the work last week. £3,000, can you believe?

7 We need to get the extension *finished/to finish* before we go away in June.

8 We had the flat *valuing/valued* the other day. Guess how much?

3 Complete the text using the correct causative form of the words in brackets.

In the UK, one in six of us like to think we are pretty good at DIY and would rather try ¹_____ (get / the job / do) ourselves than ²_____ (get / a professional / do) it. However, by ³_____ (not have / an expert / do) the work, we very often end up doing more harm than good. In fact, around 13% of DIY projects go wrong in some way, sometimes disastrously. National Insurance Association (NIA) spokesperson Ian Smith says 'People think they can easily ⁴_____ (get / the heating / work) again or ⁵_____ (get / that stuck window / unstick), but very often it's not as simple or straightforward as it seems.'

And it can be very costly. It is estimated that DIY disasters cost us £200 million a year in insurance excesses and increased premiums. 'The long bank-holiday weekends are when most DIY-related insurance claims are made. People see it as the perfect opportunity to ⁶_____ (get / those long-overdue jobs / do),' says Smith. 'Another problem is that when something goes wrong or breaks down, people often want to ⁷_____ (have / it / sort) and back up and running as soon as possible and don't have the time to wait for a professional.' According to the NIA, the most common claim is for damage to walls and ceilings, followed by damage to flooring and furnishings. Burst pipes is also high on the list. 'The sensible advice is only have a go if you know what you are doing. If not, ⁸_____ (get / a professional / do) it'.

4 🎧 **1 38** Complete the dialogues using the causative form of the words and phrases in the box. Then listen and check your answers.

get/him/see	get/it/catch	get/it/decorate
get/Jack/change	get/one/cut	get/someone/do
have/it/finish		

1 A: We need a spare key. Is there anywhere _____ round here?
   B: Yeah, there's a shop on George Road. I think they do it.

2 A: So, you finally managed _____ his mind about the flat.
   B: Well, it wasn't easy I can tell you – you know what he's like. But yeah, I finally _____ sense.

3 A: How's the nursery going? Finished it yet?
   B: Almost. I should _____ by the end of the week.

4 A: What have you done to your hand?
   B: Oh, I _____ in a car door. I was just getting out and someone closed it.

5 A: When are you moving into the new flat? Do you know yet?
   B: Well, everything's gone through and it's now ours. But we're hoping _____ before we move in, but we're not sure if we've got the time. We might have _____ it. Do you know any decorators in the area?

LANGUAGE FOCUS Expressions with *go* and *get*

5 Find 20 words that make expressions with *go* or *get*.

<u>go</u>
missing
_____
_____
_____
_____
_____
_____
_____
_____

<u>get</u>
ill
involved
_____
_____
_____
_____
_____
_____
_____

Z	M	I	S	S	I	N	G	Z	U
X	B	A	N	K	R	U	P	T	P
O	B	B	R	V	A	Y	K	I	S
Q	L	A	W	R	O	N	G	L	E
V	U	D	L	E	I	L	G	L	T
B	L	I	N	D	J	E	V	R	Z
D	J	R	E	A	D	Y	D	E	Y
E	L	O	S	T	A	R	T	E	D
A	P	R	E	G	N	A	N	T	X
F	Z	X	C	R	A	Z	Y	G	F

6 Complete the definitions with expressions from Exercise 5.

1 make a mistake _____
2 lose your eyesight _____
3 become embarrassed _____
4 stop speaking/making a noise _____
5 become not sensible/insane _____
6 become sick _____
7 lose your hair _____
8 don't know where you are _____
9 have no money (for a business) _____
10 prepare yourself _____

7 Complete the sentences with an expression using the correct form of *go* or *get* and the words in the box.

anywhere	anywhere	dark	involved
missing	a bit old	rusty	started
a new TV			

1 The office lights are programmed to come on when it starts _____. That's around three or four in the afternoon at this time of year.
2 I'll _____ with the tidying up. Can you have a go at cleaning the mess in the bathroom?
3 Some of my old records _____. You haven't lent them to anybody, have you?
4 We don't seem _____ with this. Let's have a rethink and start again. Maybe try a different approach.
5 Look at this traffic! I don't think we _____ in a hurry.
6 We need to think about _____. This one _____ now. The sound keeps cutting out.
7 Your bike chain's _____. You need to give it a bit of an oiling.
8 I wouldn't _____ if I were you. I'd leave them to sort it out themselves.

DICTATION

8 🎧 **1 39** Listen to someone talking about the term 'DIY'. Complete the sentences.

The term 'do-it-yourself', or DIY, has been in popular use since the mid-1900s. [1]_____ of a home-owner undertaking some form of home improvement, maintenance or repair themselves rather than [2]_____. The term DIY has more recently, however, taken on a broader meaning and is today used in a number of ways [3]_____, or doing something in their own way, rather than following the more traditional and established route [4]_____.
Examples of this include the music industry, where bands can now produce their own music and promote it themselves, or pay [5]_____, the recent increase in writers self-publishing, and, more generally, the myriad of websites enabling us to sell things, rent out properties and generally promote ourselves and our services on our own terms. From this has developed a more mainstream DIY ethic and culture, which refers across a whole range of areas to the idea of being self-sufficient and [6]_____ without [7]_____ it.

READING

1 Look at the title of the article. Answer the questions.

  1 What is a manifesto?
  2 Who normally publishes a manifesto?

2 Read the first paragraph describing the life of Dieter Rams. Then answer the questions.

  1 How did his background and training differ from the work he ended up doing? How was it linked?
  2 What, in the descriptions, tells you that Dieter Rams' designs were fairly 'minimalist'?

3 Read the rest of the article. Match the statements (a–h) with eight of the principles (1–10).

  a 'A well-designed object should just blend into the background.' ☐
  b 'But that's not to say it can't be attractive too – in its own way.' ☐

  c 'Good design takes time, because you have to think so carefully about how all aspects of the object function to best effect.' ☐
  d 'Really good designs surprise you because although they're fresh and new, they seem somehow obvious.' ☐
  e 'The best designs just strip things back to their bare basics.' ☐
  f 'Good designs don't just try to make something look more exclusive and up-market.' ☐
  g 'I think Apple designs are great. Even young toddlers, when they pick up an iPad, seem to know immediately how to manipulate it.' ☐
  h 'You know something's a design classic when years later people are still using (or copying) the same design.' ☐

A design manifesto

Dieter Rams is one of the most influential figures in modern industrial design. Born in Wiesbaden, Germany, in 1932, he studied and worked originally as an architect and interior designer. In 1955, he was recruited by the industrial giant and maker of electrical goods, Braun, and remained there for 40 years, becoming their Chief Design Officer. His designs ranged from record players and film projectors for Braun to shelving units and chairs for the furniture maker, Vitsoe. His own design philosophy is summed up in the phrase 'Less, but better' and, accordingly, he is often placed within the functionalist school of architecture and design, whose guiding principle is that 'form should follow function'. In other words, if you pay attention to the function of an object, good design will naturally follow.

Troubled in the 1970s and 80s by the seeming lack of co-ordination or harmony in the world of industrial and architectural design, a situation Rams called 'an impenetrable confusion of forms, colours and noises', he developed his now famous ten principles of good design. These were as follows:

1 Good design is innovative. Innovative design should never be an end in itself, but the best designs are always innovative since they achieve a harmony between form and function that has not been achieved before.
2 Good design makes a product useful. The use of the object should be immediately apparent to the user and no feature should detract from what is useful about it.
3 Good design is aesthetic. Form and function are not exclusive qualities. Beauty arises from an object's simplicity and purity.
4 Good design makes a product understandable. If the user has to struggle to understand the purpose of a particular feature or part of the design, then the designer has failed. Everything should be intuitive.
5 Good design is unobtrusive. Design for practical objects should never be showy since their purpose is not to decorate but to perform a function.
6 Good design is honest. The aim of design is not to distinguish an object as a high-quality, high-tech or high-value item, but simply to reflect an object's function.
7 Good design is long-lasting. It must stand the test of time, not only in the sense of being durable, but also in the sense of being outside the world of transient fashions.
8 Good design is thorough down to the last detail. Each detail has to be refined and each detail must work with the user in mind.
9 Good design is environmentally-friendly. Good design is respectful of the need to conserve resources, both in the object's manufacture and in its eventual disposal or recycling.
10 Good design is as little design as possible. It is the job of the designer to focus on the essential elements and produce something that is both pure and simple.

4 Find adjectives in the text that mean the same as these words (1–8).

1 comprehensible _____
2 incomprehensible _____
3 comprehensive _____
4 passing _____
5 artistic _____
6 instinctive _____
7 inconspicuous _____
8 hard-wearing _____

5 🎧 **1 40** Listen to two people discussing the 'Henry Hoover' vacuum cleaner. Do they think it fits Dieter Rams' criteria? Yes (✓), no (✗) or not clear (?).

1 ☐ 2 ☐ 3 ☐ 4 ☐ 5 ☐
6 ☐ 7 ☐ 8 ☐ 9 ☐ 10 ☐

VOCABULARY Describing objects: collocations

6 Complete the sentences with adverbs using the adjectives in the box.

> beautiful   bright   great   high   perfect
> prohibitive   reasonable   scientific   shoddy   wide

1 You can tell that they're fakes as they're so _____ built. They look like they're going to fall apart at any minute.
2 The marketing tag of '_____ proven' has become pretty common these days. But what exactly does it mean?
3 Her work is _____ admired, particularly in the US, where her _____ original pieces can fetch upwards of $100,000.
4 Today, concrete is the most _____ used building material in the world.
5 It's usually the male bird which is _____ coloured, while the female of the species is often a more drab brown colour.
6 3-D televisions were _____ expensive when they first came out, but now, like a lot of similar technology, they're pretty _____ priced.
7 The song is _____ crafted and _____ put together, with lyrics and melody combining effortlessly.

WORDBUILDING The suffix -able/-ible

7 Rewrite the sentences using an adjective ending -able/-ible to replace the words in bold. You may also need to use a negative prefix in some cases.

1 Designer Dieter Rams described the situation as a 'confusion of forms, colours and noises' that couldn't be **penetrated**.
Designer Dieter Rams described the situation as 'an impenetrable confusion of forms, colours and noises'

2 Rams said that good design makes a product easy to **understand**.
_____

3 Ibuku uses natural materials that can be **sustained** to create homes and other buildings.
_____

4 Even though it can be **broken**, carbon fibre is one of the strongest known materials currently used in manufacturing.
_____

5 His art is very hands-on and interactive with a number of exhibits with parts that can be **moved**.
_____

6 You cannot **imagine** the detail and the intricacy of the painting until you get up close and see it with your own eyes.
_____

7 The book is beyond **value** and is impossible to **replace**.
_____

8 You can instantly **recognize** the band as soon as you hear the first few bars of their songs.
_____

8 Match the adjectives (1–8) with their meanings (a–h).

1 malleable   a can be eaten
2 durable   b can burn easily
3 edible   c cannot be read
4 inflammable   d cannot be repaired
5 irreparable   e cannot be explained
6 inexplicable   f likely to last a long time
7 illegible   g can be shaped easily
8 pliable   h can be bent easily

9 Complete the sentences with the adjectives (1–8) from Exercise 8.

1 Gold is a very soft and _____ metal, which is why it has been used in jewellery making for thousands of years.
2 Modern furniture must adhere to strict safety standards and not be made of _____ material.
3 The appeal of some modern art is to me totally _____. I just don't get it at all.
4 My writing can be pretty _____ at the best of times. Even I sometimes can't read what I've written myself.
5 Fibreglass is one of the strongest and most _____ materials in the world.
6 The fire caused _____ damage to a number of the museum exhibits.
7 TVs of the future will be made from a _____ material so that you can roll them up and watch them anywhere.
8 His dishes are like _____ works of art. They're so beautiful, you don't want to eat them.

6.4 Common sense

INTERVIEW QUESTIONS

1 🎧 **1 41** Listen to four extracts from job interviews. Are these statements true (T), false (F) or unknown (U)?

Extract 1: The candidate generally works well at home. ☐
Extract 2: The candidate likes working in open-plan offices. ☐
Extract 3: The candidate would never criticize a colleague. ☐
Extract 4: The candidate's answer surprised the interviewer. ☐

2 🎧 **1 41** Complete the extracts from the interviews. Then listen again and check your answers.

1 A: D_____ you f_____
   that working at home makes it easier or harder to be
   self-disciplined?
   B: Well, t_____ d_____ ,
   I guess.
2 A: In what environment do you work best,
   w_____ you s_____ ?
   B: Mmm, I s_____ I'd
   s_____ , like, a small office or
   workspace environment...
   A: And w_____ d_____
   you s_____ t_____ ?
3 A: In a s_____ w_____
   you, for some reason, think ..., what
   w_____ you d_____ ?
   B: My f_____ i_____
   i_____ to say that I'd keep quiet and ...
   A: And how w_____ you
   g_____ a_____ doing
   this?
4 A: And one final question. I_____
   t_____ you're on a deserted island and
   can take with you just one book, w_____
   w_____ it b_____ ?
   B : Mm, t_____ 's a t_____
   q_____ . L_____
   m_____ h_____ a
   t_____ .

3 Correct the mistakes in these interview extracts. Each exchange contains two or three errors.

1 A: In situation where you felt you were being
   undervalued, what do you do?
   B: I suppose I talk to someone about it.
2 A: Would you find that you work differently at different
   times of day?
   B: Well, that's depend on what I'm working on.
3 A: Imagining a colleague is not pulling their weight, what
   do you do?
   B: That's trick question. But I guess it depends on how it
   is affecting things.
4 A: How would you go about appeal to and recruiting
   recent graduates?
   B: Let me have think. I suppose the first thing would be
   to raise our profile and presence in the universities.

5 A: Would you say are a good motivating influence?
   B: First instinct is say yes. But I suppose that's for others
   to say.
   A: And why did you say that?
   B: Well, I might think I'm helping with motivation, but that
   might not be the case.

PRONUNCIATION Word stress

4 🎧 **1 42** Read the sentences. Underline the syllables in the words in bold that you think will be stressed. Then listen and check your answers.

1 She's got a strong **imagination** and has a lot of very
   good **ideas**.
2 He's got a lot of **international** experience.
3 She's got **excellent communication** skills.
4 He's **apparently** got a **photographic** memory.
5 He's got a **background** in **economics** and **politics**.
6 What experience and **qualifications specific** to
   translation do you have?
7 We need an **effective** and **creative public** speaker.
8 A lot of what we do **requires** a strong **instinct** and
   intuition.
9 The **salary** will **depend** on **various** factors.
10 I think I'm quite **assertive** and **enthusiastic**.

WRITING SKILL Reported speech

5 Read the online post. Rewrite what you think the speaker actually said for the extracts in bold.

1 _____
_____
_____
_____

2 _____
_____
_____
_____

3 _____
_____
_____

4 _____
_____
_____

5 _____
_____
_____
_____

I'd like to share my recent interview experience. I was applying for a temporary job at a telemarketing company, or so I thought. There were two interviewers and they asked me the usual questions about why I wanted the job, what experience I had and what I could offer them. I think I answered quite well, and ¹**told them I had done it before the previous summer and that I'd managed to get some good sales figures**. Then they ²**asked me how I thought the recent changes to EU data protection law would affect the way the company operates**. I have to say I was a bit unprepared for this and couldn't really understand why they were asking me. Anyway, I said that while I was aware of the changes, I didn't know the details of the new law, and I ³**told them that I would be happy to look into it if they wanted me to**. They ⁴**said that if I was invited for a second interview, then we would probably need to talk about it**. I have to say, it threw me a fair bit and I was a bit confused why there would be a second interview. The job is basically ringing people up and reading from a script. Anyway, towards the end of the interview they ⁵**told me that because I'd just graduated in business and because I'd got experience and had done the job the year before, they thought I might be suitable as their new marketing manager**. It was nice to be considered, but I told them I wasn't interested. I did get the temporary job that I'd originally gone for though.

6 Rewrite the sentences using reported speech.

1 'What do you know about the company?'
She asked ⎯⎯⎯⎯⎯⎯⎯⎯⎯⎯⎯⎯⎯⎯

2 'What do you think the main challenges will be if you get the job?'
They asked ⎯⎯⎯⎯⎯⎯⎯⎯⎯⎯⎯⎯

3 'What do you think your colleagues would consider as your best qualities?'
They wanted ⎯⎯⎯⎯⎯⎯⎯⎯⎯⎯⎯⎯

4 'We'll be in touch if we need any further information.'
He said ⎯⎯⎯⎯⎯⎯⎯⎯⎯⎯⎯⎯⎯⎯

5 'You should look at other options before you make a decision.'
They advised ⎯⎯⎯⎯⎯⎯⎯⎯⎯⎯⎯

6 'Why aren't you applying for a more senior position?'
He questioned ⎯⎯⎯⎯⎯⎯⎯⎯⎯⎯

7 'I think it'll be a week or so before we know anything.'
They told ⎯⎯⎯⎯⎯⎯⎯⎯⎯⎯⎯⎯

8 'Do you know how many other candidates have been shortlisted?'
I asked ⎯⎯⎯⎯⎯⎯⎯⎯⎯⎯⎯⎯⎯

7 Rewrite the interview questions and answers using reported speech. Use reporting verbs (e.g. *said*, *told*, *asked*, *wanted to know*).

1 Interviewer: Why do you want to work here?
You: I see it as a positive move in my career to work for a leading company like yours.
They *asked me why I wanted to work there.* I said *that I saw it as a positive move in my career to work for a leading company like theirs.*

2 Interviewer: What can you offer us that other candidates can't?
You: I'm very experienced, I've got a lot of insight into the sector and I know the market.
They ⎯⎯⎯⎯⎯⎯⎯⎯⎯⎯⎯⎯⎯⎯⎯⎯.
I ⎯⎯⎯⎯⎯⎯⎯⎯⎯⎯⎯⎯⎯⎯⎯⎯⎯

3 Interviewer: Where do you see yourself in five years' time?
You: I hope to be heading up my own marketing team.
⎯⎯⎯⎯⎯⎯⎯⎯⎯⎯⎯⎯⎯⎯⎯⎯⎯
⎯⎯⎯⎯⎯⎯⎯⎯⎯⎯⎯⎯⎯⎯⎯⎯⎯
⎯⎯⎯⎯⎯⎯⎯⎯⎯⎯⎯⎯⎯⎯⎯⎯⎯

4 Interviewer: What do you think is the number one key to successful marketing, of any product?
You: I think the number one thing is to have a clear strategy, which is implemented consistently.
⎯⎯⎯⎯⎯⎯⎯⎯⎯⎯⎯⎯⎯⎯⎯⎯⎯
⎯⎯⎯⎯⎯⎯⎯⎯⎯⎯⎯⎯⎯⎯⎯⎯⎯
⎯⎯⎯⎯⎯⎯⎯⎯⎯⎯⎯⎯⎯⎯⎯⎯⎯

5 Interviewer: What do you see as your strengths?
You: I'm a good organizer and I plan everything in detail. I'm creative, and, as I mentioned, I know the market.
⎯⎯⎯⎯⎯⎯⎯⎯⎯⎯⎯⎯⎯⎯⎯⎯⎯
⎯⎯⎯⎯⎯⎯⎯⎯⎯⎯⎯⎯⎯⎯⎯⎯⎯

6 Interviewer: Can you think of any improvements to our products?
You: I think your products are second to none. But I do think the marketing and advertising can be freshened up a little.
⎯⎯⎯⎯⎯⎯⎯⎯⎯⎯⎯⎯⎯⎯⎯⎯⎯
⎯⎯⎯⎯⎯⎯⎯⎯⎯⎯⎯⎯⎯⎯⎯⎯⎯
⎯⎯⎯⎯⎯⎯⎯⎯⎯⎯⎯⎯⎯⎯⎯⎯⎯
⎯⎯⎯⎯⎯⎯⎯⎯⎯⎯⎯⎯⎯⎯⎯⎯⎯

Writing 3 | A REVIEW

IDEAS

You will read a review written to answer the question below.

> An English-language magazine in your local area has a regular section where people submit reviews of their favourite apps. You decide to send in a review recommending an app you enjoy using. You should briefly describe its main features and why they are useful, as well as anything users should be aware of before they download the app.
>
> Write your review in **280–320 words** in an appropriate style.

1 In the question, underline the three topics which need to be covered in the review. What points could be included in each topic?

MODEL

2 Read the article on the right. Match the functions (a–d) with the paragraphs (1–4). Are any of your ideas included?

  a Features of the app which the user likes and why they are useful ☐

  b Recommendations from the user ☐

  c Why the user wanted to download the app ☐

  d A potential problem with the app ☐

3 Correct the following statements.

  1 The user is happy with the range of recipes they already know.

  2 The user finds it easy to navigate the information available on recipe websites.

  3 You have to copy the ingredients you need to your shopping list yourself.

  4 It's easy to forget which ingredients you've used when using Recipe Record.

  5 It's a simple process to download recipes from any website.

  6 The user thinks Recipe Record is more expensive than it should be.

USEFUL LANGUAGE

4 Find phrases in the model text in Exercise 2 which mean the same as 1–6.

  1 increase the range of things I cook

  2 as far as shopping is concerned

  3 look for something without finding it

  4 a possible drawback to be aware of

  5 My £6 was well-spent.

  6 anyone who wants to

[1] I'm an avid cook and I'm constantly looking for new recipes to build my repertoire of dishes. As I'm sure is true of most people nowadays, the main way to do this is through the Internet. The problem is that recipes from different sites are all laid out in different ways, and it can be hard to find the information you need quickly.

[2] When my friend heard this complaint, she recommended Recipe Record, an app which allows you to clip recipes from websites and save them in one easy-to-search location. To use it, you simply search for a recipe within the app's browser, then tap to save it for later. When it comes to shopping, it couldn't be easier. You can automatically add ingredients from your chosen recipe to your shopping list with one tap. And no longer will you have to search in vain for your place in the recipe when you're in the kitchen: as you're cooking, cross ingredients off your list to show you've used them and use voice recognition software to listen to the step of the recipe you're on.

[3] A note of caution though: not every site allows Recipe Record to clip from it so easily. In that case, you have to manually tell the app where to find each piece of information in order to save it in the specified format. This can be time-consuming and takes a bit of practice, but it means you should be able to add recipes from any source you like.

[4] All of these functions don't come cheaply, however. Recipe Record is a mid-priced app, meaning you should be sure you're going to use it before taking the plunge. For me, it's completely changed the way I curate my recipe collection and was well worth the £6 I paid for it. I'd recommended it without hesitation to anyone looking to manage their recipes more efficiently – it really does make life easier.

5 Rewrite this review using the answers from Exercise 4.

Anyone who wants to get fit could do worse than download VidFitPlus. You can use it to increase the range of exercises you do quickly and easily. No longer will you have to look for videos showing you the safest way to stretch your quads or a new yoga breathing technique without finding them: they're all in one place within the app. Every minute you spend using VidFitPlus is time well-spent. As far as the price is concerned, it's a bargain at just 99p. It has one possible drawback though: it's addictive. Once you start using it, you won't be able to stop! I'd recommend it to all you fitness fans out there.

6 Complete the phrases so they mean the same as the sentences. Use the prompt words to help you.

1 Why is it so successful?

What _____ _____

secret _____ its _____?

2 You might think something different.

Contrary _____ _____

_____ might think…

3 It's very difficult to do this.

_____ far _____

_____ to do this.

4 The developer mostly manages to…

_____ _____ large, the

developer manages to…

5 The app I'm writing about…

The app_____ question…

6 The app deals with it in an unusual way.

The app _____ _____

_____ approach.

7 Find two replacements for the words 1–7. Use the words in the box.

> baffling   dull   entertaining   exceptional   extremely
> gripping   highly   hilarious   outstanding
> over-complicated   riveting   tedious   undeniably
> unquestionably

1 brilliant   _____ _____
2 interesting   _____ _____
3 boring   _____ _____
4 funny   _____ _____
5 confusing   _____ _____
6 very   _____ _____
7 definitely   _____ _____

PLANNING

You will answer the following question.

> Your English teacher has asked you to write a review for a blog for English learners of a TED Talk you have seen. In your review you should briefly describe the topic of the talk and say why you chose it. You should also explain the reasons why watching TED Talks can be useful for English learners.

Write your review in **280–320 words** in an appropriate style.

8 Plan your review. Write notes to answer these questions. Don't write full sentences yet.

1 Which TED Talk will you write about?
2 What is the topic of the talk?
3 Why did you choose it?
4 Why is it useful for English learners to watch TED Talks?

WRITING

9 Write a review to reply to the message in Exercise 8. In your review you should:

- Clearly identify the talk you are writing about.
- Describe the topic of the talk.
- Make it clear why you selected this talk to review.
- Explain why TED Talks are useful for English learners.

Write **280–320** words.

ANALYSIS

10 Check your review. Answer the questions.

Content: Is the talk clearly identified? Is the topic of the talk described? Is it clear why you chose this talk? Does the review include an explanation of why TED talks are useful for English learners? Is the review 280 to 320 words long?

Communicative achievement: Is it written in a neutral style? Is your opinion about the talk clear to the reader?

Organization: Is the review logically organized? Does it use clear paragraphs?

Language: Does it use correct grammar and vocabulary? Is a good range of structures used?

7 Same but different

7.1 The danger of a single story

TEDTALKS

Writer and novelist **CHIMAMANDA NGOZI ADICHIE** was born in 1977 in Enugu, Nigeria, the fifth of six children. She grew up in Nsukka, in a house formerly occupied by Nigerian writer Chinua Achebe, who later would become one of her literary idols and who would in turn become a fan of Adichie. Her parents both worked at the University of Nigeria in Nsukka – her father was a professor of statistics before becoming Deputy Vice-Chancellor and her mother was the university's first female registrar – and Adichie completed her secondary education at a school attached to the university. She was a very good student and received a number of academic prizes. Adichie then studied medicine and pharmacy at the university, where she also edited a magazine produced by the university's Catholic medical students.

When she was nineteen, Adichie went to the United States after gaining a scholarship to study communication at Drexel University in Philadelphia. She then did a degree in communication and political science at Eastern Connecticut State University, a master's degree in creative writing at Johns Hopkins University, Baltimore and, in 2008, an MA in African Studies at Yale University. In 2012, she received a fellowship of the Radcliffe Institute for Advanced Study, Harvard University.

It was in 2001, while she was at Eastern Connecticut State University, that Adichie started working on her first novel, *Purple Hibiscus*. The book was published in 2003 and received wide critical acclaim and a number of awards. She has since published several more novels and short stories, which have been translated into over 30 languages, and has received an array of literary accolades and awards. She was listed among the 'Leading Women of 2014' by CNN and among the '100 Most Influential People' by *TIME Magazine* in 2015.

Chimamanda Ngozi Adichie

CAREER PATHWAYS

1 Read the text. Answer the questions.

1 What links with the University of Nigeria do Adichie and her parents have?
2 What connects Adichie and Chinua Achebe, both within and outside their professional lives?
3 In what subjects does Adichie have academic qualifications?
4 Was her debut literary publication successful? What tells us this?
5 In what ways has Adichie been honoured?

TED PLAYLIST

2 Other TED speakers are interested in topics similar to Chimamanda Ngozi Adichie's TED Talk. Read the descriptions of four TED Talks at the top of page 65. In your opinion, which is the best title for this playlist, a, b or c?

a Celebrating diversity and difference
b Where we come from and who we are
c A journey to a better place

3 Read the TED playlist again. Find a speaker who ...

1 examines how people from different backgrounds co-exist.
2 is primarily interested in questions of identity.
3 looks at the effects of migration.
4 is trying to promote women's rights in their country.

4 Read the TED playlist again. Which verbs or verb phrases describe a speaker who:

1 is forcing people to question things
2 is using a pool of knowledge
3 made an observation
4 is drawing attention to something

5 Which talk would you most like to see? Why? Watch the talk at TED.com.

▶ **Nadia Al-Sakkaf: See Yemen through my eyes**

In this 2011 TED Talk, given soon after political protests began in her country, the editor of the *Yemen Times*, Nadia Al-Sakkaf, talks at TEDGlobal with host Pat Mitchell, highlighting how the independent English-language newspaper is vital for sharing a new vision of Yemen and of that country's women as equal partners in work and change.

▶ **Yassmin Abdel-Magied: What does my headscarf mean to you?**

What do you think when you look at this speaker? Well, think again. (And then again.) In this funny, honest, empathetic talk, Yassmin Abdel-Magied challenges us to look beyond our initial perceptions, and to open doors to new ways of supporting others.

▶ **Rich Benjamin: My road trip through the whitest towns in America**

As America becomes more and more multicultural, Rich Benjamin spotted a phenomenon: some communities were actually getting less diverse. So he got out a map, found the whitest towns in the USA – and moved in. In this funny, honest, human talk, he shares what he learned as a black man in Whitopia.

▶ **Colin Grant: How our stories cross over**

Colin Grant has spent a lifetime navigating the emotional landscape between his father's world and his own. Born in England to Jamaican parents, Grant draws on stories of shared experience within his immigrant community – and reflects on how he found forgiveness for a father who rejected him.

AUTHENTIC LISTENING SKILLS
Weak forms

6 🎧 2 01 You are going to hear a podcast in which a member of the *Keynote* team talks about Yassmin Abdel-Magied's TED Talk, *What does my headscarf mean to you?* Read the sentence and underline the words you think are weak forms. Then listen and check your answers.

Yassmin's talk makes me question how I can still have biases and how I can overcome them.

7 🎧 2 02 Guess what the missing grammatical words (pronounced as weak forms) are in this sentence. Then listen and check your answers.

I _____ worked in _____ field _____ second-language learning _____ over 35 years, exposed _____ students _____ educators _____ many different cultures _____ perspectives.

LISTENING

8 🎧 2 03 Listen to the full podcast. Choose the correct words or phrases to make true sentences.

1 Laura travels and encounters different cultures *in her work / in a search to broaden her mind*.
2 Laura feels that *she has managed to overcome her biases / she is still influenced by her biases*.

9 🎧 2 03 Listen again. Answer the questions.

1 Why did Yassmin Abdel-Magied change her outfit while talking, according to Laura?
2 What does seeing someone as 'different' often imply, according to Laura?

3 Why should Laura have 'no excuse' for having cultural biases?
4 What did Laura assume the Saudi woman thought of her?
5 What was the lesson of Laura's story about the Saudi woman in the plane?
6 What idea of Yassmin Abdel-Magied's does Laura find particularly true?
7 What is Yassmin Abdel-Magied's simple solution to overcoming bias?

VOCABULARY IN CONTEXT

10 Read the extracts from the podcast. Choose the correct meaning of the words in bold.

1 The unconscious bias is something I have **grappled with** for a long time.
   a argued against ☐   b struggled with ☐
   c had to live with ☐
2 We all have these inner biases and, no matter how much we realize intellectually that they are **unfounded** and wrong, …
   a without sense ☐   b without benefit ☐
   c without basis ☐
3 … yet I still sometimes have the **gut reaction** of 'my way' being the right way versus 'their way'.
   a certainty ☐   b theory ☐   c instinct ☐
4 Then during the flight, we hit **turbulence**.
   a loss of cabin pressure ☐   b electrical storms ☐
   c uneven atmospheric movement ☐
5 When I see people really **living hand to mouth** …
   Surviving: a from day to day ☐   b on donations ☐
   c by doing basic manual jobs ☐

7.2 No better, no worse

GRAMMAR Comparative forms

1 Find and correct the mistake in each sentence.

1 You're by far more likely to stand out if you dress like that.
2 Learning the language is the best far way to get to know a culture.
3 The differences between the two are so slight to be negligible.
4 I always feel whole lot better after a good night's sleep.
5 Invite as many people as you like. More, the merrier.
6 I'm not as open-minded you are, but I'm happy to try most things once.
7 This one's not nearly interesting as that one, don't you think?
8 I think the population is bit bigger, but I'm not sure.

2 🎧 2 04 Read the table and the extracts from a student presentation. Complete the text with the words in the boxes and any other words necessary. Then listen and check your answers.

> about 40 times/big   considerably/big   ~~far/big~~
> far/big   high/percentage/land used for agriculture
> much/great   only about/a third/short
> over five times/people   slightly/high/urban population

	USA	UK
area	9,857,000km²	243,610km²
coastline	19,924 km	12,430 km
total population	320 million	62 million
urban population	81%	90%
agricultural land	44%	71%
life expectancy	79 (76m, 81f)	81 (79m, 83f)
happiness index	71%	70%
world wealth rank (GDP)	2nd ($17.9 trillion)	9th ($2.6 trillion)

As we can see in the table, the USA is ¹ *far bigger than* the UK, ² _____ in fact. However, and perhaps surprisingly, the coastline of the UK is ³ _____ than that of the USA. But, if you look at what's called the total tidal shoreline, which takes into account rivers and other inlets, then the difference is ⁴ _____.

In terms of population, the USA is ⁵ _____ , with ⁶ _____ the UK. The majority of people in both countries live in urban areas, with the UK having ⁷ _____ the USA, as a percentage of total population. At the same time, the UK has a ⁸ _____ the USA. However, the total land used for agriculture is ⁹ _____ in the USA.

3 Rewrite the sentences so the meaning is similar.

1 Staying in touch was much more difficult even just ten years ago compared to these days.
Staying in touch is a whole *lot easier these days compared to even just* ten years ago.
2 As technology advances, it gets easier and easier.
The _____ , the _____ .
3 That was the best lecture yet by a long way.
_____ far _____ .
4 It was nothing like as expensive as we thought it would be.
_____ far _____ .
5 There were far more people here last week.
_____ not nearly _____ .
6 We need to leave and if we do it soon, it will be better.
We need _____ and the _____ .

4 Complete the quotations with the words and phrases in the box.

a whole lot	by far	nearly	twice

1 There are books of which the backs and covers are _____ the best parts.
Charles Dickens (writer)
2 I like surfing in Mexico _____ better than sitting with people in Washington that I don't even like.
Jesse Ventura (politician)
3 Ignorance per se is not _____ as dangerous as ignorance of ignorance.
Sydney J. Harris (journalist)
4 A wide screen just makes a bad film _____ as bad.
Samuel Goldwyn (film producer)

LANGUAGE FOCUS Expressing preferences

5 Choose the correct option to complete the sentences.

1 Research has shown that most school children *would rather / would prefer* learn to code *than to / rather than* to speak a foreign language.

2 Most people *would rather / would prefer* to have a bigger smartphone with better battery life, *than / rather than* a smaller one with shorter battery life.

3 According to a survey, most savers generally *like / favour* investing in property *than / over* paying into a pension.

4 People tend to *rather / prefer* dogs *than / to* cats as they consider them better companions.

5 Some people think we would be *sooner / better* off *to have / having* fewer men in positions of power.

6 Would it be better *have / to have* the Olympics every two years *to / rather than* every four?

7 Research suggests that a growing number of people *would prefer / would sooner* text *to / than* speak on the phone if they have the choice.

8 A lot of people say they would just *as soon / rather* watch a sporting event on TV *as / to* actually go to the event.

6 🎧 **2 05** Complete the dialogues using the correct form of the words in brackets. Then listen and check your answers.

1 A: Shall we sit here?
B: I _____ (rather/sit) a bit further from the door, if that's OK. Is that table over there free?

2 A: There's a flight at about eight in the morning and another at eleven.
B: I think we _____ (be/better off/get) the earlier one. The second one might be cutting it a bit fine. What do you think?

3 A: Do you mind if I smoke?
B: I _____ (rather/you/not/do), if you don't mind.

4 A: I'll email you tomorrow.
B: It _____ (might/be/better/speak) on the phone, if possible. I think it would keep things easier.

5 A: I generally _____ (prefer/listen) to music through speakers rather than headphones. It's sometimes a bit too intense through headphones.
B: Yeah, I know what you mean.

6 A: We _____ (prefer/you/pay) in Swiss francs rather than euros, if that's OK.
B: Sure, no problem.

7 A: Is it OK if I tell Jenny?
B: I _____ (rather/you/keep) it to yourself for the time being.

8 A: Are you a big cinema-goer?
B: Not really. To be honest, I _____ (just as soon/watch) a film at home as _____ (go) to the cinema.

DICTATION

7 🎧 **2 06** Listen to part of a student presentation comparing the highest and lowest ranking countries in the Global Gender Gap index. Complete the sentences.

The Global Gender Gap index, which is produced by the World Economic Forum, rates countries, among other criteria, according to women's economic participation and opportunity, their political empowerment and whether [1] _____ to have access to education and healthcare. The latest report shows that Iceland [2] _____ and Yemen the least, of the 145 countries in the study. In Iceland, [3] _____ are in work or looking for work, 83% compared to 87%, and their earnings [4] _____ men's. In Yemen, female employment [5] _____ compared to 74% for men. Women's earnings are also [6] _____, for a comparable job. In Yemen, only one in ten senior officials, managers and legislators are female, and just one in ten government ministers are women. By comparison, in Iceland the proportion of women in these jobs [7] _____, with 44% of government ministers being women.

7.3 Why more is less

READING

1 Look at the title of the article. What do 'clues' mean in this context?

   a solutions   **b** evidence   **c** examples

2 Read the article. Tick (✓) the clues that the researchers discovered about why people make stereotypes. Stereotypes arise because of:

   1 the way we communicate   ☐
   2 negative feelings to others   ☐
   3 our need to connect with others   ☐
   4 our need to classify things   ☐

3 Read the article again and choose the best answer.

   1 The research at Aberdeen suggests that
     a negative stereotypes are not made deliberately
     b no stereotypes are made deliberately
     c all stereotypes are made deliberately

   2 The writer suggests that
     a no-one wants to use stereotypes
     b no-one can help using stereotypes
     c everyone enjoys using stereotypes

Scientists find clues to how stereotypes develop

Recent research at the University of Aberdeen suggests that cultural stereotypes are not a concerted effort by one group of people in society to marginalize another, but rather an unintentional consequence of the way that human beings share information. The study, conducted by Dr Doug Martin and his team at the University of Aberdeen's Person Perception Lab, sought to investigate how stereotypes came about and how, once formed, they evolved.

Like it or not, we all have stereotypes in our minds: people in their 20s (Generation Y) feel a sense of entitlement, people who play computer games are geeky, people who work in sales are confident and pushy. But where did such opinions originate and how did they become widespread? Dr Martin's theory is that they developed and spread in much the same way as language does.

In an experiment originally devised to examine the evolution of language, Dr Martin's team invented groups of aliens, each group with a different colour, body shape and set of characteristics. Volunteers were asked to learn the attributes associated with each group and after that were given a test to see what they could remember. The details they recalled were then passed on to be learned by another volunteer. This process was repeated from volunteer to volunteer. With each step of information-sharing, the attributes of each alien group became distilled into a standardized (and simplified) picture of colour, shape and personality traits; in other words, into stereotypes.

Dr Martin believes that these stereotypes evolve because of humans' natural tendency to want to make sense of new information. Categorization is a natural way to do this. Just as we process language by fitting it into a framework of knowledge about how language works – e.g. words that come between an article and a noun are likely to be adjectives – so we fit other information into convenient categories or ready-made frameworks.

Such stereotypes can, of course, be very negative, since they can have no basis in fact. The association of people from a particular region of the world with red hair and freckles could originate from valid observation. But the idea that the same people are generally mean with their money is likely to be completely untrue, however widely that view is shared by another social group. According to Dr Martin, both types of stereotyping are common. 'Where a genuine relationship exists between social categories and attributes, people are very good at detecting this, remembering it and then passing this information on. Equally, however, where there is no existing relationship between social categories and attributes, we see this association emerging spontaneously over time as the social information evolves.'

So is there any hope of changing mistaken associations and perceptions? Dr Martin's next project is to try to understand better how such cultural stereotypes form and evolve, so that their content can be manipulated and influenced in a positive way.

3 In the experiment conducted at the University of Aberdeen all the volunteers
  a depended on another volunteer for information about the aliens
  b got their information about the aliens from the researchers
  c learned about the aliens either from researchers or another volunteer
4 Dr Martin thinks that stereotypes with no basis in fact
  a are less likely to become widespread than those based on fact
  b are just as likely to become widespread as those based on fact
  c are more likely to become widespread than those based on fact
5 Dr Martin's view of negative and incorrect stereotypes is that
  a they could be changed for the better
  b it is not the job of scientists to change them
  c they are naturally occurring and must not be changed

4 Choose the definitions (a–c) for the words (1–5) from the text.

1 concerted (paragraph 1)
  a combined   **b** strong   **c** planned
2 marginalize (paragraph 1)
  a treat as insignificant   **b** get power over
  c define the characteristics of
3 entitlement (paragraph 2)
  a needing to work only if they want   **b** being wiser
  than their parents   **c** deserving to have what they want
4 distilled (paragraph 3)
  a transformed   **b** condensed   **c** expanded
5 valid (paragraph 5)
  a authentic   **b** occasional   **c** incorrect

VOCABULARY Idioms related to choice

5 Rewrite the idioms by changing the words in bold.

1 I think I'm going to have to sit on the **cherry** on this one. I really can't make a decision.
2 Well, despite our terrible run of form, I don't think we should be looking for a new manager just yet. Better the **evils** you know, I say.
3 Companies like Google and Apple can pretty well **plunge** pick whoever they like.
4 A romantic weekend in Paris or a weekend paintballing? It's a no-**judgement**.
5 I'm going to hedge my **fence** and put a bid on two or three items. Hopefully I'll win one of them.
6 House prices are going up and up, so it's time to take the **devil** and get on the property ladder before it's too late.
7 Well, I voted for him against my better **brainer**. But as I've got reservations about both candidates, I guess it's a case of the lesser of two **bets**.

WORD FOCUS *choice*

6 Complete the phrases and expressions in bold. Use the words in the box.

by	freedom	Hobson's	left	matter
of	of	~~spoilt~~		

1 Being *spoilt* **for choice** means you have a lot of things to choose from.
2 Doing something _____ **choice** means you choose to do it yourself.
3 Something _____ **choice** (e.g. *my drink* ...) is your favourite or preferred option.
4 If you **have no choice in the** _____ , it means you have to accept the situation.
5 _____ **of choice** means that you are free to make a choice.
6 If you are _____ **with no choice but to** (or **have no choice but to**) do something, it means you have no other options remaining.
7 If something is _____ **your choice** (e.g. *a side dish of your choice*), it is the alternative that you choose.
8 If you have _____ **choice**, it means despite having a choice, only one option can in reality be chosen.

7 Complete the sentences with the phrases and expressions from Exercise 6.

1 Well, I'm not here on this course _____ , that's for sure. My ever-so thoughtful boss thought it would be a good idea.
2 I'm a bit _____ by this menu. It all looks so delicious. I don't know what to choose.
3 A Rolls Royce used to be the car _____ for any self-respecting 1960s pop star, TV star or actor.
4 I'm sorry, but you _____ . A decision has been made and that's that.
5 Having already shown him the yellow card, the referee was _____ send him off.
6 It's important to have _____ when it comes to choosing a school for your children.
7 All the other hotels were either full or too expensive, so it was a case of _____ .
8 First prize in the competition is a weekend for two in a European capital city _____ .

7.4 Having said that ...

USING DISCOURSE MARKERS

1 🎧 **2 07** Listen to two people presenting an argument, each about a different topic. Are the statements true (T) or false (F)?

Speaker 1 ...

1 thinks online social media is a good way to keep in touch. ☐

2 likes seeing the everyday little details about people's lives. ☐

3 agrees he might post things that irritate other people. ☐

Speaker 2 ...

4 thinks people generally accept that the news in their own country is accurate and truthful. ☐

5 thinks it's inevitable that news stories are sometimes presented very differently in different parts of the world. ☐

6 thinks that the different viewpoints of the press in different parts of the world is always a positive thing. ☐

2 Complete the extracts using the words in brackets.

1 Immigration is _____ (large) a good thing for most countries. In some areas _____ (least), it has resulted in a significant change in local demographics which can impact quite significantly on the traditions of the local community.

2 _____ (whole), I tend to agree with the idea that taxes need to increase to fund any free health care. _____ (same time), we could introduce health insurance to help minimize any tax rises.

3 Today, we have more understanding of genetics than ever before. _____ (result), we can now screen for and prevent many hereditary and congenital conditions. However, _____ (said), such screening is only usually used in a very few high-risk cases.

4 Information is pretty well instantly accessible to anyone at all times and _____ (because) a key life skill today is not so much remembering information, but knowing how to find information. _____ (consequence), the nature of human memory made over time may change significantly.

5 _____ (broadly), I personally agree with the notion that there are just two types of people, in the world of business _____ (rate). And that is those who lead and those who follow. _____ (having), I do think there is an important distinction between natural leaders and those who have been appointed.

6 Capitalism in many parts of the world has been very successful, _____ (grant/ that). However, the fundamental laws of economics say that one person's gain is another person's loss. _____ (reason), you can understand why historically, and in the present day, capitalism is a dirty word and doesn't work for everyone.

PRONUNCIATION Linking in discourse markers

3 🎧 **2 08** Mark the linking in the words in bold. Then listen and check your answers.

1 **By and large**, the project was a great success.

2 Things improved **as far as exam results are concerned**.

3 There was no noticeable difference, among the 11–14 age range **at any rate**.

4 **As a result**, demand increased significantly.

5 New security measures were introduced **as a consequence**.

6 **In spite of** the marketing campaign, sales continued to fall.

7 **On top of that**, attendance increased by almost 5%.

8 **Because of the** delay, extra costs were incurred.

WRITING SKILL Describing graphs

4 Read the description of a graph and underline the following.

1 Three phrases saying what the graph shows.

2 Four phrases that draw our attention to what we see.

3 Two verbs that describe an increase or decrease.

4 Two adverbs and two adjectives that describe the rate or degree of increase or decrease.

The graph shows the number of students in different sectors of education in the USA. It compares participation at high school, undergraduate, master's and doctoral level and also includes those who did not finish their studies. The graph also compares the number of males and females in each of the different levels of education. What we observe is that participation in education decreases steadily from high school to those obtaining a doctorate. Around 88% of Americans graduate from high school, with around 35% going on to achieve a first degree. The number then falls sharply to around 10% for a master's degree and to around 3% for a doctorate. It is also worth noting that around 50% attend higher education, but without obtaining a final qualification. Looking at participation by gender we can see that more females than males achieve first degrees and master's degrees. While the difference is slight for first degrees, it is more significant at master's level at around 19% participation for males and 24% for females.

5 Rewrite the sentences using the adverb or adjective form of the words in italics.

1 *sharp*
Enrolment increased.
Enrolment increased sharply.
There was an increase in enrolment.
There was a sharp increase in enrolment.

2 *gradual*
Attendance declined. _____
There was a decline in attendance.
_____

3 *slight*

Sales dropped. _____

We can see a drop in sales.

4 *significant*

The graph shows that results improved.

_____

The graph shows an improvement in results.

_____

5 *steady*

Temperatures rose. _____

There was a rise in temperature.

_____

6 Complete the sentences describing graphs using the words in the box.

compares	consider	constant	declined
observe	looking	rose	see
shows	significant	steadily	worth

1 Literacy levels _____ from 89% to 95% over a 50-year period.

2 What we _____ is a resurgence in the sales of vinyl records in 2015.

3 The graph _____ university fees in ten European countries.

4 It is also _____ noting that the increase in school attendance was higher in pupils from lower socio-economic backgrounds.

5 _____ at the figures for 2012, we can _____ that sales were consistently higher than in earlier and later years.

6 Enrolment on the course has remained _____ for the past three years.

7 If we _____ GDP per capita, there is a _____ difference in China's ranking on the global wealth index.

8 The graph _____ that the president's popularity rating _____ _____ from 75% to around 50% over the course of his final term of office.

7 Complete the description of the graph using the words in the box.

steady rise	decreases steadily	we can see
we can observe	it compares	looking at
it is worth noting	if we look	the graph
shows		

[1] _____ the unemployment rates and average earnings in the USA relative to educational level. [2] _____ these figures at high school, first degree, master's degree and doctoral degree level. First, [3] _____ unemployment rates, [4] _____ that this correlates with level of education and [5] _____ from around 10% of the workforce with just a high school education to 2.5% for those with a doctorate. [6] _____ that the average unemployment rate for all workers is about 8%. [7] _____ at weekly earnings, [8] _____ a [9] _____ from around $630 per week for those with a high-school education to around $1,500 per week for those with a doctorate.

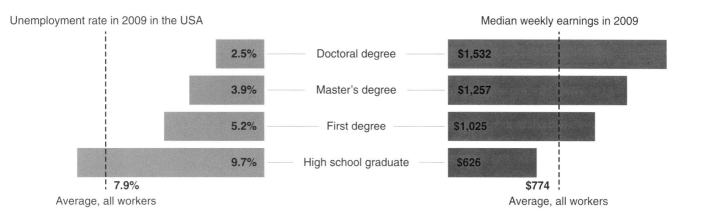

Unemployment rate in 2009 in the USA

2.5%	Doctoral degree	$1,532
3.9%	Master's degree	$1,257
5.2%	First degree	$1,025
9.7%	High school graduate	$626

7.9% Average, all workers

Median weekly earnings in 2009

$774 Average, all workers

YOUR IDEA

1 Read three descriptions of people's homes. Are the statements (a–f) true (T) or false (F)?

1 Weronika: I love where I live. It's just an average-sized apartment on the eighth floor, but the location is perfect. There is a fantastic view out over the river, and you can see bridges and the island in the middle. It's a very green city and my balcony overlooks a park with lush greenery that goes all the way down to the riverbank. The rent is very expensive, even though it isn't the biggest place. I can only really afford to live here now that I have a more senior position where I work. But, for me, to live in such a beautiful part of the city is worth the price.

2 Samira: In my culture, it's quite common for members of extended families to live close together. Well, in my family we actually take it a bit further – in the same building we have me, my brothers and sister, my parents, and my grandparents. We have quite a big property, five bedrooms with a front yard, a garage and a back garden big enough to have a marquee. We even had all my cousins to stay for a big party last summer. We had to get some huge temporary decking put up in the garden next to the French windows. It was quite expensive, but it was definitely worth it. Although it was crowded with so many people, we had a great day with all the family.

3 Angelo: This is actually the second place where I've lived in the UK. When I first moved here, I rented a studio flat. I didn't need anywhere bigger than that really. But then I met my wife and pretty soon we didn't have enough space. So we bought a detached house in a town near Manchester. We're expecting our second child now, so we're having one of our back rooms converted. Eventually it will become a separate bedroom for our daughter, and we can have the cot for our new baby in the bedroom with us. We're doing it ourselves this time, with some help from family and friends. But I think if we have any more work done on the house, we'll get professionals in for it.

a All three people are happy where they live. ☐
b Weronika had to have work done on her home. ☐
c Angelo moved to a bigger home because of his work. ☐
d Samira talks about an event that happened at her home. ☐
e All three people mention the location of their home. ☐
f Angelo's family is going to get bigger soon. ☐

2 Write notes about your home. Include both good and bad things about your home.

_____

_____

_____

_____

3 Match the sentence halves to make contrasts.

1 Even though the location is not perfect, … ☐
2 It may not have everything, … ☐
3 The rent is quite expensive. ☐
4 I haven't lived here very long, … ☐

a … although I did visit a lot before I moved.
b However, I wouldn't live anywhere else.
c … I still think it is a great place to live.
d … but it is good enough for me.

4 Practise your presentation out loud. Focus on sounding persuasive during your presentation. Try to use …

- emotive words and phrases (e.g. *such a beautiful place*).
- contrasts (e.g. *It may not be cheap, but it is a wonderful place to live*).
- imagery and metaphor (e.g. *It unlocks the door to a whole world of opportunities*).
- rhetorical questions (e.g. *Who wouldn't want to live in such an amazing place?*)

ORGANIZING YOUR PRESENTATION

5 Match the four steps of a presentation with two examples of useful language (a–h).

1 Introduce yourself and the topic of your presentation ☐ ☐
2 Tell the audience the good things about your home ☐ ☐
3 Contrast the good things with other information about your home ☐ ☐
4 Thank the audience and finish the presentation ☐ ☐

a One of the best things is the location. I mean, in the city centre you have everything you need nearby.
b Thank you for listening. Are there any questions?
c Hello, I'm Anna. Today I'm going to be talking about my home.
d While it may be a lively place to live, I just can't stand how noisy it is on Friday and Saturday nights.
e They say 'Home is where the heart is'. My name's Peter and that's what my talk is about.
f You might think everything is perfect, but there are actually things I don't like about living here.
g Well, that's all I've got to say. So, let's open the floor for questions.
h There are a few things I truly love about where I live.

6 Read the useful language on the left and make notes for your presentation.

1 Introduce yourself and the topic of your presentation Hi, I'm … Today's talk/presentation … I'm going to …	
2 Tell the audience the good things about your home One of … It's good to live here because … I (truly) love …	
3 Contrast the good things with other information about your home While it may …, but … Even though … … However, …	
4 Thank the audience and finish the presentation Thank you … Are there …? Let's open …	

7 Film yourself giving your presentation or practise in front of a mirror.
Give yourself marks out of ten for …

- making your talk sound persuasive.   ☐ /10
- following the four steps in Exercise 6.   ☐ /10
- using correct grammar.   ☐ /10

8 Food and sustainability

8.1 How I fell in love with a fish

TEDTALKS

DAN BARBER was born in 1969 and grew up in New York City's Upper East Side. He learned about farming and agriculture at a young age while helping out on his grandparents' farm in Massachusetts. Barber studied Political Science and English at Tufts University and graduated in 1992. He then worked at the renowned Chez Panisse restaurant in Berkeley, California, before returning to New York City to attend the French Culinary Institute. Barber then worked briefly for the Michelin-starred chef Michel Rostang in Paris before he returned once more to New York City to work in another top restaurant, Bouley.

In 1996, Barber took the decision to go it alone and started Dan Barber Catering. Four years later, having teamed up with his brother, he opened Blue Hill Restaurant in Greenwich Village, New York City, and the company was renamed Blue Hill Catering. Barber soon began to develop his signature approach to cooking, blending innovative new American cuisine with locally sourced and sustainable ingredients. Philanthropist David Rockefeller, impressed with what Barber was achieving, hired him to oversee the development of his 3,500-acre estate in Westchester, New York, and invested $30 million for Barber to open another Blue Hill restaurant.

In 2002, *Food & Wine Magazine* named Barber one of the Best New Chefs in the country and he has since won a number of other awards, including James Beard Foundation Outstanding Chef in 2009. Barber has advised Harvard Medical School's Center for Health and Global Environment and has served on President Obama's Council on Physical Fitness, Sports, and Nutrition. His first book, *The Third Plate*, was published in 2014 and he has also written for publications such *as TIME Magazine*, *The New York Times*, and *Gourmet Magazine*.

Dan Barber

CAREER PATHWAYS

1 Read the text. Answer the questions.

1 What initially inspired Dan Barber's interest in food?
2 Where did Barber gain experience of the food industry before setting up his own business?
3 What is meant by 'go it alone'? (paragraph 2)
4 What is meant by 'signature approach'? (paragraph 2)
5 What is Barber's culinary philosophy?

TED PLAYLIST

2 Other TED speakers are interested in topics similar to Dan Barber's TED Talk. Read the descriptions of four TED Talks at the top of page 75. In your opinion, which is the best title for this playlist, a, b or c?

a Alternatives to industrial farming
b Eating for good health
c Ingenious ideas for feeding the world

3 Read the TED playlist again. Find a speaker(s) who ...

1 is concerned about animal welfare.
2 believes in less transportation of food.
3 believe there are ways to eat fish sustainably.

4 Find words or phrases in the TED playlist that mean the same as the words and phrases (a–f).

a a difficult choice   b a saying   c kind
d revealing and amazing   e a perspective
f favourable

5 Which talk would you most like to see? Why? Watch the talk at TED.com.

▶ **Barton Seaver: Sustainable seafood? Let's get smart**

Chef Barton Seaver presents a modern dilemma: seafood is one of our healthier protein options, but overfishing is desperately harming our oceans. He suggests a simple way to keep fish on the dinner table that includes every mum's favourite adage – 'Eat your vegetables!'

▶ **Dan Barber: A foie gras parable**

At the Taste3 conference, chef Dan Barber tells the story of a small farm in Spain that has found a humane way to produce foie gras. Raising his geese in a natural environment, farmer Eduardo Sousa embodies the kind of food production Barber believes in.

▶ **Jackie Savitz: Save the oceans, feed the world**

What's a marine biologist doing talking about world hunger? Well, says Jackie Savitz, fixing the world's oceans might just help to feed the planet's billion hungriest people. In an eye-opening talk, Savitz tells us how we can help our global fisheries heal, while making more food for all.

▶ **Birke Baehr: What's wrong with our food system**

Eleven-year-old Birke Baehr presents his take on a major source of our food – far-away and less-than-picturesque industrial farms. Keeping farms out of sight promotes a rosy, unreal picture of big-box agriculture, he argues, as he outlines the case to green and localize food production.

AUTHENTIC LISTENING SKILLS
Word recognition

6 🎧 **2 09** You are going to hear a podcast in which a member of the *Keynote* team talks about Birke Baehr's TED Talk, *What's wrong with our food system*. Look at the words and a) circle the syllables that are stressed b) write how you think the highlighted sounds are pronounced. Then listen and check your answers.

controversial	*include*	*pesticides*	*preservatives*
diabetes	*prove*	*threats*	*among*

LISTENING

7 🎧 **2 10** Listen to the full podcast. Tick (✓) the items (1–4) that Paul says Birke Baehr covers in his talk.

1 The health risks posed by the food we eat. ☐
2 The problem of poor food distribution in the world. ☐
3 Ways to lobby the agriculture sector for change. ☐
4 Practical advice on what food to buy and eat. ☐

8 🎧 **2 10** Listen again. Complete the statements.

1 Paul was impressed by this eleven-year-old's _____ and passion.
2 One of the main problems Baehr mentions is food companies' false _____ .
3 One of Paul's favourite quotes in the talk is 'we can either pay the _____ , or we can pay the _____ '.
4 Another reason Paul is impressed by Baehr is that he acts on his _____ .
5 Baehr was the one in his family who got everyone to change their eating, consuming and _____ habits.
6 Baehr's ambition is to become an _____ farmer.

VOCABULARY IN CONTEXT

9 Read the extracts from the podcast. Choose the correct meaning of the words in bold.

1 ... and I was **blown away** by both his confidence and obvious passion.
  a very surprised ☐   **b** very charmed ☐
  c very impressed ☐
2 'You are what you eat', but the sad thing is that many people are **turning a blind eye to** this.
  a failing to recognize ☐   **b** pretending not to see ☐
  c hoping to notice ☐
3 ... this child of eleven years has not only figured out how to **work around** the system.
  a improve elements of ☐
  b navigate a way past ☐   **c** make the best of ☐
4 He led. They followed. I think this **speaks volumes about** him.
  a says a lot about ☐   **b** shows hidden parts of ☐
  c reveals everything about ☐
5 This kid **rocks**!
  a is talented ☐   **b** is brave ☐
  c is amazing ☐

8.2 Mind what you eat

GRAMMAR Modal verbs

1 Complete the sentences with the words in the box.

can't	could've	couldn't	can't have
didn't need to	had to	've just got to	might
might've	ought to	should've	
shouldn't have			

1 He _____ been very hungry. He hardly touched his food.

2 I _____ go to the market and get a few things for dinner tonight. I'll be back shortly.

3 How kind of you! Tulips, my favourite. Thanks. But you really _____ .

4 I _____ book. They said around 6.30 should be fine to get a table.

5 I didn't realize you were vegetarian, sorry. You _____ told me and I _____ prepared something else for you.

6 Sorry I _____ join you for drinks last night. I _____ work late.

7 This _____ be the right place, surely. It doesn't look anything like the photo, does it?

8 You really _____ try that new place on Union Street. It's very good.

9 _____ it be possible to have a seat nearer the window?

10 Excuse me. The bill's not right. I think you _____ added on another table's food.

2 Choose the correct option to complete the text.

Easy healthy eating

With a minimum of effort, healthy eating ¹ *shall / can / might* be really easy. You really ² *can't / mustn't / don't have to* work hard at eating healthily and you more than likely ³ *won't need to / shouldn't / mustn't* make much change to what you already eat. However, we ⁴ *do need to / do have / do ought to* be aware of the basics of healthy eating. Balance and eating foods in the right proportions is the key and if we get this right, we ⁵ *might / can / could* eat a wide variety of foods. Essentially, our diet ⁶ *shall / could / should* be based on starchy foods such as rice, pasta and potatoes, which is supplemented with plenty of fruit and vegetables. We also ⁷ *can / could / need to* make sure we eat plenty of protein-rich foods and some dairy products. And while fat, salt and sugar are important in our diet, we ⁸ *couldn't / mustn't / don't have to* consume too much of them. Below, we take a look at these foods in more detail.

3 Complete the text with the best modal verbs. More than one answer may be possible.

Starchy food

Starchy foods ¹ _____ ideally constitute around a third of all we eat and ² _____ be the basis of our meals. And even though you ³ _____ find the wholegrain or wholemeal varieties of rice, pasta and bread less appealing, they are much better for us as they generally contain more fibre, and minerals and vitamins.

Fruit and vegetables

We ⁴ _____ try to eat at least five portions of fruit and vegetables each day as these are an important source of vitamins and minerals. Research suggests that people who eat five or more portions a day ⁵ _____ have a lower risk of heart disease and other related health issues.

Protein

For our body to grow and repair itself efficiently, we ⁶ _____ eat plenty of protein-rich foods, such as meat, fish, nuts and pulses. These foods also give us essential vitamins and minerals.

Fat

While we ⁷ _____ stop eating fatty foods altogether, as they are a vital source of energy for the body, eating too much fat ⁸ _____ lead to weight gain or too high levels of cholesterol, both of which in turn ⁹ _____ lead to a range of health issues. We ¹⁰ _____ eat less unhealthy saturated fat, found in foods like cheese and butter and eat more unsaturated fat, which is present in nuts, seeds and vegetable oils.

Sugar

Sugar, which is another vital source of energy for the body, occurs naturally in a range of foods such as fruit and milk. But we generally ¹¹ _____ cut down on these types of foods as they ¹² _____ have great benefits. It is the sugar which is added to drinks, biscuits and cakes and some ready-meals which we ¹³ _____ try to avoid.

4 Rewrite the extracts by replacing the phrase in bold with a phrase using a modal verb.

1 **We were made to queue** for ages before they let us in.
We had to queue for ages before they let us in.

2 **It is a possibility that we'll be going out** this weekend.
_____

3 As it turned out, **it wasn't necessary for me to go** to the meeting after all.
_____
_____

4 She **maybe told** me, but I really can't remember.
_____
_____

5 **It's not possible that you saw** him last night. He's in Paris at the moment.
_____
_____

6 **I expected them to be** here by now. **Perhaps they've missed** the bus.
_____
_____

7 **Surely he realized** what was happening. How **was it possible that he didn't realize**.
_____
_____

8 **I'm obliged to go** to a meeting this evening. But it**'s very likely to be finished** by 7.30. So **it's possible for us to meet** then if you like.
_____
_____

LANGUAGE EXTRA Expressions with modal verbs

5 🎧 **2 11** Choose the correct option to complete the expressions. Then listen and check your answers.

1 A: You haven't by any chance got any fresh basil, have you?
B: **As luck _would / might_ have it**, I have. I got some this morning.

2 A: I had the cheese and spinach calzone and salad.
B: **I _may / might_ have guessed**. Do you ever have anything different?

3 A: There are way too many coffee shops round here. How many do we need?
B: **You _can / should_ say that, but** they're all always pretty busy.

4 A: How do you make parkin?
B: Parkin! **How on earth _should / must_ I know**!

5 A: Did you say anything to him?
B: Yes, but **I _mustn't / needn't_ have bothered**. He didn't seem the slightest bit interested.

6 A: I don't think we need to book. They usually have tables.
B: **I _mightn't / wouldn't_ bet on it**. Not on a Friday.

7 A: I heard that new bar's closing down already.
B: **You _may / can_ well be right**. There was never anyone in there, was there? **I _might / can_ well believe it**.

8 A: You ate whale steak! **How _would / could_ you**?
B: Well, a lot of restaurants sell it there. It's quite normal. So I thought **I _might / could_ as well give it a try**. Why not?

DICTATION

6 🎧 **2 12** Listen to the opening to a lecture about global food waste. Complete the sentences.

How much food have you wasted today, or at least in the last week? I'm sure all of us must have thrown something away that [1] _____.
On its own, it might not amount to much, but multiply that by [2] _____ and the figures are quite shocking. It's something that we, as individuals and governments, [3] _____
_____.

Here are a few basic facts about the food we waste. Each year, about one third of the food produced for human consumption is lost or wasted. That's around 1.3 billion tonnes. And [4] _____.
Fruits and vegetables, [5] _____,
are the most wasted food types and may account globally for as much as 50% of all food thrown away. This is primarily because these foods generally
[6] _____ and can also be more susceptible to physical damage. And there are some interesting and important differences when it comes to when, at which stage from farm to consumer, food is lost or wasted. In developing countries, around 40% of food wastage occurs during processing.
[7] _____ issues in harvesting techniques as well as inadequate storage and transportation facilities.

8.3 A contradiction in terms

READING

1 Look at the title of the blog. Which of the foods below do you think fall into the 'truly sustainable' category? Then read the blog and check.

    a a carton of orange juice   **b** an apple   **c** some steak from a local farm   **d** a loaf of bread made with local flour   **e** a Spanish tomato

2 Read the blog again. Answer the questions.

    1 What is the author's answer to the question: is any food truly sustainable?
    2 What sentence(s) in the blog best sums up this view?
    3 What are the two important rules to follow in trying to eat sustainably?

3 Read the blog again. What is the author referring to in each case?

    1 something else (line 5) _____
    2 that (line 12) _____
    3 it (line 17) _____
    4 these (line 19) _____
    5 a good alternative (line 31) _____
    6 this (line 36) _____
    7 what (line 39) _____
    8 here (line 40) _____
    9 there (line 41) _____
    10 which (line 51) _____

I give up! Is any food truly sustainable?

1 As Kermit the Frog once pointed out, 'It isn't easy being green!'. As well as trying to make healthy eating choices for ourselves, we constantly have to keep an eye on what foods are sustainable too. Not a week goes by without news that something else needs to be struck off the menu: sea-life that's being fished to extinction, nuts that take huge amounts of water to cultivate, fruit whose production is heavily dependent on pesticides. What's an environmentally-concerned person to do?

10 The fact is that unless you are going to be satisfied with a diet of cactus and insects – and, personally, you can count me out of that – you're going to have to compromise. So rather than looking for food that is 100% sustainable, look for what's least damaging to the environment. Here's a start:

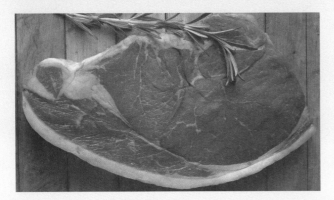

Meat: Poultry has the lowest carbon footprint, less than a quarter of that of beef or lamb. Try to buy local and, if you can afford it, organic to ensure minimal use of antibiotics.

Cereals: Crops such as wheat, barley and oats use relatively little water in their production. Among these,
20 buckwheat is particularly hardy and resistant to drought. Rice is also good because it returns a high number of calories relative to its footprint.

Vegetables: Beans, peas and lentils are leguminous – that means they enrich the soil they grow in, doing away with the need for (fossil fuel-based) fertilizers. Green-leaf vegetables like kale and spinach grow fast and are also extremely rich in minerals and nutrients.

Fruit: Seasonal berries like strawberries are great, with only 300 grams of carbon emissions per kilo of fruit. (Compare that to 2–3kg of CO_2 per kilo of tomatoes). They 3 also make a good alternative as a sugary treat. Of all the fruit-bearing trees, the least water-consuming are the pomegranate and the olive tree.

Fish: Which fish are OK to eat varies from year to year as fish stocks rise and fall, so check a website for up-to-date information on this. Since a lot of bought fish is now from farms, one good option is to go for herbivorous varieties like carp or tilapia, because you can never be quite sure what the fish on your plate has been fed.

Dairy: Not much good news here, I'm afraid. Cheese is right up there with beef in carbon footprint terms, since most dairy products come from cattle and sheep, whose heavy footprint isn't just from the water and energy used in meat production, but also from their emissions!

Sorry if the menu is a little more limited than you would have liked. But there's actually nothing wrong with rice and beans followed by some fruit – it's what a lot of people get by with as their staple diet all over Central America.

Two last points to note. First, worry less about food miles than the amount of energy and water used in food production, which makes up a much more significant part of the equation. Secondly, buy only what you're going to eat – food waste is the main reason that our current eating habits are unsustainable.

4 🎧2 13 Listen to someone describing ways to cut down food waste. Complete the table.

Food item to be used	Dish it creates	Method
1 _____	_____	Bake in hot oven with _____, salt and pepper
2 _____ cores and _____	_____	_____, then strain
3 Old _____ and _____	Frittata	_____ eggs, add to _____ and bake for _____
4 Leftover _____ and _____	_____	Cook in _____ with _____
5 Meat _____ and _____ carcasses	_____	_____ with a few

VOCABULARY Synonyms -able and -ible

5 ~~Cross out~~ the word which does not have a similar meaning to the other two.

1 Her commitment to her veganism is *amenable/laudable/commendable*.

2 Unfortunately, in some parts of the world, an insufficient diet is *unavoidable/unattainable/inevitable*.

3 My local café is 'pay what you want' for a coffee every Monday. It's a great idea, but only really *workable/viable/agreeable* for the one day a week.

4 The idea that we will all one day be living entirely on pills is simply not *plausible/credible/negligible*.

5 It's a great restaurant and the owner is very *agreeable/amenable/laudable*.

6 A diet where you consume just 500 calories a day for five days a week? Is that *feasible/commendable/doable*?

7 I think you need to be realistic regarding any weight-loss plan and aim for what is *amenable/attainable/achievable*.

8 Environmental damage and destruction due to industrial scale agriculture is not always *unavoidable/irreparable/irreversible*.

9 Research suggests that any correlation between vegetarianism and longevity is *negligible/unattainable/insignificant*.

WORDBUILDING Multi-part verbs with *up, down, on* and *off*

6 Complete the sentences with the correct form of the verbs in the box.

chop	cut	dish	drink	go
~~heat~~	live	top	whip	wolf

1 I'll leave your dinner in the fridge and you can *heat* it **up** in the microwave.

2 We haven't got much time. I'll _____ **up** an omelette if you like.

3 I see your glass is nearly empty. Can I _____ you **up**?

4 I really need to _____ **down on** the amount of sugar I eat.

5 Dinner's ready. I'm just about to _____ it **up**.

6 Come on, _____ **up**. We need to be going.

7 Could you _____ some veg **up** for me?

8 He must've been starving. He _____ it **down** in no time.

9 He'll _____ **on** fresh fruit given half the chance. He'd have it for breakfast, lunch and dinner.

10 Yuk! The milk's _____ **off**. I'll just go and get some more.

7 Match the words and phrases with the multi-part verbs from Exercise 6.

1	warm	*heat up*
2	eat only	_____
3	make quickly	_____
4	finish your drink	_____
5	serve it	_____
6	reduce	_____
7	ate quickly	_____
8	cut into small pieces	_____
9	fill	_____
10	gone bad	_____

8 Rewrite the sentences using a multi-part verb from Exercise 6.

1 Let me fill your glass.
_____

2 Finish your drink and let's go.
_____

3 He virtually eats only ready-meals.
_____

4 He made this amazing meal in no time at all.
_____

5 I was starving. I ate it very quickly.
_____

6 I'm serving it in two minutes.
_____

7 You need to warm it in a pan for a few minutes.
_____

8 I've been trying to eat less cheese.
_____

8.4 I'll try anything once ...

ATTITUDE TO FOOD

1 🎧 2 14 Listen to three people talking about their attitude to food and answer the questions.

> **1** Who would you say is the most and least open to trying new foods?
>
> **2** What types of food would each speaker prefer to avoid when it comes to trying out new food?
>
> Speaker 1 _____
> Speaker 2 _____
> Speaker 3 _____

2 🎧 2 14 Look at these extracts from Exercise 1 and write the words in the correct order in the space provided. Then listen again and check your answers.

Speaker 1

I guess on the whole ¹ *eat / what / pretty / with / I'm / I / cautious* _____
and I generally like to ² *know / what / with / I / stick* _____ and ³ *option / take / safe / the* _____ .

⁴ *I / experiment / am / to / happy* _____

and ⁵ *something / a / new / give / go* _____ ,

but ... ⁶ *it / generally / safe / like / to / I / play* _____ . But if I'm confident that something is OK, then ⁷ *to / try / happy / I'm / out / it* _____ .

Speaker 2

⁸ *I'd / adventurous / I'm / say / quite* _____ when it comes to food and ⁹ *to / open / new / always / experiences* _____ ...

I suppose ¹⁰ *anything / try / generally / I'm / to / happy* _____ ,

though I ¹¹ *line / draw / might / at / the* _____ some of the more extreme things ...

Speaker 3

I think ¹² *conservative / I'm / quite / really* _____ when it comes to food ...

I suppose ¹³ *quite / I'm / my / traditional / tastes / in* _____ .

3 Complete the sentences.

> **1** I'm quite adventurous when it _____ to trying out new foods and I'm generally _____ to try anything, within reason. I will draw the _____ at some things though.
>
> **2** My parents are really quite conservative _____ it comes _____ food. Whenever we go out for a meal, they always take the safe _____ , usually something quite traditional.
>
> **3** I'm always happy to _____ out something new. My attitude is like, I've never seen this before and might not ever again, so let's _____ it _____ go.
>
> **4** I have a gluten allergy, so I always need to _____ it safe when I'm eating out and _____ with what I know. So, yeah, I am pretty _____ in what I eat. I have to be.

PRONUNCIATION Assimilation and elision

4 🎧 2 15 Look at the words in bold and mark where the linking of two sounds creates a new sound (assimilation) or causes a sound to be 'lost' (elision). Then listen and check your answers.

> **1** I don't **understand why** anyone would want to eat that.
> **2** Can you **ask what's** in it?
> **3** I'll eat **most things**, within reason.
> **4** I **used to** be vegetarian, but I started **eating meat** a couple of years ago.
> **5** Do you know *Meals for five pounds*? It's a **good book**.
> **6** The whole meal was less than **ten pounds**.
> **7** Is this the **first time** you've eaten here?
> **8** A table for one, please. It's **just me**.

WRITING SKILL Participles

5 Underline the participles in the text.

> <u>Having been</u> for many years just a treat for the weekend, a new survey has revealed that the average Briton now spends over £100 per month on take-away meals. Not having the time or the inclination to cook, or being too tired are the biggest reasons for having a take-away. Picking up the phone or ordering online and having something delivered is quite the norm according to the survey. Men are the biggest fast-food consumers, and get through around 150 take-aways a year, while the figure for women is around 125, with 25- to 34-year-olds being the biggest consumers of take-away food.
>
> Having been overtaken by Chinese and Indian food, the traditional British take-away meal of fish and chips has gone from being the nation's most popular take-away to its third favourite. Closely followed by pizza in fourth place. These foods make up around 85% of all take-away meals.

6 Complete the extracts using the correct participle form of the verbs in brackets.

1 _____ (derive) from the Tamil word *kari*, which means spiced sauce, curry, was originally a soup-like dressing served in southern India. It is the Portuguese, _____ (include) a *kari* recipe in a 17th-century cook book, who are credited with popularizing it in Europe.

2 _____ (live) in the UK for several years, one of the things I miss most is al fresco dining.

3 _____ (open) in 2005, the restaurant gained its first Michelin star only two years later.

4 _____ (weigh) 2.3 kg, the truffle, _____ (buy) anonymously at auction, fetched over $1 million.

5 _____ (spend) over five million pounds on the revamp, they needed to run at at least 75% capacity seven days a week.

6 The EU has a total rice-growing area of around 450,000 hectares, with 80% of this _____ (grow) in Italy and Spain.

7 Complete the text using the correct participle form of the verbs in the box.

be	be	~~constitute~~	cook
eat	refer	supply	vary

> [1] *Constituting* a dominant portion of a standard diet in a given population, staple foods, often [2] _____ to as just *staples*, are at the heart of the human diet, [3] _____ a large fraction of our energy needs. [4] _____ from region to region and [5] _____ as often as at least once every day, staples typically include tuber- or root-crops, grains and legumes and include one or more of the three essential macronutrients of carbohydrate, protein and fat. Globally, just fifteen crop plants provide 90 per cent of the world's food energy intake with rice, maize and wheat [6] _____ the staple food of over 4 billion people and comprising two thirds of human food consumption. Rice alone is the staple for almost half of the world's population, [7] _____ the predominant staple not only in a number of countries in Asia and the Pacific, but also in the Americas and in Africa. And [8] _____ correctly, rice is the highest provider of energy (kJ) per weight of all the world's common staple foods.

8 Rewrite the sentences using a participle clause.

1 He was known affectionately as General Chef and he always found time to chat with the customers.
Known affectionately as General Chef, he always found time to chat with the customers.

2 They had no idea what the food was like as they hadn't eaten there before.
_____
_____

3 The lively little restaurant is known for its quirky menu and attracts visitors from miles around.
_____
_____

4 She decided to give the snails a miss on this occasion as she had tried eating them before.
_____
_____

5 We didn't know the area so we had no idea where was the best place to eat.
_____
_____

6 The food is inspired by the local landscape and the character of its people and the restaurant is usually fully booked for up to six months in advance.
_____
_____
_____

Writing 4 | A REPORT

IDEAS

You will read a report written to answer the question below.

> A literary festival was recently held in your town for publishers to promote new books and for local people to meet authors. You have been asked to write a report for the organizers. You should briefly describe the festival and identify two or three events of particular interest and relevance. You should also evaluate the extent to which such events contribute to the cultural life of your town.

Write your report in **280–320 words** in an appropriate style.

1 In the question, underline the three areas which need to be covered in the article. What kind of events could be included? How might a literary festival contribute to a town's cultural life?

MODEL

2 Read the report on the right. Which heading and section deals with each area you identified in Exercise 1? Does it include any of your ideas?

3 Read the report again. Answer the questions.

  1 What was the theme of the festival?
  2 What statistics does the writer give to show that the festival was popular?
  3 What does the report writer suggest might be one result of Marshall's talk?
  4 According to the writer, why was the talk about becoming a travel writer different to normal?
  5 Which places did festival goers visit that they might not normally go to?

USEFUL LANGUAGE

4 Find phrases in the model text in Exercise 2 which have the same meaning as 1–6. The number in (brackets) tells you how long the phrase is.

  1 lots of (3 words)
  2 was very popular (4 words)
  3 interested me (3 words)
  4 which we probably would have no other chance to learn (9 words)
  5 providing for the needs of (2 words)
  6 learn that something is good (5 words)

This report relates to the recent 'Around the world in 80 books' festival organized by the city library service.

¹Overview

The week-long festival incorporated over 50 events, covering a wealth of topics related to travel writing. They included question-and-answer sessions, book signings, and four book launches. There were guest appearances from ten different authors and six publishers were represented.

The travel theme went down very well, with the majority of events sold out before the festival began. Those which didn't sell out had at least 80% attendance.

²Highlights

There were two events that drew my attention: the first featuring William Marshall and the second offering tips for potential travel writers.

Marshall's hour-long question-and-answer session allowed the audience to delve deeply into the stories behind his wide range of travel books. His answers were informative and amusing, and included insights into cultures that we might not otherwise have been aware of. I have no doubt that there will be an upsurge in the number of his books borrowed from the library as audience members were left wanting to read more of his work.

It was no surprise to see that the presentation on how to set yourself up as a travel writer was completely full. The presenter covered a range of possible avenues into writing, no matter what your experience of travelling, catering for everyone from adventurous backpackers to staycationers*. Since so many people believe that you can only be a travel writer if you visit far-flung places, this made a refreshing change.

³Effects

As indicated above, 'Around the world' was a success, providing opportunities for local people to gain a positive impression of the world of publishing, as well as encouraging them to go to many, sometimes neglected, libraries and museums in our city. The benefits to the city mean that another such festival should definitely be organized again as soon as possible.

staycationers = people who take holidays in their own countries, e.g. a Brit taking a holiday in the UK.

5 Add an adjective or adverb from the box to the appropriate place in the sentences to create emphasis. Make any other necessary changes to the sentences.

ably	ample	careful
general	huge	personally

1 I will begin by providing an overview of the festival.
2 Consideration should be given to whether we can afford to run a similar festival again.
3 I found her talk to be one of the highlights of the whole event.
4 The organizers were assisted by a team of volunteers.
5 There were opportunities for audience members to participate in the discussion.
6 Overall, the festival was a success.

6 Match the verbs (1–6) with their collocates (a–f).

1 highlight ☐
2 make ☐
3 pay ☐
4 cover ☐
5 find ☐
6 interpret ☐

a close attention to
b something particularly problematic
c the importance of
d something in a number of ways
e a refreshing change
f a range of issues

7 Put the phrases in the correct order. They can all be used to signpost the structure of your report.

1 covered / aspects / suggest / the / earlier

_____

2 findings / in / our / of / light

_____

3 appear / it / then / that / would

_____

4 mentioned / as / outset / at / the

_____

5 from / following / previous / the / point / on

_____

6 it / whether / questioned / therefore / be / should

_____

PLANNING

You will answer the following question.

> You work for the tourist office in your area. Your manager has asked you to write a report in English on the food scene where you live. You should briefly describe the types of establishment that are currently available to visitors. Your report should also recommend two or three changes that could be made to the food industry in the area and explain why these would attract even more visitors.

Write your report in **280–320 words** in an appropriate style.

8 Plan your report. Write notes to answer these questions. Don't write full sentences yet.

1 Where can tourists go to eat in your area?
2 What is good or bad about the range of eating establishments currently available and the service they provide?
3 What changes could be made?
4 How will these changes attract more visitors?

WRITING

9 Write a report to reply to the question in Exercise 8. In your report you should:
- state the aim of the report.
- describe the types of eating establishments in your area.
- recommend changes that could be made to improve on what is already available.
- explain why these changes would attract more visitors to the area.

Write **280–320 words**.

ANALYSIS

10 Check your report. Answer the questions.

Content: Does the report describe where people can eat in the area? Are two or three changes recommended? Is the potential impact of these changes on visitor numbers included? Is the report 280 to 320 words long?

Communicative achievement: Is it clear to the reader what you would like them to do as a result of the report? Is it written in a neutral or formal style?

Organization: Is the report logically organized? Does it use headings? Are the ideas and paragraphs appropriately linked?

Language: Does it use correct grammar and vocabulary? Is a good range of structures used?

9 Internet sensation

9.1 Why videos go viral

TEDTALKS

KEVIN ALLOCCA was born in 1964 and grew up in Fort Lauderdale, Florida. He studied Communication and Film Studies at Boston College, where he was also a columnist for a humorous university publication and was a performer, writer and the director of a university comedy sketch show. Allocca was a state champion in duo interpretation, in which a pair of performers acts out a play or poem or other literary piece under certain constraints, such as using no props and not touching or making eye contact with each other. Allocca has been coaching duo interpretation professionally since becoming state champion.

After university, Alloca had a number of jobs, including production assistant and producer for filmmakers Etoile Productions, a political satire writer, producer and editor at *The Huffington Post* and editor at the media and jobs resource site mediabistro.com. He then joined YouTube as part of their News and Politics team before becoming Trends Manager from 2010 to 2012 and then Head of Culture and Trends. As an expert on popularity and cultural phenomena, he tracks the latest viral videos, identifies what is popular and oversees community programming, connecting YouTube users who can benefit from each other.

Allocca has made numerous TV appearances, including Good Morning America, CNN and Fox News and has been frequently quoted in various publications, including major newspapers such as *The New York Times* and the *LA Times*. He has spoken at events around the world on the subjects of web video, social media, entertainment and breaking news. His TED Talk has been watched over one million times.

Kevin Allocca

CAREER PATHWAYS

1 Read the text. Answer the questions.

   1 How are Kevin Allocca's university studies and his extra-curricular activities related to his subsequent career?

   2 How is duo interpretation different from more conventional acting?

   3 What roles in filmmaking and media production has Allocca had?

   4 How does Allocca's role at YouTube help its users?

   5 How might people who don't watch YouTube have heard about Allocca?

TED PLAYLIST

2 Other TED speakers are interested in topics similar to Kevin Allocca's TED Talk. Read the descriptions of four TED Talks at the top of page 85. In your opinion, which is the best title for this playlist, a, b or c?

   a Popular media

   b Reality TV

   c Internet fame

3 Read the TED playlist again. Find a speaker who …

   1 gives a lesson in how to create an internet sensation.

   2 helped ordinary people to express their creativity.

   3 looks at the adoption of media phenomena.

   4 doesn't talk about music.

▶ **Eric Whitacre: A virtual choir, 2,000 voices strong**

In a moving and madly viral video in 2010, composer Eric Whitacre led a virtual choir of singers from around the world. He talks through the creative challenges of making music powered by YouTube, and unveils his new work, 'Sleep', with a video choir of 2,052.

▶ **Adam Sadowsky: How to engineer a viral music video**

Adam Sadowsky's team was charged with building a machine for the band OK Go's music video. He tells the story of the effort and engineering behind their labyrinthine creation that quickly became the YouTube sensation 'This Too Shall Pass'.

▶ **Alexis Ohanian: How to make a splash in social media**

In a funny, rapid-fire four minutes, Alexis Ohanian of Reddit tells the real-life fable of one humpback whale's rise to Web stardom. The lesson of Mister Splashy Pants is a shoo-in classic for meme-makers and marketers in the Facebook age.

▶ **Cynthia Schneider: The surprising spread of Idol TV**

Cynthia Schneider looks at two international 'American Idol'-style shows – one in Afghanistan, and one in the United Arab Emirates – and shows the surprising effect that these reality-TV contests are creating in their societies.

4 Find words or phrases in the TED playlist that mean the same as the words and phrases (a–e).

a shows for the first time   **b** given the responsibility of   **c** intricate   **d** certain to win   **e** competitions

5 Which talk would you most like to see? Why? Watch the talk at TED.com.

AUTHENTIC LISTENING SKILLS Dealing with accents: British and American

6 🎧 2 16 You are going to hear a podcast in which a member of the *Keynote* team talks about Eric Whitacre's TED Talk, *A virtual choir, 2,000 voices strong*. Listen to this sentence from the talk said by two speakers, one British and one American. Underline four words that are pronounced differently.

I liked this talk. It starts off modestly and quietly and then it builds.

7 🎧 2 17 Now listen to this sentence. Is the speaker British or American?

I've seen a few talks about viral videos and YouTube sensations …

LISTENING

8 🎧 2 18 Listen to the full podcast. Choose the statement that sums up the main message of Whitacre's talk, according to Karen.

The power of the Internet is its ability to …

1 help us make meaningful art.
2 help us realize our dreams.
3 help us form human connections.

9 🎧 2 18 Listen again. Complete these key ideas from the podcast.

1 Eric Whitacre's talk starts quietly, but it builds to a moment of _____.
2 Eric Whitacre wanted to be a pop star, but he ended up getting involved with _____ music.
3 He set up an online choir, but he had no _____.
4 Karen's friend wanted to take a comedy routine to the Edinburgh Festival, but he felt _____.

VOCABULARY IN CONTEXT

10 Read the extracts from the podcast. Choose the correct meaning of the words in bold.

1 while the content of the videos themselves can be amusing, often they're fairly **inane** and trivial.
a offensive ☐   **b** childish ☐   **c** senseless ☐

2 I don't want to **give too much away**, suffice to say it features a collaborative online singing project.
a reveal too much ☐   **b** get too much wrong ☐   **c** give too much credit ☐

3 I don't want to give too much away, **suffice to say** it features a collaborative online singing project.
a it's necessary to say ☐   **b** it's enough to say ☐   **c** it's important to say ☐

4 When he put a post about his **predicament** on Facebook, ….
a difficult situation ☐   **b** proposed plan ☐   **c** embarrassing story ☐

5 And he went, and his routine **went down really well**.
a was well rehearsed ☐   **b** was well received ☐   **c** was well rewarded ☐

9.2 Completely lost without it

GRAMMAR Gradability

1 Choose the correct option to complete the extracts.

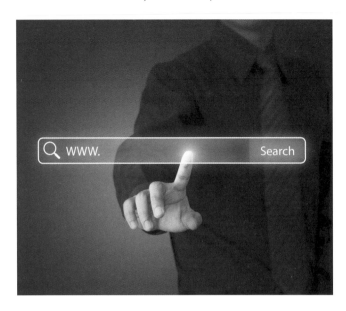

1 The Internet is an *absolutely/incredibly* extensive network infrastructure, in which *absolutely/completely* any computer can normally communicate with any other computer providing they are both connected to the Internet.

2 Web browsers have made the Internet *incredibly/absolutely* accessible to almost anyone with a computer and today there are over a billion regular users. And now that internet access is becoming *very/pretty* standard on mobile phones, we should *quite/a bit* soon see a *totally/fairly* rapid increase in the number of users.

3 The *totally/very* first retailer to offer online ordering was Pizza Hut in 1994. Other commercial websites and online banking *very/really* quickly followed later the same year. The first search engines, AltaVista, Lycos and Yahoo were also launched in 1994, but all were *a bit/rather* limited in their search capabilities.

4 The Internet can be *somewhat/absolutely* prone to misinformation and information overload, so users need to be *very/totally* careful about what they select for use.

5 The Internet has *deeply/totally* transformed our lives in *very/virtually* many ways and has *entirely/extremely* revolutionized the way we conduct our social lives, shop, do business and even educate ourselves.

2 Complete the quotations with the adverbs in the box.

absolutely	a little bit	extremely	highly	practically
pretty	quite	really	strongly	very (×2)

1 The Internet could be a _____ positive step towards education, organization and participation in a meaningful society.
Noam Chomsky, linguist

2 The new information technology ... Internet and e-mail ... have _____ eliminated the physical costs of communications.
Peter Drucker, author and consultant

3 In the internet industry, it's not about grand innovation, it's about a lot of little innovations: every day, every week, every month, making something _____ better.
Jason Calacanis, businessman

4 I _____ believe the Internet is passing from its free days into a paid system. Inevitably, I promise you, it will be paid.
Barry Diller, businessman

5 For a _____ motivated learner, it's not like knowledge is secret and somehow the Internet made it not secret. It just made knowledge easy to find. If you're a motivated enough learner, books are _____ good.
Bill Gates, businessman and founder of Microsoft

6 Regarding social media, I _____ don't understand what appears to be the general population's lack of concern over privacy issues in publicizing their entire lives on the Internet for others to see to such an extent... but, hey, it's them, not me, so whatever.
Axl Rose, rock singer

7 I'm so thankful for the Internet because actors and singers and performers now have a way to connect with their fans on a _____ personal level which I think is _____ special.
Ariana Grande, singer and actress

8 While I _____ encourage my readers to take advantage of the Internet and social networking platforms to gain a greater understanding of their personal finances, it is _____ important to be safe, smart, and responsible when it comes to sharing, discussing, and managing your finances online.
Alexa Von Tobel, businesswoman

3 Replace the gradable adjectives in bold with their ungradable equivalents in the box.

awful	deafening	fantastic	filthy	flabbergasted
furious	hideous	loaded	mortified	packed
soaked	spotless	starving		

Hey, I got the job. I couldn't believe it, I was **surprised** [1]_____ when they phoned me. Everyone else seemed so much more experienced than me.
I am so sorry about the other day. I was **embarrassed** [2]_____ when I realized what I'd said.
What a **nice** [3]_____ apartment your friend's got. He must be **rich** [4]_____ . It's **totally clean** [5]_____ too – how does he do it?

How was the weekend? Well, the hotel was right next to the airport runway and the noise was **loud** [6]_____ 24/7.

The hotel was **dirty** [7]_____, the food was **bad** [8]_____ – we were **hungry** [9]_____ most of the time – and the decor was **pretty ugly** [10]_____, to be honest. Tom was **angry** [11]_____. And the beach was **crowded** [12]_____, which wasn't fun at all. And the one time we decided to get away from it all and go for a walk along the coast, it started raining, can you believe, and we got **wet** [13]_____. Not the best weekend!

4 🎧 **2 19** Complete the dialogues using ungradable adjectives from Exercise 3. Then listen and check your answers.

1 A: The screen is really dirty.
B: Dirty? It's absolutely _____. How can you even see anything?

2 A: Were there many people at the convention?
B: It was totally _____. You could hardly move at times.

3 A: Is this clean enough?
B: Keep going. It needs to be completely _____.

4 A: Is he rich?
B: Too right. Absolutely _____.

5 A: That's the loudest gig I've ever been to.
B: Yep, absolutely _____.

6 A: Were you surprised?
B: Yep, I was utterly _____!

7 A: I was _____!
B: Well, it was quite embarrassing, I suppose.

8 A: What an ugly building!
B: Totally _____. Yuk!

LANGUAGE FOCUS Collocations with intensifying adverbs

5 Match the adverbs (1–12) with their collocates (a–l).

1	painfully	☐	**a**	committed
2	wildly	☐	**b**	slow
3	widely	☐	**c**	accepted
4	deeply	☐	**d**	exaggerated
5	highly	☐	**e**	admit
6	readily	☐	**f**	appreciate
7	fully	☐	**g**	disadvantaged
8	severely	☐	**h**	controversial
9	distinctly	☐	**i**	gifted
10	desperately	☐	**j**	remember
11	sincerely	☐	**k**	in need of
12	extraordinarily	☐	**l**	believe

6 Complete the sentences with collocations from Exercise 5.

1 The concept of internet addiction has become _widely accepted_ and the long-term effects of this are _desperately in need_ of study.

2 Research suggests that internet search engines can give people a _____ and inflated view of their own intelligence.

3 People in areas of low internet accessibility or reliability can be _____ or even penalized in both their professional and social lives. As a result, many governments are _____ to providing internet access for all.

4 That governments can now legally monitor anyone's online movements is _____.

5 Many students _____ to copying and pasting from the Internet, and even do not see this as wrong, even though many sources are unverifiable and this is also usually classified as plagiarism.

6 People generally don't ever _____ fast Internet and take it for granted until they are stuck with _____ Internet.

7 Research shows that almost all people _____ their first mobile phone.

8 Just a few _____ and pioneering individuals have shaped the way we use the Internet.

DICTATION

7 🎧 **2 20** Listen to a lecture extract about how people get their news online. Complete the sentences.

Recent research in the United States suggests that the majority of people who get their news online use [1]_____. It revealed that while most internet users are interested in [2]_____, they tend to be [3]_____ of internet sites they use to obtain that information. Around 20% say they generally receive their news from just one main website, while around 60% tend to use up to five websites. According to the study, most of those using just [4]_____ that this most likely gives them a narrower view of events, but the majority also believe their favoured source to be [5]_____ of the news.

These users also tend to have [6]_____ news interests and are [7]_____ with keeping updated with the major news stories of the day. On the other hand, most of those using several websites to get their news say they do so specifically to get [8]_____ and emphasis on different kinds of news. They are also more open to what is known as 'accidental news consumption', which is when you come across things you weren't specifically looking for and didn't know would interest you.

The word 'meme' comes from the Greek 'mimeme' meaning an imitated thing.

μίμημα

History of the meme

The term was first used by the scientist, Richard Dawkins, in 197 to describe units of expression – catchphrases, melodies, clothes fashions, pieces of technology – that carry a cultural idea. Meme could change and evolve or they could become extinct.

YOLO
(You only live once)

An internet meme is an idea, often expressed as an image or video (but also in words), that spreads quickly or goes 'viral'. Many internet memes are commentaries on or parodies of other internet memes or events.

Don't look too hard for the cultural message within an internet meme. Two of the earliest internet memes were 'dancing baby' (1996) and the 'hamster dance' (1999) – a group of cartoon hamsters set to music – the latter received 15,000 visits a day, a lot of traffic for its day.

Among the most famous memes of the 2000s was the 'Dancing Inmates of Cebu', a video showing a large number of Filipino prisoners doing synchronized dancing to the music of Michael Jackson's 1982 song *Thriller*. The dance was part of a programme to keep prisoners mentally and physically fit. But why did so many watch it? Nostalgia? A way of feeling good about people we lock up? Or something else?

Some internet memes have made people better off. Antoine Dodson from Chicago, who was filmed telling the world to "Hide yo' kids, Hide yo' wife" after his house was broken into by an intruder, is estimated to have earned $50,000 out of his internet fame – enough to help him move out of his home to a better neighbourhood.

$50,000

Other memes have made people unhappy. Ghyslain Raza, also known as the **'Star Wars kid'** for a clumsy display on stage with a pole supposed to be a light sabre, was so picked on at school subsequently that he was forced to drop out. (He later sued his persecutors).

You Tube

4chan and YouTube are the main sites for starting and spreading internet memes, because it is relatively simple to upload videos onto them. This has given rise to enormous numbers of home-made videos being uploaded.

One of the most successful homemade videos was called 'David after dentist' in which a young boy, disorientated by the effects of the anaesthetic, explains his feelings to a parent in the car on the way home. The family is reported to have made $150,000 from the video and related marketing.

Cats rule the Internet. There are vast numbers of memes involving cats, the most famous – and lucrative for the cat's owner – of which is 'Grumpy Cat', a cat whose expression has become a byword for annoyance or bad-tempered-ness. The cat's owner, Tabetha Bundesen, is involved full-time in advertising campaigns for cat-related products and has even been offered book and movie deals.

READING

1 In your opinion, are these statements true (T) or false (F)?

1 A meme is just another word for a viral video. ☐ ☐
2 Viral videos are a 21ˢᵗ century phenomenon. ☐ ☐
3 Memes are a reflection of cultural trends. ☐ ☐
4 Ordinary people can make a lot of money from viral videos. ☐ ☐
5 YouTube is the home of the viral video. ☐ ☐
6 Viral videos are harmless fun. ☐ ☐

2 Read the infographic. Are the statements in Exercise 1 true (T), false (F) or unknown (U)?

3 Find words or phrases in the infographic that mean the same as the words and phrases (1–8).

1 memorable sayings
2 disappear completely
3 occurring at the same time
4 physically awkward
5 bullied
6 provoked
7 confused
8 profitable

4 Look at the infographic and find examples of the memes (1–8).

1 unexplained cultural messages
2 animals behaving like humans
3 children being themselves
4 a catchphrase
5 amateur performances
6 an early viral video
7 reactions to misfortune
8 profitable videos

5 🎧 **2 21** Listen to Naomi and her friend discussing a meme. Answer the questions.

1 What was the meme that Naomi liked?
2 What did she like about it?

6 🎧 **2 21** Listen again and write the adjectives that Naomi uses to describe the following.

1 the videos reaching 1 billion views _____
2 the raising of hundreds millions of dollars _____
3 most internet memes _____
4 being aware of problems in the world _____

VOCABULARY New internet words

7 Complete the definitions.

1 _____ = a website, web page or article usually written in an informal style and generally regularly updated
2 _____ = a downloadable audio file available on the Internet which is usually part of a themed series
3 _____ = sending emails purporting to be from reputable companies in order to entice individuals to reveal personal information online
4 _____ = a physical location that has good wi-fi
5 _____ = a way of raising finance by asking a large number of people each for a small amount of money
6 _____ = not connected to or using the Internet
7 _____ = to post a deliberately provocative or insulting message to a public space online. Also, a person who does this
8 _____ = unsolicited messages usually sent to large numbers of users for the purposes of advertising, phishing or spreading malware

WORDBUILDING The prefix *inter-*

8 Complete the sentences using *inter-* and the words in the box.

connected	cut	dependent	disciplinary	face
locking	~~net~~	play	weaves	

1 The *Internet* is essentially a vast network of _____ computers.
2 The website has a simple user-friendly _____, which makes it easy to navigate.
3 The story cleverly _____ the lives of a number of characters who all eventually end up becoming friends online.
4 The conference provided an opportunity for _____ discussion on the legal, social and economic aspects of the Internet.
5 The podcast was constantly _____ with excerpts of music from his childhood.
6 A crossword is a word puzzle made up of _____ words.
7 The website is immediately impressive with a modern design and stunning _____ of colours.
8 e-commerce websites such as eBay and Gumtree and the people who sell on them have become totally _____, both relying on and needing each other.

9.4 Online presence

GIVING AND EXPLAINING OPINIONS

1 🎧 **2 22** Listen to two people answering the question 'does the Internet need censorship?'. Answer the questions.

1 Which speaker is broadly against and which is broadly for the censorship of the Internet?

2 Which speaker thinks that censoring the Internet would be difficult to implement?

3 Which speaker believes those doing the censoring may use the opportunity to promote their own ideas?

2 🎧 **2 22** Are the following mentioned by speaker 1 or speaker 2? Listen again and check your answers.

a blocking individuals and organizations ☐
b The USA's First Amendment ☐
c influence and incitement ☐
d who will censor the censors ☐
e existing internet censorship ☐
f flaming and cyberbullying ☐
g users monitoring themselves ☐

3 🎧 **2 22** Read and complete the extracts from Exercise 1 with the words in the boxes. Then listen again and check your answers.

allowing	concerned	fact	far
insofar	personally	say	

Speaker 1

Well, ¹_____, I think that there should ideally be freedom of expression ...

... I don't think there should be absolute freedom, ²_____ as there should be limits to what is acceptable ...

Also, as ³_____ as the individual is ⁴_____, some people can be victims of abusive content and things like flaming, you know, insulting people online, and cyber-bullying.

But ⁵_____ for the ⁶_____ that no-one actually controls the Internet as such, I'm not so sure how we can actually control things, really ...

But, in a word, I'd ⁷_____ that censorship would probably be a good thing.

accept	different
inasmuch	just

Speaker 2

... the First Amendment prohibits any laws that infringe freedom of speech. So, why should it be any ⁸_____ with the Internet? ...

I know in some countries, internet content is controlled, ⁹_____ as the government allows or disallows access to certain websites ...

I think we ¹⁰_____ have to ¹¹_____ that that's the reality and that it isn't really going to change.

4 Put the words in the correct order to complete the sentences.

1 *that / I / personally, / think* _____ we just have to accept that there are always going to be people who want to post things we don't like.

2 All in all, *say / considering / I'd / that* _____ the Internet essentially manages itself, it's a truly amazing tool.

3 *just / that / to / have / we / accept* _____ online theft is getting more and more sophisticated all the time.

4 Any responsible parent wouldn't let their child watch endless hours of TV, so *be / with / different / should / why / it / any* _____ the Internet? *screen time / screen time / is* _____ .

5 Actually being talented in the traditional sense *it / doesn't / into / come / really* _____ . These days, almost anyone can have their fifteen minutes of internet fame.

6 *fact / allowing / the / that / for* _____ a lot of online reviews are most probably made up by competing businesses, I think most review sites are very helpful.

7 The Internet is a great academic research tool *as / it / can / insofar* _____ point you in the right direction.

8 *far / is / as / your public / concerned / online presence / as* _____ , just make sure you'd be happy for any potential employer to see it.

PRONUNCIATION Stress in opinion giving

5 🎧 **2 23** Underline the most stressed parts of the answers to the question 'Is internet censorship a good thing?'. Then listen and check your answers.

1 Personally, I think it is.
2 As far as I'm concerned, it's a good thing.
3 Our opinion doesn't really come into it.
4 We just have to accept that it's inevitable.
5 In my opinion, it's fair enough.
6 If you ask me, it's not a good idea.
7 Freedom of speech is freedom of speech.
8 Well, it's not a bad thing.

WRITING SKILL Compound nouns, adjective + noun, and noun + noun collocations

6 Underline the compound nouns (adjective + noun, and noun + noun) in the professional profile.

Tom Gardener, waiter and duty manager

Professional waiter with duty management experience in a number of high-end restaurants and hotels. Team player, but capable of using own initiative. Hard worker, but knows the importance of having fun. Focusses on the detail, but can see the big picture. Works to high standards and expects the same. Quick learner and doesn't need telling twice. Proven track record of getting things done. Degree in business studies. Looking to take career to the next level in the catering or hospitality sector.

7 Rewrite the sentences using a compound noun.

1 Our events offer opportunities for networking.
Our events offer networking opportunities.
2 The hotel has got several rooms for meetings.
_____
3 We place a great deal of importance on training for staff.
_____
4 She's fanatical about fitness.
_____
5 She's an author who has written some best-sellers.
_____
6 He's a person with lots of ideas.
_____
7 He put forward an argument that was equally compelling.
_____
8 She has a track record that impresses.
_____
9 It was an exercise in building relationships.
_____
10 She specializes in ethics in the field of medicine.
_____

8 Rewrite the phrases in bold as compound nouns.
Suzy Nader, marketing manager

I am a Marketing Manager for SoftEd, [1]~~a company that develops educational software~~ *an educational software developer*, with over 100 [2]**products that are innovative** _____ currently being used in schools and universities in a number of countries. I head the company's marketing team. Oversee [3]**a team which is dynamic and deals with marketing and sales** _____ .
I conceptualize, plan and develop new [4]**strategies for marketing** _____ and I also manage the [5]**budget for marketing** _____ . I have [6]**a track record which is proven and unrivalled** _____ of getting our software adopted by educational establishments. Before joining SoftEd, I worked for [7]**an agency which is well-known and which is concerned with the marketing of educational services** _____ and I personally worked with [8]**clients who are high-end and exacting** _____ such as Kaplan, Newton and NovaLabs.
Ultimately professional, passionate about my work and [9]**someone who is good at listening** _____ , I particularly enjoy working with clients to understand their needs and requirements in order to find solutions and to establish [10]**relationships that last a long time** _____ .
I see marketing as [11]**a process of collaboration** _____ between provider and end-user.
I have a first degree in computer studies and an MBA in Marketing and Human Resources Management.

YOUR IDEA

1 Read about the changes people have made (1–3) on the right. Are these statements (a–e) true (T) or false (F)?

a If people bought local produce, it might help the environment. ☐

b Roberta talks about how her restaurant could have won an award. ☐

c Akbar is impressed by what people can achieve by coming together. ☐

d All three people talk about how food can change a situation. ☐

e Paolo thinks that most people could become vegan easily. ☐

2 Write notes about how someone could make their life more sustainable. Think about things like food, travel and waste.

_____

_____

_____

_____

3 Match the sentence halves to describe the possible effects of some sustainable lifestyle changes.

1 If more people were vegetarian, … ☐

2 If you provide a space for people to work together, … ☐

3 We would have been able to cut greenhouse gas emissions sooner … ☐

4 There would be much less need for landfill sites … ☐

a … if more drivers had switched to electric cars.

b … if only more people recycled their waste.

c … demand would increase for fruit and vegetables.

d … they could achieve some remarkable things.

4 Practise talking about a change that could be made out loud. Try to vary the pace of your talk. Try …

- not to speak too quickly or slowly – you don't want to confuse your audience or make them get bored.
- to speak slowly and clearly when you are explaining something complicated or serious.
- to use pauses in your talk – these can be effective just before you make an important point.

1 Paolo: I suppose it's quite trendy to be a vegan nowadays. It's true that not eating meat or dairy products makes life challenging sometimes – you know, it can be difficult to find vegan food in some places. If you make the effort, vegan diets can be quite nutritious, so a lot of people make this change for the good of their health. But I actually decided to change my diet because I suddenly realized its impact on the environment – did you know that the consumption of processed meat is one of the biggest contributors to carbon emissions? All the machinery involved in intensive farming spews out a lot of greenhouse gases. It's something I've become quite passionate about. I'm not saying we should all become veggies – just that if people ate a lot less meat, perhaps it would be much better for the environment.

2 Roberta: I'm a big believer in supporting the local community and small businesses. That's why I always knew I wanted to run a restaurant that served locally sourced food. It's not always easy to manage – sometimes getting good quality produce can be difficult and you might have to pay over the odds to get what you want. And it's amazing that it actually matches what a lot of my customers want! They're not really interested in exotic fruit and veg, as they'd much rather have a really nice and tasty apple pie with fruit from the local orchard! In fact, our turnover has almost doubled and customer satisfaction is up since we switched to buying locally. Who knows – if we had done this sooner, we might have even won a Michelin star by now!

3 Akbar: People have been affected quite badly here. You could see it around, you know. People didn't look as though they were taking care of themselves. They probably didn't have the most stable of lives at home. This wasn't a case of people being on the streets, more of a struggling, low quality of life. So we took the plunge and decided to set up a soup kitchen – people could come here, have a hot meal if they couldn't get one at home. But more importantly, they could be with other people. We thought 'if people could just come together, perhaps this would help'. And it actually did. We've supported people in need; we gave them a space to come, without pretensions, to share with each other. What's amazing is that some people have even taken it further and started to set up their own local initiatives. Just goes to show what can be done when people come together.

ORGANIZING YOUR PRESENTATION

5 Match the four steps of a presentation with two examples of useful language (a–h).

1 Starting the presentation ☐ ☐
2 Explaining the change you are going to talk about ☐ ☐
3 Describing the impact of this change ☐ ☐
4 Finishing the presentation ☐ ☐

a I hope you have found this presentation interesting. Are there any questions?

b What is sustainable living? Over the next few minutes I am going to talk about a change people can make to live a more sustainable life.

c One easy change we can all make to reduce our impact on the world is to use public transport more. If fewer people travel in private vehicles like cars, the environment can only benefit.

d It is much easier, nowadays, to reuse and recycle things like paper, plastic and metal. We should all make an effort to recycle these whenever we can. It will mean that far fewer resources are used up.

e Not only will travelling less by car help reduce your carbon footprint, you could get healthier too – walking every day is a form of sustainable exercise!

f That brings us to the end of this presentation. Let's open this up for you to add your thoughts.

g If we want to live more sensible and sustainable lives, we should think about what happens to our rubbish. We really need to recycle a lot more.

h Hello, everyone. How can we live more responsibly and not use up too much of the world's resources? Well, here's my suggestion.

YOUR PRESENTATION

6 Read the useful language above and make notes for your presentation.

1 Start the presentation What is … ? In this talk … Over the next few minutes … How can we … ?	
2 Explain the sustainable change you are going to talk about A/An/One (easy) change … If …, we should … If we could …, then it would …	
3 Describe the impact of this change It is (much) easier to … Not only will …, it could also … If we could do this, …	
4 Finish the presentation That brings us … I hope … Let's open …	

7 Film yourself giving your presentation or practise in front of a mirror. Give yourself marks out of ten for …

- varying your pace. ☐/10
- following the four steps in Exercise 6. ☐/10
- using correct grammar. ☐/10

10 The meaning of success

A kinder, gentler philosophy of success

TEDTALKS

ALAIN DE BOTTON was born in 1969 in Zurich, Switzerland. He spent his early childhood in Switzerland and spoke French and German. In 1981, his family moved to London, where he continued his education, first at a boarding school in Oxford, where English became his main language, and then at Harrow School. He then studied history at the University of Cambridge and, in 1992, completed a master's degree in philosophy at King's College, London. He began a PhD in French philosophy at Harvard University, but did not complete this. Around this time, de Botton started writing his first novel *Essays in Love*, which was published in 1993. To date, the book has sold two million copies worldwide. He has since written a number of books on love, travel, architecture and literature and on what has been described as 'the philosophy of everyday life'. His works have been bestsellers in 30 countries.

In 2008, de Botton co-founded The School of Life, which offers a variety of classes and workshops on 'developing emotional intelligence' and addressing such issues as 'how to find fulfilling work, how to develop relationships and how better to understand the world'. The school's headquarters are in London, with branches in a number of countries worldwide. In 2009, de Botton co-founded and became the Creative Director of Living Architecture, an organization which uses some of the world's leading architects to build homes for rent around the UK.

De Botton is a regular contributor to several UK newspapers and has contributed to and presented television programmes, including several by his own production company, Seneca Productions, which he set up in 2003. He also lectures extensively on his areas of interest. He has won a number of awards and, in 2011, was elected as a Fellow of the Royal Society of Literature.

Alain de Botton

CAREER PATHWAYS

1 Read the text. Are these statements true (T), false (F) or unknown (U)?

1 Alain de Botton is trilingual. ☐
2 De Botton has a first degree, a master's degree and a PhD. ☐
3 De Botton's first book was an instant bestseller. ☐
4 The main aim of The School of Life is to make people more employable. ☐
5 De Botton has appeared in and makes his own TV programmes. ☐

TED PLAYLIST

2 Other TED speakers are interested in topics similar to Alain de Botton's TED Talk. Read the descriptions of four TED Talks at the top of page 95. In your opinion, which is the best title for this playlist, a, b or c?

a The road to success
b Creating a happy work environment
c The key to a happy life

3 Read the TED playlist again. Find a speaker who ...

1 examines our real motivations for working.
2 reassures us that we can be happy in spite of not realizing our goals.
3 examines what we really want from life.

▶ Dan Gilbert: The surprising science of happiness

Dan Gilbert, author of *Stumbling on Happiness*, challenges the idea that we'll be miserable if we don't get what we want. Instead, he claims, our 'psychological immune system' lets us feel truly happy even when things don't go as planned.

▶ David Brooks: Should you live for your résumé, or your eulogy?

Within each of us are two selves, suggests David Brooks in this meditative short talk: the self who craves success, who builds a résumé, and the self who seeks connection, community, love – the values that make for a great eulogy. Brooks asks: can we get the right balance between these two selves?

▶ Scott Dinsmore: How to find work you love

Scott Dinsmore quit a job that made him miserable, and spent the next four years wondering how to find work that was joyful and meaningful. He shares what he learned in this deceptively simple talk about finding out what matters to you – and then getting started doing it.

▶ Barry Schwartz: The way we think about work is broken

What makes work satisfying? Apart from getting a nice pay cheque, there are intangible values that, Barry Schwartz suggests, our current way of thinking about work simply ignores. It's time to stop thinking of workers as cogs on a wheel.

4 Find words or phrases in the TED playlist that mean the same as the words and phrases (a–d).

a upset   **b** is hungry for   **c** having a purpose
d difficult to describe

5 Which talk would you most like to see? Why? Watch the talk at TED.com.

AUTHENTIC LISTENING SKILLS Hedging

6 🎧2 24 You are going to hear a podcast in which a member of the *Keynote* team talks about David Brooks's TED Talk, *Should you live for your résumé, or your eulogy?* Look at the sentence from Leila's description. Then listen and complete the sentence with hedging words.

Most people who watch this talk for the first time have probably never pondered their own two selves.

LISTENING

7 🎧2 25 Listen to the full podcast. Choose the statement that best describes why Leila thinks this talk teaches us an important lesson.

1 It shows us how we can better balance our lives inside and outside work.
2 It goes to the heart of what we all, and especially young people, consider 'success' to be.
3 It shows how we can improve ourselves so that we can achieve our true goals in life.

8 🎧2 25 Listen again. Are these statements true (T) or false (F)? If false, say why.

1 Leila thinks that most people try to avoid thinking about their 'eulogy' self in case they fail to achieve their ambitions. ☐
2 She thinks it is very difficult to balance these two 'selves'. ☐
3 According to Leila, David Brooks thinks that volunteering or doing charity work can help you find a balance. ☐
4 Leila thinks that these ideas are very relevant to people like her who are very career-driven and work-focussed. ☐
5 Leila would like to see what people of different ages and backgrounds thought about Brooks's ideas. ☐

VOCABULARY IN CONTEXT

9 Read the extracts from the podcast. Choose the correct meaning of the words in bold.

1 ... most people who watch this talk for the first time have probably never **pondered** their own two selves.
a liked ☐   **b** considered ☐
c distinguished between ☐
2 Balancing your two lives is a dynamic and often **baffling** task.
a very tiring ☐   **b** very difficult ☐
c very confusing ☐
3 I think, in practice, this is a **tall order** for the majority of people.
a difficult task ☐   **b** great achievement ☐
c threatening situation ☐
4 I am also interested to better understand David Brooks's take on how charitable and **selfless** acts ...
a unselfish ☐   **b** anonymous ☐   **c** unthinking ☐
5 I actually think the talk may be more important or **pertinent** for a younger generation.
a practical ☐   **b** positive ☐   **c** relevant ☐

10.2 Self-help

GRAMMAR Verb and adjective patterns

1 🎧 2 26 Complete the dialogues with the correct form of the verbs in the boxes. Then listen and check your answers.

deal	get	~~persuade~~	talk

1 A: We finally managed *to persuade* him to _____ to someone about it.

B: I imagine it was a relief for him _____ it off his chest.

A: Yes, he couldn't go on _____ with it himself any longer.

find	find	get

2 A: The programme has enabled over ten individuals _____ full-time employment in the local area, and helped over twenty others _____ part-time work.

B: That's great. And it's brilliant that so many local businesses were willing _____ involved.

be	speak	take	talk	work

3 A: My boss won't let me _____ any more time off work. I even offered _____ an extra half day to make up for it.

B: You'd expect him _____ a bit more understanding of your situation. Have you tried _____ to someone else? Is it worth _____ to someone above him?

apologize	be	see	upset	upset

4 A: Well, I spoke to Patrick, but he failed _____ the funny side. He even wanted me _____ for _____ unprofessional. Can you believe? I really didn't mean _____ him.

B: Oh, I wouldn't worry about _____ him. He's not got much of a sense of humour at the best of times.

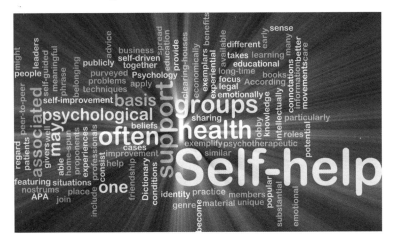

2 Choose the correct options to complete the text.

A brief history of self-help books – the 1800s

In the early 1800s, self-help publications were essentially concerned [1]*to advocate / with advocating* personal responsibility and tended [2]*promoting / to promote* the idea that it was possible [3]*to achieve / achieving* self-improvement through self-awareness and education. In the mid-1800s, the American essayist and lecturer Ralph Waldo Emerson espoused ideas such as individuality and freedom and that humans were capable [4]*to realize / of realizing* almost anything. In an essay in 1841, Emerson suggested that 'every man in his lifetime needs [5]*thanking / to thank* his faults' and that everyone should try [6]*acquiring / to acquire* 'habits of self-help'. In 1859, a bestselling book by the Scottish author Samuel Smiles simply entitled *Self-Help* opened with the line 'Heaven helps those who help themselves'. The book encouraged people [7]*raising / to raise* themselves 'from poverty to social eminence and even wealth' through self-education and by creating and capitalizing on new opportunities. It was with some irony then that, after the book had become successful, it eventually went on [8]*to sell / selling* over a quarter of a million copies, Smiles met the publisher George Routledge who, after congratulating Smiles [9]*to have written / on having written* the book, asked if he would be interested [10]*in writing / to write* for him. Smiles took great pleasure [11]*to inform / in informing* the unknowing Routledge that his company had in fact refused [12]*to publish / publishing Self-Help* a few years earlier.

3 Put the verbs into the correct form. In some cases you need to add a preposition.

In the 1900s, self-help publications [1] **start / become** _____ more fashionable as people realized it [2] **be possible / take** _____ more control of their destinies. In 1903, the British philosophical writer, James Allen, published *As a Man Thinketh*, which postulated that 'a man is literally what he thinks'. The main theme of the book was that through patience and careful thought any person [3] **be able / transform** _____ his or her circumstances. The book claims that 'noble thoughts make for a noble person, while lowly thoughts make for a miserable person'. Allen described his work as 'a book that [4] **help / you / help** _____ yourself'. In the mid-1930s, two of the most influential and best-selling self-help books of all time were published. In 1937, writer and journalist Napoleon Hill published *Think and Grow Rich*, which advocated a simple formula [5] **base / have** _____ belief in oneself and which anyone [6] **be capable / understand** _____ and [7] **achieve** _____.
Published around the same time, Dale Carnegie's bestseller *How to Win Friends and Influence People* probably [8] **do / more than any other book / put** _____ the self-help genre firmly into the mainstream.

4 Find and correct the mistakes.

1 She's very easy get along with.
She's very easy to get along with.

2 He was reluctant opening up at first, but he's more expressive now.

_____

3 I'm not convinced he's suited to work in management.

_____

4 Are you serious to look for another job?

_____

5 Do you think it's worth to try to contact her again?

_____

6 It's useless to phone them. They never answer.

_____

7 I'm interested to knowing what they thought about it.

_____

8 My parents never let me to stay up late during the week.

_____

LANGUAGE FOCUS Patterns using adjective + *that*

5 Complete the comments with the words in the box.

adamant	amazed	aware	~~convinced~~
convinced	disappointed	had	proud
regret	surprised		

1 My friends *convinced* me that I should try it. They were all _____ that it works.

2 I was _____ and _____ that I managed to stop smoking. I really quite surprised myself.

3 I wasn't _____ that it had sold so many copies. It's incredible.

4 I was _____ that it didn't really work for me. I _____ high hopes that it would.

5 I'm not _____ that it works that well. I'm quite _____ that it's so successful, to be honest.

6 I _____ that I didn't come across it sooner.

6 Rewrite the sentences using the words given.

1 I wasn't aware that there was a deadline at all.   *of*
I wasn't aware of there being a deadline at all.

2 I'm determined not to get behind with things again.   *that*

_____

3 She was upset that she wasn't told any sooner.   *about*

_____

4 He's not so keen on us going on the training course.   *that*

_____

5 I was pleased that I was given the opportunity.   *to*

_____

6 I'm not conscious of any decision being made.   *that*

_____

7 I was delighted to be even considered for the post.   *that*

_____

8 We have decided that we are not going ahead with the project.   *against*

_____

PRONUNCIATION Prepositions as weak forms

7 🎧 **2 27** Look at the sentences and underline the prepositions that include the weak form /ə/. Then listen and check your answers.

1 I wasn't aware **of** there being a deadline **at** all.

2 I'm determined not **to** get behind **with** things again.

3 She was upset **about** not being told any sooner.

4 He's not so keen **on** us going **on** the training course.

5 I was pleased **to** be given the opportunity.

6 I'm not convinced that we should hold the conference **in** July.

7 I was delighted **to** be even considered **for** the post.

8 We have decided **against** going ahead **with** the project.

DICTATION

8 🎧 **2 28** Listen to someone from student services talking about preparing for an interview. Complete the sentences.

I'd like to start by saying that it's vitally important to prepare for any interview. That might seem a bit obvious, but you'd be surprised how many people turn up for an interview and have clearly not [1] _____ at all. So, first, do as much research as possible about the company and the job you're applying for. It's [2] _____ a little about their origins, any major landmarks in their history and, if applicable, who their main clients are. Also, visit their website and social media profiles and search any news to make sure you're up-to-date. You're [3] _____ about this, but it is useful to be able to ground some of your responses in this. For the actual interview itself, [4] _____ and have some ready-made answers. Of course, you need to be prepared to improvise on these answers, but [5] _____ at the ready. Also, be prepared to explain aspects of your CV, such as why you left a job. But make sure to avoid openly criticizing any previous employers. So, it's definitely [6] _____ with the details of your CV.

10.3 What generations want

READING

1 You are going to read three short essay answers to the question 'What is success?'. Before you read, match the words (1–6) from the essays with their synonyms (a–f).

1 legitimate	☐	**a**	fundamental
2 empowered	☐	**b**	off course
3 underlying	☐	**c**	superficial
4 fulfilled	☐	**d**	valid
5 shallow	☐	**e**	satisfied
6 astray	☐	**f**	strengthened (in authority)

2 Read the three student essay answers. Say which two answers are most similar in the view they express.

3 Match the views (a–f) with the essay answers (1–3).

a Accepted definitions of success are not always correct. ☐ ☐

b Money or wealth is not a good measure of success. ☐

c Success and happiness are closely linked. ☐ ☐

d Success is about earning the respect of other people. ☐

e Definitions of success are subjective / made by the individual. ☐ ☐

f What you consider to be success evolves as you grow and change. ☐

What is success?

Answer 1

Literally, the definition of success is the achievement of set goals or targets, set by you or set by others. No-one would disagree with that definition. Disagreements about what success means arise because we disagree about what the goals or targets should be. A lot of people are critical, in theory at least, of those who make earning money their goal. But I think that is unfair, because their underlying goal is financial security for themselves and their families, which is a perfectly legitimate aim. The problem, as I see it, is that many people do not adjust their goals as circumstances change. Someone who started out by making money the measure of their success will inevitably, at some point in their life – when they find they have no time for family or friends or when they become sick from stress and overwork – question this: 'Why did I define success as having a lot of money? It hasn't made me happy.' So a better definition of success would be: the understanding of what the correct goals are for you and the achievement of these goals.

Answer 2

When we think of success we generally think of fame, wealth and power – all the obvious things that make other people notice us and think we are important. Being admired by others is a great boost to our self-confidence; it tells us that we have value. Fame, wealth and power are all recognition of our worth to other people, but they are a shallow kind of recognition, a definition of success that society has created. The definition I think is the true one is the recognition from other people that you have helped them or inspired them in some way. So for me, success is being a good human being: being kind to other people, helping people in difficulty, showing love where people lack love and putting people on the right course when they have gone astray.

Answer 3

Before she started raising a family, my mother was a successful athlete. She represented her country in the triathlon many times and won two bronze medals at international events. Then she became pregnant with me and has since had two other children. She gave up her athletics career to focus on raising a family. Does that mean that she achieved success in the past, but is not successful now? I asked her these two questions: did you feel fulfilled as an athlete and that the effort you put in empowered you and rewarded you? Do you feel empowered, fulfilled and rewarded as a mother? The answers she gave me tell you all you need to know about success. She was encouraged to do athletics as a teenager, and although she liked competing, she disliked the training and the travelling to events, which took over her life. Now, she says, she loves her life. She has three healthy children, good friends and neighbours, a lovely home and a garden where she grows plants and vegetables.

4 🎧 **2 29** Listen to two teachers discussing the students' essay answers. Answer the questions.

1 Which of the essays in Exercise 2 do they mention?

2 What impressed the female teacher about the students' answers?

5 🎧 **2 30** Listen again to the second part of the conversation and complete the summary.

The male teacher says we all reach a point when we need to _____ our ambitions, but the female teacher thinks that our _____ change.

VOCABULARY Success and failure

6 Complete the news extracts with words from the box.

ambition	dropping	fall	heart	it	make
out	realizing	set	throw	towel	wayside

Mark Zuckerberg, Steve Jobs and Bill Gates are well documented for [1] _____ [2] _____ of university to pursue their ambitions. But, according to a recent study, for every success story, there are many who say they regret the decision to not finish their studies. The research suggests that if you want to [3] _____ [4] _____ in your chosen field or profession, then a university education is still the best start you can get.

Local hero Ella Franklin [5] _____ her [6] _____ on becoming a professional footballer and playing for her country at the age of eight and today, is on the verge of [7] _____ her [8] _____ . She has for the first time been named in the provisional national squad to play Germany next week. 'It feels great,' she said. 'It's been a hard journey and I've seen many players [9] _____ by the [10] _____ or for various reasons [11] _____ in the [12] _____ , but for me it's all I've ever wanted to do. It's been hard work and there have been a lot of sacrifices along the way, but if I get selected, then it's all been worth it.'

WORD FOCUS *success*

7 Match the expressions (1–10) with the phrases (a–j).

1 achieve success ☑

2 proven success ☐

3 overnight success ☐

4 limited success ☐

5 secret of one's success ☐

6 key to one's success ☐

7 confident of success ☐

8 without success ☐

9 success story ☐

10 success rate ☐

a an unknown factor in someone's success

b the main reason for someone's success

c success that comes suddenly

d some success, but not much

e success that is undisputed

f certain you will succeed

g frequency of success

h example of success

i unsuccessfully

j be successful

8 Complete the sentences with the words from Exercise 7.

1 It has been said that you have *achieved* success when you don't know whether what you're doing is work or play.

2 With the last known case in Bangladesh in 1975, the eradication of smallpox is one of the great success _____ of our time.

3 The game Angry Birds became an _____ success after its release in 2009, with 15 million official downloads in its first year. However, its creator, Rovio Entertainment, had previously launched 50 similar games with _____ success.

4 Comedienne Joan Rivers said the _____ of her success was that she put into words what people were secretly thinking.

5 Sir Alex Ferguson, the most successful football coach of all time, believed that his risk-taking mentality was _____ to his success. He also claimed that if a team is genuinely _____ of success, it is far more likely to win.

6 Harry Potter author J.K. Rowling approached a dozen publishers _____ success before she was offered a publishing deal.

7 In vitro fertilization (IVF) has a success _____ of about 35% for younger women. This drops steadily with age.

8 The model of starting something simply and building a community around it, as demonstrated by the likes of Facebook and Twitter, has been a _____ success.

How did you get on?

TALKING ABOUT SUCCESS

1 🎧2 **31** Listen to six short dialogues. For each, did the second speaker achieve success (✓), not achieve success (✗) or achieve partial success (-)?

1 ☐   2 ☐   3 ☐   4 ☐   5 ☐   6 ☐

2 🎧2 **31** Complete the words in the questions and responses from Exercise 1. Then listen again to check your answers.

1 A: H_____ d_____ i_____
   g_____ w_____ Silvia? D_____
   y_____ m_____ to get things sorted?
   B: Yeah, it's a_____ s_____ now.

2 A: D_____ y_____ h_____
   a_____ l_____ getting that extension for
   your assignment?
   B: Well, it c_____ h_____
   b_____ b_____ .

3 A: H_____ d_____ y_____
   exam g_____ ?
   B: I m_____ a b_____ of a
   m_____ of it, actually.

4 A: H_____ d_____ y_____
   g_____ o_____ w_____
   booking those flights?
   B: Well, w_____ g_____
   t_____ .

5 A: D_____ y_____ g_____
   a_____ w_____ that refund?
   B: As w_____ as c_____ be
   e_____ , I guess.

6 A: H_____ w_____ the meeting?
   D_____ i_____ g_____ OK?
   B: It a_____ w_____ very
   s_____ , thanks.

3 Put the words in the correct order to complete the dialogues.

1 A: *go / did / your tutor / how / with / it*
   _____?

   B: Well, *better / been / it / could've*
   _____

   She wants me to almost totally rewrite the essay.

2 A: *you / with / the insurance / luck / did / have / any*
   _____?

   B: *hoped / well / could / as / be / as*
   _____ .

   They'll pay us for the things we've got receipts for, but nothing else.

3 A: *with / how / you / get / did / the team-building day / on* _____?
   B: I really enjoyed it, actually. I think most people did. *say / I'd / success / was / it / a*
   _____ .

4 A: *your boss / get / you / with / anywhere / did*
   _____?

   B: Well, there are still a few things we need to sort out. But *did / make / we / headway / some*
   _____ .

5 A: *convincing / you / have / them / did / any / trouble*
   _____?

   B: No, surprisingly. *all / smoothly / very / went / it*
   _____

   I was sure they'd be against the idea, but they were fine with it. *sorted / it's / all*
   _____ .

6 A: *go / how / did / your presentation*
   _____?

   B: *a / of / made / it / a / I / of / bit / mess*
   _____

   actually. I got my timing totally wrong and basically ran out of time.
   A: That's a shame. *you / adjust / manage / to / did*
   _____

   and cover the key points?
   B: A bit, but it was too rushed. It really wasn't good.

PRONUNCIATION Elision

4 🎧**2 32** Read the dialogues. Underline the words where you think elision will occur. Then listen and check your answers.

1 A: How did your exam go?
   B: It could have been better.
2 A: Do you think it will work?
   B: Depends if we have any trouble convincing people.
3 A: How did it go this morning?
   B: It all went smoothly, thanks.
4 A: Did it go OK with your boss?
   B: It's all sorted now.

WRITING SKILL Phrases in report writing

5 Choose the correct prepositions to complete the extracts.

1 An interim report will be prepared while the audit is **on / in progress**.
2 We remind all employees that they are **subject to / for** the company's code of conduct.
3 **At / To some extent**, the timing of the launch was fortuitous with unusually warm weather boosting sales.
4 The report has been commissioned **by / at the request of / from** the board of directors.
5 **In / At the time of / in** writing, the marketing strategy is being finalized and is awaiting approval.
6 The research will determine how the company is perceived **by / in comparison of / with** its competitors.
7 We need to ensure that all operational procedures are **in / on line with / to** company policy.
8 It was an ambitious project **in / by relation with / to** the company's size.
9 **By / On behalf of / from** the HR Department, we would like to thank everyone for their participation in what was a very successful training day.

6 Rewrite the phrases in bold using the prepositional phrases in the box.

~~as a result of~~   in collaboration with   in contrast with
in keeping with   in view of   on account of
under the circumstances   with reference to

1 **Owing to** *As a result of* new compliance regulations, all staff travel will need to be authorized by Paul Davis.
2 All transactions must be authorized and approved **adhering to** _____ company policy.
3 Online performance is improving **compared to** _____ high-street sales.
4 We have launched the study **working together with** _____ the University of Oxford.
5 **Considering** _____ the recent IT security issues, the sending of personal emails is now prohibited.

6 There is a possibility of market risk **because of** _____ recent interest-rate instability.
7 This report summarizes our operations **regarding** _____ the Health and Safety at Work Act.
8 **Considering the situation** _____, we think that the right decision has been made.

7 Use the words to write extracts from business reports.

1 This report / commissioned / the request / our parent company, TechEd / relation / sales performance / falling market share.

_____
_____
_____
_____
_____
_____

2 This interim report finds / the prospects / the company / some extent / not positive. While / analysis / still / progress, / we / identified / number / areas / weakness, / particularly / relation / customer relations and after-sales service. / view / this, / Stephanie Amilhat / asked / oversee / customer relations team / foreseeable future.

_____
_____
_____
_____
_____

3 I / writing / behalf / board of directors / reference / next year's planned relocation / our production facility / from / current location in Cambridge / to / new location in Nottingham. / As / result / new land-use legislation, / move / put on hold / enable us / modify / plans / the new facility.

_____
_____
_____
_____
_____
_____

101

IDEAS

You will read an essay responding to the two sources below.

Source 1

> Technology has democratized knowledge by allowing anyone, regardless of where they live, to study business analysis with Harvard University or nanotechnology with the University of Oxford through courses made freely available on the web. Experts in many fields are also easier to reach than ever before through email and social media channels, allowing people to enter into debate with them on a variety of subjects, or just to indulge their own curiosity about a subject.

Source 2

> With all the information we now have available for free at our fingertips, many people no longer feel the need to learn the research skills necessary to exploit a library properly. Within just a few decades, these skills will all but die out. We are outsourcing our memory to the Internet and just because we can search for it online, we believe we know more than we really do.

Write your essay in **240–280 words** in an appropriate style.

1 In the essay you need to address the four points covered in the sources. List them in the order they appear in the sources.

a _____
b _____
c _____
d _____

MODEL

2 Read the essay on the right. Match the four sections with a description (a–d) from Exercise 1.

1 ☐ 2 ☐ 3 ☐ 4 ☐

3 Correct the following statements. According to the author…

1 … it's more expensive to study online than face-to-face.
2 … if you study online, you don't get the benefits of being part of a university community.
3 … you can find any documents you need to on the Internet.
4 … everybody knows about what information you can access in libraries and archives.
5 … traditional research skills are no longer necessary.

USEFUL LANGUAGE

4 Find phrases in the model essay which match the definitions (1–6).

1 the arrival of a new technology
2 a large amount of something
3 an issue which continues for a very long time or happens again and again
4 using one cost or payment to cancel or reduce the effect of another
5 emphasizing that more is available than ever before
6 have a belief or an idea that is based on incorrect information or that is not fully understood

With the advent of the Internet, we now have a wealth of knowledge available to us at the click of a button, in a way which was never possible before.

[1]One of the perennial problems that governments have been particularly concerned with over the past few decades is access to higher education. The expense of a university education can now be offset by following cheap or free open online courses from prestigious universities. [2]While it is undoubtedly true that a large part of the university experience is about being surrounded by other students and academics who you can discuss and debate with, the unparalleled access that social media offers to these same communities means that working towards a degree online is not much less stimulating than doing so in a face-to-face environment.

[3]Having said that, it may also be true that the Internet has had negative effects on our education system. Some people labour under the misconception that everything can be found on the Internet. [4]It may be the case that many documents are being digitized, but there are still countless resources that can only be accessed in their original form. There is a general lack of awareness of the riches of libraries and archives among many young people. Only by incorporating a focus on research skills into education will these skills continue to be available to future generations. It would be impossible to truly research the history of the Dark Ages, for instance, without examining original documents from the period.

I strongly believe that while the democratization of knowledge that the Internet has brought with it is widely regarded as being positive, it is vital that we continue to educate people in how to access information offline, too.

5 Complete the sentences using the emphasis words in the box.

deeply   immensely   strongly   undeniably
vehemently   widely

1 I _____ believe that employers should not look at our social media profiles before interviews.
2 The Internet is _____ regarded as being a beneficial tool for society.
3 It is _____ true that success means different things to different people.
4 The desire to fit into society is _____ ingrained in the human psyche.
5 They are _____ opposed to all university education being free.
6 Their contribution is _____ enriching to society.

6 Put the words in order to create phrases which can introduce points in an essay.

1 indisputable / it / that / fact / is / an
_____

2 dispute / would / the / that / nobody / fact
_____

3 case / may / that / it / the / be
_____

4 be / also / that / it / might
_____

5 raises / the / of / issue / this
_____

6 important / consider / that / of / to / is / an / question
_____

7 Match the phrase halves. The phrases can all be used to add contrasting ideas.

1 While this may ☐
2 At the ☐
3 This is not ☐
4 Set against ☐
5 Be that ☐
6 Having ☐

a same time …
b said that …
c be true up to a point …
d as it may …
e to say that …
f this is …

PLANNING

You will respond to the following two sources.

Source 1

In the past, many societies venerated their elders, but now they are often forgotten. Those without families may be left to rely on the state to look after them, if there is even such a support system in place, rather than being supported by their communities. Another problem is that governments are moving towards being 'digital only', so older people can feel left behind or neglected by society as a whole.

Source 2

Thanks to advances in modern healthcare, our aging population is staying fitter for longer, able to enjoy working well past retirement age if they so choose, or have an active retirement if not. Older family members also provide valuable support to their younger counterparts, for example through providing childcare which enables both parents to go to work. This reliance on older members of society is a valuable asset.

Write your essay in **240–280 words** in an appropriate style.

8 Plan your essay. Identify the four key points from the sources. Write notes to decide how you will respond to them. Don't write full sentences yet.

1 _____
2 _____
3 _____
4 _____

WRITING

9 Write an essay to respond to the sources in Exercise 8. In your essay you should:

- refer to all four of the key points you have identified
- make your own opinion on the topic clear in the conclusion
- use a neutral or formal style

Write **240–280** words.

ANALYSIS

10 Check your essay. Answer the questions.

Content: Does the essay respond to all four points in the sources? Is it 240 to 280 words long?
Communicative achievement: Is it written in a neutral or formal style? Is it clear to the reader what your opinion on the topic is?
Organization: Is the essay logically organized? Does it use appropriate linking devices?
Language: Does it use correct grammar and vocabulary? Is a good range of structures used?

11 Learning and memory

11.1 Build a school in the cloud

TEDTALKS

SUGATA MITRA was born in Kolkata, India, in 1952. After finishing his schooling in Delhi, he completed a degree in physics at Jadavpur University, Kolkata. He then studied at the Indian Institute of Technology (IIT) in Delhi, first receiving an MSc in physics, in which he specialized in quantum biology and acoustic holography, and then, in 1978, earning a PhD in the theoretical physics of organic semiconductors. Over the next few years, Mitra held a number of academic positions at IIT, including Research Associate, Senior Scientific Officer and Product Development Manager.

On leaving IIT in 1983, Mitra became Head of Technology and then Director of Publishing Systems at two of India's leading publishing companies. Following this, from 1990 to 2006, he was Chief Scientist at NIIT Limited, a training and software services company, where he was responsible for research and development in education, media and communications technology. In 2006, Mitra returned to academia and became Professor of Educational Technology at the School of Education, Communication and Language Sciences at Newcastle University, UK.

Mitra has been credited with over 25 inventions and innovations in the area of cognitive science and education technology, for which he has received a number of awards. He is perhaps most widely known for his and NIIT's groundbreaking 1999 'Hole in the Wall' experiment, in which a computer was placed in a kiosk in a wall in a slum area in Delhi for children to use freely and which demonstrated that children can learn on their own very easily without any formal guidance or training. Mitra subsequently termed this Minimally Invasive Education (MIE) and he has become internationally recognized as a leading proponent of this. Research in MIE has led to The School in the Cloud, an educational programme which Mitra started in 2013 and which he describes as a 'global experiment in self-organized learning'. To help get The School in the Cloud off the ground, Mitra was awarded the $1 million TED Prize in 2013.

Sugata Mitra

CAREER PATHWAYS

1 Read the text. Are these statements true (T) or false (F)? Correct the sentences that are false.

1 Mitra's early academic background was in IT and education. ☐

_____

2 Mitra worked at the Indian Institute of Technology until 1983 and then again from 1990 to 2006. ☐

_____

3 The 'Hole in the Wall' experiment was designed to test MIE. ☐

_____

4 Mitra received the $1 million TED Prize to support The School in the Cloud. ☐

_____

TED PLAYLIST

2 Other TED speakers are interested in topics similar to Sugata Mitra's TED Talk. Read the descriptions of four TED Talks at the top of page 105. In your opinion, which is the best title for this playlist, a, b or c?

a Pupil power in learning
b Beyond the classroom
c Learning from children

3 Read the TED playlist again. Find a speaker who …

1 realized the power of online learning.
2 wants us to change our adult perspective on the world.
3 isn't interested in exams.
4 encourages students to have more faith in their own abilities.

▶ **Shimon Schocken: The self-organizing computer course**

Shimon Schocken and Noam Nisan developed a curriculum for their students to build a computer, piece by piece. When they put the course online, thousands jumped at the opportunity to learn, working independently and organizing their own classes in the first Massive Open Online Course (MOOC). A call to forget about grades and tap into the self-motivation to learn.

▶ **Adora Svitak: What adults can learn from kids**

Child prodigy Adora Svitak says the world needs 'childish' thinking: bold ideas, wild creativity and especially optimism. Kids' big dreams deserve high expectations, she says, and grownups must be as willing to learn from children as to teach.

▶ **Kiran Sethi: Kids, take charge**

Kiran Bir Sethi shows how her groundbreaking Riverside School in India teaches kids life's most valuable lesson: 'I can.' Watch her students take local issues into their own hands, lead other young people, even educate their parents.

▶ **Sugata Mitra: The child-driven education**

Education scientist Sugata Mitra tackles one of the greatest problems of education – the best teachers and schools don't exist where they're needed most. In a series of real-life experiments from New Delhi to South Africa to Italy, he gave kids self-supervised access to the web and saw results that could revolutionize how we think about teaching.

4 Find words or phrases in the TED playlist that mean the same as the words and phrases (a–d).

a programme of learning   **b** revolutionary
c addresses   **d** genius

5 Which talk would you most like to see? Why? Watch the talk at TED.com.

AUTHENTIC LISTENING SKILLS
Understanding mid-sentence changes

6 🎧 2 33 You are going to hear a podcast in which a member of the *Keynote* team talks about Sugata Mitra's TED Talk, *The child-driven education*. Listen to the opening sentence and put the elements (a–e) in the order that you hear them. Then indicate the two places where the speaker changes direction mid-sentence.

a but I have to say that he was ☐
b before watching *The child-driven education* ☐
c his talk immediately grabbed my attention ☐
d I'd never come across the TED speaker Sugata Mitra ☐
e heard his theories of education before ☐

LISTENING

7 🎧 2 34 Listen to the full podcast. Choose the word or phrase (a–c) that best describes Harry's opinion of Sugata Mitra's ideas.

a convinced   **b** sceptical   **c** in two minds

8 🎧 2 34 Listen again. Tick (✓) the things that Harry mentions about Sugata Mitra's ideas:

1 The best results were gained where people had had bad teachers. ☐
2 Results were obtained simply by giving children access to the Internet. ☐

3 The experiments had the same results all over the world. ☐
4 This way of learning teaches people English at the same time. ☐
5 This represents a revolution in the way people can learn. ☐
6 This way of learning can fit into the existing examination system. ☐
7 The idea extends education to those who could not afford it before. ☐

VOCABULARY IN CONTEXT

9 Read the extracts from the podcast. Choose the correct meaning of the words in bold.

1 … it was at the same time entertaining, compelling and most of all, extremely **credible**.
  a systematic ☐   **b** clever ☐   **c** convincing ☐
2 His own experiences of providing children with the **bare necessities** for learning.
  a most important things ☐   **b** most basic things ☐
  c most obvious things ☐
3 More importantly, the results were outstanding **no matter** the circumstances of the child.
  a regardless of ☐   **b** according to ☐
  c with no effect on ☐
4 In my mind, there is no doubt as to the **efficacy** of his approach, …
  a effectiveness ☐   **b** morality ☐
  c significance ☐
5 Teachers take note, because the implications could be **far-reaching**!
  a very dangerous ☐   **b** very significant ☐
  c very long-term ☐
6 I am excited to see how Sugata's project will **play out** …
  a be received long-term ☐   **b** help long-term ☐
  c develop long-term ☐

11.2 The value of education

GRAMMAR Conditionals

1 Match the quotation halves. Do the quotations express something real and/or possible (R) or something unreal, hypothetical or imaginary (U)?

1 If I had my choice, ☐ ☐

2 If you think education is expensive, ☐ ☐

3 I love teaching. If I made a trillion dollars, ☐ ☐

4 If teaching isn't rewarding and challenging, ☐ ☐

5 I didn't know what to do with myself. I wasn't excited by the teaching of the school. If they'd been intent on really teaching you things, ☐ ☐

6 Teaching is a very noble profession that shapes the character, calibre, and future of an individual. If the people remember me as a good teacher, ☐ ☐

a try ignorance. (Derek Bok, lawyer and educator)

b we're going to continue to lose our best teachers to work in other fields. (Michael Bennet, businessman, lawyer and politician)

c every high school would be teaching financial literacy along with math and science. (Gregory Meeks, politician)

d I would have been a little more attentive. (Diane Cilento, actress)

e I would still teach. It's different every day. You get to meet intelligent people all the time – or at least most of the time. (Richard Bausch, author)

f that will be the biggest honour for me. (A. P. J. Abdul Kalam, former President of India)

2 Complete the text with the correct form of the words in brackets.

It is well documented that you don't have to have a university education to be a success. And even if you ¹_____ (go) to university, you ²_____ (not / have to) see it through to graduation to become successful. We all know that if the likes of Bill Gates, Paul Allen, Steve Jobs and Steve Wozniak ³_____ (finish) their studies instead of dropping out to start Microsoft and Apple respectively, then the world ⁴_____ (may / not / quite / be) the place it is today. But here are four people who have made their mark and who have become successful, rich and famous without completing their university courses.

Things ⁵_____ (may / be) very different for Warren Buffett if he ⁶_____ (not / drop) out of the University of Pennsylvania in 1949 to pursue a more business-oriented course at the University of Nebraska. Buffett went on to become the world's most successful investor and one of the greatest and most generous philanthropists of all time. If it ⁷_____ (not / be) for his generosity, the Bill and Melinda Gates Foundation ⁸_____ (not / benefit) from the $37billion donation he made in 2006.

3 Complete the text with the correct form of the verbs in the box.

be	be	not/carry out	enter
have	have	leave	record
may/subject	wish		

If you ¹*are* a parent or guardian, you ²_____ a responsibility to ensure that your child receives school education for the years in which it is compulsory. Should you, without good reason, ³_____ this duty, there ⁴_____ a number of measures that can be taken to make sure that they are carried out. A child must stay on the school register until they are legally allowed to leave school. If a child were for any reason ⁵_____ school before that date, this ⁶_____ as taking unauthorized absence and ⁷_____ to legal action. Even though the school-leaving age is 16, a young person must by law continue in education or training until their 18th birthday. This means that if a child ⁸_____ to leave school at the age of 16, he or she ⁹_____ a choice of either undertaking work-based learning, such as an apprenticeship, or undertaking part-time education or training if they ¹⁰_____ employment.

4 Rewrite the sentences in a more formal style, beginning with the word or words in italics.

1 If I'd known about the seminar, I most certainly would've gone. *had*

Had I known about the seminar, I most certainly would've gone.

2 If the lecture theatre is unavailable, we'll book a different room. *should*

_____

3 If you'd been paying attention, you'd know what to do. *had*

_____

4 If he was here, I'm sure he'd have a lot to say about the matter. *were*

_____

5 If her housemates hadn't woken her up, she would've probably slept through the whole exam. *had it*

_____

6 If I reapplied for the course, do you think I'd have a chance? *if I were*

_____

LANGUAGE FOCUS Conditional conjunctions

5 ~~Cross out~~ the word or phrase that is not possible in each sentence.

1 *If I don't / As long as / Unless I* call you, let's meet in the library at 2.30.
2 *In the event that / Providing that / Assuming that* I don't fail the final assignment, I should pass the course.
3 *Supposing / Imagine / Unless* you failed the exam, would you be able to retake it?
4 *On condition that / In the event of / In case of* the fire alarm sounding, leave the lecture room by the exit here.
5 *Whether or not / But for / If it hadn't been for* my old maths teacher, Mrs Riley, I probably wouldn't have gone to university.
6 We'll have the tutorial in room 212 *in case of / as long as / providing* it's free. *Otherwise / If not / Assuming that*, we'll meet in my office.

6 Complete the sentences with the words or phrases in the box.

| assuming | but for | in the event that | otherwise |
| unless | whether or not | | |

1 _____ you get accepted on the course will depend as much on the interview as on your exam results.
2 _____ we get enough participants, the course will run in the second week of July.
3 We'd better get a move on, _____ we'll be late.
4 _____ one or two areas where you could have gone into a bit more depth, this is a very good essay. Well done.
5 _____ the course is cancelled, you will receive a full refund.
6 You can't normally teach at a university _____ you have at least a master's degree.

DICTATION

7 🎧 **2 35** Listen to someone talking about the importance of their academic qualifications in their career. Complete the sentences.

Well, I think my education and qualifications have had a direct effect and influence on my career. And quite simply, if ¹_____ the qualifications I have, I ²_____ _____ the position I am now. First and foremost, you need a master's degree as an absolute minimum to teach in a UK university, so if ³_____ in the university. Also, I have a PGCE, a Postgraduate Certificate in Education, which is ⁴_____ _____ , on top of your first degree, to teach in a school if ⁵_____ _____ a BEd as your first degree. So, ⁶_____ a PGCE a couple of years after my first degree, I ⁷_____ in the first place. As well as that, the PGCE got me really interested in teaching and education. And before that, of course, you can only do a PGCE ⁸_____ _____ a first degree.

11.3 How to remember

READING

1 Look at the title of the article. Answer the questions.

  1 What things make you feel more mentally alert?

  2 What things make you feel mentally tired and slow?

2 Read the blog and say which of these areas offer real help in boosting memory and brain power, according to the author.

  a food in general

  b superfoods

  c exercise in general

  d yoga

  e neuro-enhancing drugs

3 Read the article. Are these statements true (T) or false (F)? If they are false say why.

  1 There are now more ways to improve memory and brain-power than in the past, because there is more scientific knowledge available about the brain. ☐

  2 If you need a quick energy boost, processed food is one possible option. ☐

  3 The best types of exercise for the brain are those activities that demand you think hard about what you are doing. ☐

Can you really **boost brain power?**

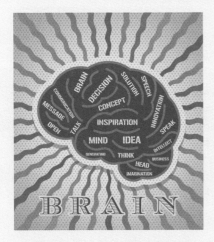

Advertisements for shortcuts to a better memory and a sharper mind – questionable promises about what a ten-dollar 30-day programme can achieve – are nothing new. While the 1980s and 90s saw the emergence of some more scientific, tried and tested methods – like 'Brain Gym', it is only recently, against the background of increased life expectancy and a corresponding rise in the incidence of dementia and other mental illnesses, that the demand for ways to maintain a healthy and active mind has become more urgent. Consequently, today we see a wide range of options on offer: 'eat your way to cleverness'; 'eight effective yoga poses to increase your brain power'; 'boost memory with natural neuro-enhancers'. But do these routes offer any greater promise than the programmes of the past?

Brain food and superfoods

Evidence suggests that a balanced diet, including a lot of fresh and unprocessed foods, is good for you in many ways, helping you maintain your energy levels and regulate your mood. (Processed foods tend to give you energy rushes, but are followed by energy crashes.) There is also evidence that eating the correct type of fats, such as Omega 3, can be beneficial, aiding short-term or working memory. But the bold claims made for so-called 'superfoods', like Goji berries, are more dubious. One thing which is known to help concentration and consolidation of memories is coffee! A recent study at Johns Hopkins University in Baltimore showed that a dose of caffeine equivalent to a double espresso significantly increased subjects' memory retention for up to 24 hours.

Exercise

Aerobic exercise is not only great for your body, it's also good for your mind, helping blood-flow to the brain and reducing the risk of Alzheimer's and dementia in the elderly. Exercising 'mindfully' – as is the case with yoga, for example – is better still. This is because an awareness of one's actions and observation of what is around you at a given moment, both without any judgement or criticism, reduces mental stress, induces a feeling of calm and compassion, and helps you to see things more clearly.

Neuro-enhancers

The idea of drugs which can enhance your mental acuity came to public attention in the film *Limitless*, starring Bradley Cooper, in which the hero becomes a super-successful business advisor – until his supply of the drugs dries up and side-effects start to kick in. The film was based on a real product, Addium, which some still claim works wonders for them and others rubbish as nothing more than glorified caffeine tablets. There are various other products on the market to help concentration, many used by students, which do temporarily improve alertness and cognitive ability. But they do not make you smarter as such and there is also evidence now emerging that longer-term users can experience a 'crash' or prolonged depression when they stop using them.

4 The writer suggests that he doesn't enjoy drinking coffee, even though it helps concentration. ☐

5 Public opinion is divided on the question of whether Addium is an effective brain power booster or not. ☐

6 Although he expresses reservations, the writer is optimistic about the potential of neuro-enhancers. ☐

4 🎧 **2 36** Listen to this extract from a radio phone-in show and complete the table, including the advice that the psychologist gives the caller.

Name of caller	Jordan
Occupation	_____
Problem	Not concentrating, feeling _____
Current habits	Sitting at a _____ for _____; getting to bed at _____; _____ on Facebook and WhatsApp
Advice	**1** Get back into _____ **2** Get rid of _____ **3** Prioritize _____ **4** Spend time _____

VOCABULARY Learning and memory

5 Complete the sentences with the verbs in the box.

acquire	assimilate	called	commit	evoked
get	hone	learning	recall	recite

1 Do you _____ what number our old house was on Southgate Lane, when we were students?

2 When I was at school, we all had to stand up and _____ our multiplication tables by heart.

3 According to research, the older you get, the harder it is to _____ new skills.

4 Learning the basics is often quite easy, but it usually takes a long time to _____ a skill to a high standard.

5 What you just said _____ to mind something that happened to me a few years ago.

6 You can do it. You'll soon _____ the hang of it.

7 There's a lot of information there, so it might take me a while to _____ it and work out exactly what I need to do.

8 I have to say, looking at those photos _____ a lot of memories of the good old days.

9 There was a lot of rote _____ when I was at school – historical dates and that kind of thing, that we just had to _____ to memory.

WORD FOCUS Memory

6 Match the words (1–7) with their definitions (a–g).

1 memorable ☐   **a** an official note sent within an organization

2 memento ☐   **b** learn something so you can remember it exactly

3 memoir ☐   **c** a statue, or similar, built in order to remind people of an important past event or person

4 memo ☐   **d** special, good or unusual and therefore easy to remember

5 memorabilia ☐   **e** an item that you keep to remind you of a place or person

6 memorial ☐   **f** an account written by someone about their life and experiences

7 memorize ☐   **g** items that people collect because they are associated with a famous person, event or time

7 Complete the sentences with the words from Exercise 6.

1 Did you get that _____ yesterday about the restructuring of the marketing department?

2 Have you ever read *This Boy's Life*? It's basically the _____ of the author, Tobias Wolff.

3 I've been collecting Beatles _____ for years. I've got hundreds of items: records, posters, models, books.

4 I think the Arc de Triomphe in Paris was built as a _____ to the French soldiers who died during World War I.

5 I just don't know anyone's phone numbers any more. I think I might need to _____ a few important ones, just in case.

6 The most _____ place I've stayed in? I'd say the Lake Palace Hotel in Udaipur in India. It's basically a palace built in the middle of a lake.

7 I always like to get some little _____ of the places I go to. Just something small I can put on the shelf.

8 Complete the dialogues with the 'memory' expressions in the box.

brought back a lot of memories	from memory
if my memory serves me well	in living memory
trip down memory lane	

1 A: Do you remember the name of our history of science professor at uni?
   B: _____ , it was Dr Johnstone, wasn't it?

2 A: Isn't this weather amazing? So warm for this time of year!
   B: Well, we've had the warmest December _____ , apparently. In fact, maybe even since records began.

3 A: What did you have to do in the experiment?
   B: It was interesting, actually. We had to draw a number of famous brand logos _____ and then we had to assess how close we'd drawn them to the real ones.

4 A: It was great to see you after all these years. It _____ .
   B: You too. A real _____ . We must get together again soon.

11.4 I'll get the hang of it

DESCRIBING CAPABILITIES

1 🎧**2 37** Listen to someone talking about how they were thrown in at the deep end and answer the questions.

1 What was the job?
2 How much notice did the person get?
3 How did the person prepare for the first session?
4 How did the person feel they coped? (a) brilliantly
   (b) quite well   (c) terribly
5 What specific aspect did the person have difficulty with?
6 What did the job inspire the person to do?

2 🎧**2 37** Match the two parts of the sentences. Then listen again and check your answers.

1 I could do it with ☐   a my depth.
2 I had no idea what ☐   b daunting.
3 I was totally out of ☐   c through.
4 It was pretty ☐   d I was doing.
5 I struggled ☐   e my eyes shut.
6 I'm a pretty ☐   f on top of it.
7 I soon got the ☐   g straightforward.
8 I started to feel ☐   h quick learner.
9 It all seemed pretty ☐   i clueless.
10 I was pretty ☐   j hang of it.

3 Match the two parts of the sentences.

1 I've got it off ☐   a ear and out the other.
2 I'm sure it'll come ☐   b rusty.
3 I'm not quite up ☐   c back to me.
4 I'm a bit ☐   d to speed.
5 It just goes in one ☐   e pat.

4 Rewrite the phrases in bold with expressions and phrases from Exercises 2 and 3.

1 A: You're a quick learner. I'm sure you'll ~~understand what to do~~ *get the hang of it* in no time.
   B: Maybe, but ~~I don't fully understand~~ *I'm not quite up to speed* just yet.
2 A: You'll be fine teaching him. In fact, you used to teach maths, didn't you?
   B: Well, I haven't taught for over ten years now, so I'm sure **I won't be as good as I used to be** _____ . But I'm sure **I'll remember** _____ pretty quickly.
3 A: I've no idea what I should be doing. It's been explained to me several times, but **I can't keep anything in my head** _____ .
   B: Let me help you. I'm sure it's all **quite simple and easy** _____ , really.

4 A: Hey, how was your first day back at work?
   B: Well, it was **quite intimidating** _____ , to be honest. There was a time when I could've done it **incredibly easily** _____ , but a lot's changed since I've been away. I'm sure I can **make the effort and just about manage** _____ though.
5 A: I **knew nothing** _____ when I started here. Totally **lacking in the necessary experience** _____ .
   B: Me too. But I'm starting to feel **that I understand things** _____ now.

PRONUNCIATION Linking vowel sounds

5 🎧**2 38** Read the sentences. Which consonant sounds do you think link the underlined vowel sounds, /w/, /j/ or /r/? Listen and check your answers.

1 He <u>j</u> asked me if I wanted to do some English teaching to<u> </u>earn some money.
2 They w<u>ere a</u> group of teenagers.
3 So<u> </u>anyway, I got to th<u>e </u>end of the morning.
4 I wasn't great, by<u> </u>any means.
5 That's how I got int<u>o </u>it as a career.
6 It goes in one ear<u> </u>and out the <u>o</u>ther.
7 I used to be<u> </u>able to do<u> </u>it with my eyes shut.
8 I've n<u>o </u>idea what I should be doing.

WRITING SKILL Preposition + participle

6 Underline the preposition + participle phrases in the extracts.

1 After seeing an 8.2 per cent increase in sales for the period leading up to the start of October, the increase dropped to 3.7 per cent for the following six months. With other firms similarly reporting a distinct seasonal difference in sales, it seems a new trend is emerging.
2 Hanson Industries is planning to reduce its debt by passing it on to the holding company and by doing so will be in a better position to make acquisitions as opportunities arise.
3 Written sources are of prime value to the historian and, without devaluing the important contribution made by other kinds of evidence, such as archaeology, by providing an unparalleled depth of insight into human conduct, offer us so much more information about the past.
4 On completing the claim form, please email it directly to us at the address at the bottom of this page. Before sending, please ensure that the form has been electronically signed as forms without a signature cannot be accepted.

7 Complete the extracts with the correct preposition.

1 _____ arriving at the conference, please go to the welcome desk to collect your badge.

2 _____ waiting for over one hour, we still had not received our food. Only _____ threatening to leave the restaurant did we attract the attention of your staff.

3 _____ interest rates being as low as they are at the moment, this may be a good time to take out a loan.

4 We are beginning to make steady progress and _____ spending more on resources, we are confident of making further progress.

5 The miscalculations have been costly and _____ wishing to apportion blame, there has clearly been an element of human error in the process.

6 _____ accepting your kind invitation to speak at the conference, I have a few questions.

8 Rewrite the extracts using preposition + participle phrases.

1 Please make sure that you satisfy the participant criteria **before you apply** for a place on the training programme.
*Please make sure that you satisfy the participant criteria **before applying** for a place on the training programme.*

2 **When you leave** the building, please ensure that you sign out and return your pass.

_____

3 **After an employee has completed** the required probationary period, annual leave will accrue at an initial rate of half a day per week worked.

_____
_____

4 **As we don't know** all the facts, it is difficult for us to make a judgement at this time.

_____
_____

5 We help small businesses grow **because we provide** expert assistance with Social Media Search Engine Marketing.

_____
_____

6 **If you accept** these terms and conditions you also agree to the terms of our Privacy Policy.

_____

7 **Although I don't want to get** too technical at this stage, I do have a few concerns regarding the data collection methodology. **If you use** counterbalancing rather than randomization, there could be an element of bias.

_____
_____
_____

8 As you may be aware, over 75% of consumers research a service or product online **before they make** a purchase. And **because such a high proportion of potential customers come** from search engines, a user's first impression is critical. In fact, research shows that **when they visit** a website, a consumer forms an opinion of it within 0.2 seconds.

_____
_____
_____
_____
_____

YOUR IDEA

1 Read three paragraphs about learning and studying. Which speakers say statements a–c?

1 Pietro: Sometimes it's really difficult to remember things when you need to. Revising for exams always does this to me. I find it hard to keep all the facts and figures in my memory so that I can recall them when I sit down to write a paper. I was in real danger of failing my course at university, so I knew something needed to be done. I tried not to get discouraged by any tests I had already failed and I committed myself to making a change. I took a course about improving memory and they taught me a very useful thing to do. Basically, the key is to put all the things you have to remember – the facts, numbers, people – into a story in your head. It does sound a bit crazy and unbelievable, but it really helped me. ☐

2 Hina: I'm a real fan of memory puzzles and games – you know like they have sometimes in the newspaper. Crosswords, Sudoku, logic puzzles – I love them. And I also think they have an effect on how good your memory is and what you're able to concentrate on at any particular time. I used to be terrible at remembering my friends' birthdays and other bits and pieces. But after I bought a book of memory games and tried a few out, I really noticed a difference. I don't think it's a case of being too obsessed with remembering things. It's more that you will remember important things more easily if you keep your mind active. ☐

3 Ivana: If there's one thing I've come to realize over the last few years it's how important it is to have a system. I used to keep lots and lots of notes, but they weren't organized. Then a friend suggested to me that I start using sticky notes and putting them in strategic places. It's so simple, but now that I can write reminders and put them in useful places I remember things much more easily. For example, I now put my shopping list up on the door of my fridge. I put notes about work by my mirror – since I look in the mirror every day, I'm not going to miss those reminders. ☐

a I changed my behaviour to improve my memory.
b I learned a new technique to help my memory.
c I use an imaginative activity to help improve my memory.

2 Write notes about the things you do to help you learn and remember things. Think about how habit, routine, techniques and technology can help you.

_____
_____
_____
_____

3 Complete these sentences about learning and memory techniques using the words in the box.

set	strategic	test	train

1 _____ your brain by completing logic puzzles and crosswords.
2 Be _____ when you make notes – use colours to make them easier to understand.
3 Use technology – _____ yourself reminders on your smartphone.
4 _____ your memory to see if you are improving at remembering things.

4 Practise your presentation. Practise different techniques to make sure you do not forget what you want to say. Try to …

- rehearse your presentation a lot. Say it aloud so you know what sounds right and practise in front of other people.
- memorize the opening lines and the last few lines so that you can establish eye contact with your audience at these points.
- avoid reading from slides.

ORGANIZING YOUR PRESENTATION

5 Match the six steps of the presentation with the examples of useful language (a–f).

1 Start the presentation ☐
2 Tell a brief personal story about learning and memory ☐
3 Talk about what you do that helps you learn and remember things ☐
4 Explain how this has helped you in your life ☐
5 Suggest how others can benefit from this ☐
6 Conclude ☐

a This may particularly help people who like information presented visually.
b So, one thing that helps me is to remember things as an image. For example, to remember a fact about a poem, I'll imagine a picture of the poet in their house.
c Thank you for being here. Today I'm going to be talking about my learning and memory techniques.
d So, that's all I have to say. Are there any questions from the floor?
e This has allowed me to approach the task of memorizing things in a different way. I can remember facts and numbers much more easily now.
f I've always had trouble remembering things when I'm studying. Sometimes there is just too much and I find it difficult to recall everything.

YOUR PRESENTATION

6 Read the useful language on the left and make notes for your presentation.

1 Start the presentation Thank you for … I'm going to … This talk … I'll suggest …	
2 Tell a brief personal story about learning and memory I've always … Something that … This is …	
3 Talk about what you do that helps you learn and remember things One thing that … What I do is … To help me I … The key is to …	
4 Explain how this has helped you in your life This allows me to … When I do this I can … It enables me to …	
5 Suggest how others can benefit from this This may … Other people could … Benefits for others could be …	
6 Conclude That's it … Are there … from the floor? What are … ?	

7 Film yourself giving your presentation or practise in front of a mirror.
Give yourself marks out of ten for …

- memorizing the opening and closing lines of your presentation.   ☐/10
- not reading from your slides.   ☐/10
- following the six steps in Exercise 6.   ☐/10
- using correct grammar.   ☐/10

12 Invention or innovation

12.1 Creative problem-solving in the face of extreme limits

TEDTALKS

NAVI RADJOU is a French national who was born in Pondicherry, India, in 1970. He studied information systems at École Centrale, Paris, and, after that, attended the Yale School of Management.

Radjou was an analyst for ten years and, later, Vice President at US-based technology research and consulting firm Forrester Research. Here, drawing on his native India and other emerging markets, such as China, he investigated how globalized innovation drives new market structures and organizational models, for which he coined the business concept of 'Global Innovation Networks'. At this time, he also started to develop his core interest in creating 'new practical business frameworks that integrate Western and Eastern perspectives on innovation and leadership'. Also, while at Forrester, he advised leading organizations worldwide, including General Motors, Fujitsu, IBM and Microsoft, on innovation, leadership and breakthrough growth strategies. Radjou then became Executive Director of the Centre for India & Global Business at Judge Business School, University of Cambridge and, in 2011, became a Fellow of Judge Business School. Radjou has also served as a member of the World Economic Forum's Global Agenda Council on Design Innovation and has been a columnist for *Harvard Business Review*.

Radjou has authored and co-authored a number of books, including *Frugal Innovation: How To Do More With Less* and the 2012 bestseller *Jugaad Innovation*. The latter is based on the Indian concept of Jugaad, which shows how businesses can find solutions to problems using limited resources and how they can, at the same time, become more efficient and cost-effective by utilizing the 'grassroots ingenuity' in their organization. *The Economist* called it 'the most comprehensive book' yet to appear on the subject of frugal innovation and, in 2013, Radjou received the Thinkers50 Innovation Award, which is given to a management thinker who is re-shaping the way we think about and practise innovation. Radjou is a sought-after conference speaker and his 2014 TED Global Talk on frugal innovation has had over 1 million views.

Navi Radjou

CAREER PATHWAYS

1 Read the text. Answer the questions.

1 How has Radjou's native India had a role in shaping his career?

2 What work has Radjou done as:
   a a researcher   **b** an academic   **c** an advisor/consultant

3 Which words in the text mean the following?
   a created or invented a new word or phrase (paragraph 2)
   b the ordinary members of an organization (paragraph 3)
   c using only as much as is needed (paragraph 3)

TED PLAYLIST

2 Other TED speakers are interested in topics similar to Navi Radjou's TED Talk. Read the descriptions of four TED Talks at the top of page 115. In your opinion, which is the best title for this playlist, a, b or c?

a Seeking out talent in unlikely places
b Making technology accessible
c New routes to innovation

▶ **R.A. Mashelkar: Breakthrough designs for ultra-low-cost products**

Engineer R.A. Mashelkar shares three stories of ultra-low-cost design from India that use bottom-up rethinking, and some clever engineering, to bring expensive products (cars, prosthetics) into the realm of the possible for everyone.

▶ **Bunker Roy: Learning from a barefoot movement**

In Rajasthan, India, an extraordinary school teaches rural women and men – many of them illiterate – to become solar engineers, artisans, dentists and doctors in their own villages. It's called the Barefoot College, and its founder, Bunker Roy, explains how it works.

▶ **Anil Gupta: India's hidden hotbeds of invention**

Anil Gupta is on the hunt for the developing world's unsung inventors – indigenous entrepreneurs whose ingenuity, hidden by poverty, could change many people's lives. He shows how the Honey Bee Network helps them build the connections they need – and gain the recognition they deserve.

▶ **Manu Prakash: A 50-cent microscope that folds like origami**

Perhaps you've punched out a paper doll or folded an origami swan? TED Fellow Manu Prakash and his team have created a microscope made of paper that's just as easy to fold and use. A sparkling demo that shows how this invention could revolutionize healthcare in developing countries.

3 Read the TED playlist again. Find a speaker who ...

1 talks about inventions made using limited resources.
2 is interested in helping people to develop their skills.
3 is interested in people who can help their own communities.
4 is interested in improving medical care.

4 Find nouns in the TED playlist that mean the same as the words (a–d).

a domain/territory   b craftspeople   c appreciation
d presentation

5 Which talk would you most like to see? Why? Watch the talk at TED.com.

AUTHENTIC LISTENING SKILLS
Discourse markers

6 🎧 2 39 You are going to hear a podcast in which a member of the *Keynote* team talks about Manu Prakesh's TED Talk, *A 50-cent microscope that folds like origami*. Complete the sentences with discourse markers. Then listen and check your answers.

The speaker starts off by explaining the importance…
He ¹ _____ goes on to say that most microscopes that can accurately identify such microbes are too bulky or complicated to be used out in the field. ² _____
³ _____ ⁴ _____ , many people are waiting too long for a diagnosis.

LISTENING

7 🎧 2 40 Listen to the full podcast. Tick (✓) the words that you think describe Jon's reactions to the talk.

slightly confused ☐   professionally interested ☐
sceptical ☐   curious to know more ☐

8 🎧 2 40 Listen again. Complete the statements using one word.

1 Microscopy can be used to detect _____ in the blood that cause diseases like malaria.
2 The 'foldscope', with its built-in projector, is made of _____ .
3 Jon couldn't work out if the photo used in the demonstration was taken in _____ time or not.
4 The photos that Prakash showed also seemed to be on a _____ scale than the level needed to detect microbes.
5 Overall Jon thinks this cheap microscope has enormous _____ in the field and in schools.

VOCABULARY IN CONTEXT

9 Read the extracts from the podcast. Choose the correct meaning of the words in bold.

1 Most microscopes that can accurately identify such microbes are too **bulky** or complicated to be used out in the field.
   a large ☐   b expensive ☐   c heavy ☐
2 … a functioning microscope … which has micro-optics **embedded** in the paper …
   a lying flat ☐   b set inside ☐   c activated ☐
3 I find this very interesting and am **eager** to see the device in action.
   a curious ☐   b keen ☐   c optimistic ☐
4 After part-demonstrating the construction, the speaker then **dims** the lights.
   a turns up ☐   b turns down ☐   c turns off ☐
5 … would … have given the presentation much more impact – it would have **swayed** me more anyway.
   a persuaded ☐   b pleased ☐   c woken up ☐

12.2 Patent pending

GRAMMAR Adverbs and word order

1 Complete the text with the adverbs in the box.

also	exactly	famously	globally
however	increasingly	in turn	likely
often	therefore		

When we think about contemporary innovative companies, we are ¹ _____ to think of companies such as Google, Apple, Microsoft and the like. ² _____, there are many much smaller, less well-known companies that are ³ _____ developing or advancing state-of-the-art technologies. And these companies ⁴ _____ remain unknown because their innovations are not always consumer oriented. But the world needs companies like this and, as many nations continue to lose their competitive advantages in traditional industries like manufacturing, their ability to compete ⁵ _____ is ⁶ _____ dependent on their ability to innovate. But what ⁷ _____ is innovation and what makes a company innovative? Steve Jobs once ⁸ _____ said that 'innovation distinguishes between a leader and a follower'. ⁹ _____ , for companies to be more innovative, there needs to be more innovative leadership, which can oversee turning new ideas and technologies into assets that will, ¹⁰ _____ , help to transform the country's economy.

2 Choose the correct options to complete the list of characteristics of great innovators.

1 Being innovative means *differently doing things / doing things differently* or doing things that *never have before been done / have never been done before*.
2 Innovators are leaders who create dynamic and *highly productive / productive highly* organizations which have loyal employees who feel valued and respected and who *towards the company's aim work passionately / work passionately towards the company's aim*.
3 Innovators know that innovation *happens never in a vacuum / never happens in a vacuum*. They *highly value / value highly* networks of people, assets and organizations and *view positively collaboration / view collaboration positively*.

4 Innovators understand it takes many different points of view *to fully grasp / fully to grasp* the complexity of the business and technological challenges that we *today face / face today*.
5 Innovators *never take / take never* shortcuts and *will usually seek / usually will seek* more complex solutions, *even if / if even* it means taking *higher considerably / considerably higher* risks.
6 Innovators understand that all companies, old and new, *have to continuously reach above and beyond / have to reach above and beyond continuously* what they *have before done / have done before* in order to remain competitive.
7 Innovators *never are / are never* afraid to break with the norm and *to outside the box think / to think outside the box*. They are aware that customers *do not always know / do not know always* what they want.

3 Rewrite the sentences with the adverbs in the correct place.

1 Research has shown that we think.
when we are lying down / faster, more creatively and more innovatively
Research has shown that we think faster, more creatively and more innovatively when we are lying down.
2 Lying down can boost thinking speeds.
by up to 10% / significantly / according to the research,
_____
_____
3 This is due to the chemical noradrenalin, which is produced and which slows mental activity and reduces our attention to detail.
when we are stressed / by the brain
_____
_____
4 The mind has more to process, and the brain produces more noradrenalin.
thus / considerably / when we are standing up,
_____
_____
5 The brain has less to process and it produces less noradrenalin.
when we are lying down, / usually / therefore / conversely,
_____
_____
6 We can process information and think.
more clearly and innovatively / as a result, / when lying down, / at greater speeds / generally
_____
_____

4 Rewrite the quotations by putting the adverbs in italics in the correct place.

1 Innovation can occur where you can breathe free.   *only*
Joe Biden (politician)

_____

_____

2 Change is the law of life. And those who look to the past or present are certain to miss the future.   *only*
John F. Kennedy (US president)

_____

_____

3 Companies have too many experts who block innovation. True innovation comes from perpendicular thinking.   *really*
Peter Diamandis (engineer and entrepreneur)

_____

_____

4 The biggest risk is not taking any risk … In a world that is changing quickly, the strategy that is guaranteed to fail is not taking risks.   *really*   *only*
Mark Zuckerberg (founder of Facebook)

_____

_____

5 Radical innovation is difficult to fund. It seems scary. And the radical things seem more scary.   *really*   *even*
Nolan Bushnell (engineer and entrepreneur)

_____

_____

LANGUAGE FOCUS Adverbial phrases

5 Complete the adverbial phrases with the correct prepositions.

1 *To* everyone's disappointment, the proposal was not accepted.
2 _____ put it bluntly, it was a stupid thing to do.
3 _____ coincidence, they both studied first at Oxford and then Harvard.
4 _____ his defence, he did actually tell us that he wasn't going to be here.
5 _____ be fair, it was only his second time playing the game.
6 _____ their credit, they persevered with the idea despite all the knock backs.
7 _____ reflection, we should've been a bit more proactive.
8 _____ the whole, everything went as well as could be expected.
9 _____ hindsight, I think we should've waited a bit longer.

10 _____ respect, you don't quite seem to understand.
11 _____ the top _____ my head, I'd say there were about two hundred there.
12 _____ interest, did you see Jenny at the conference?

6 Rewrite the adverbial phrases in bold using the words or phrases from Exercise 5.

1 **Disappointingly for him**, he didn't even make the shortlist. *To his disappointment*
2 **Not having thought about it**, I'd say it'll be about £5,000 altogether. _____
3 **Respectfully**, you don't know what you're talking about. _____
4 **To be fair**, she did warn us that this might happen. We can't blame her. _____
5 **To be completely frank**, I think we might have a bit of a problem here. _____
6 **Coincidentally**, both products were launched on the same day. _____
7 **Good for them**, they stuck to their principles and didn't give in to pressure. _____
8 **In hindsight**, we should've re-advertised the post. _____
9 **All in all**, I think you have a good point there. _____
10 **I'm just wondering**, did Harry say anything about the meeting last week? _____

DICTATION

7 🎧**2** **41** Listen to a student in a seminar taking about a new energy technology. Complete the sentences.

I read something really interesting the other day about some new technology that can use the energy in the radio waves that are all around us to charge small, low-energy electronic devices. I think it's called Freevolt, or something like that, and [1] _____ is it absorbs, or 'harvests', all the radio waves [2] _____ around us, from, say wi-fi, mobile phones and broadcast networks and they reckon that, with a bit more development, this energy can [3] _____ to power devices like our mobiles, or lighting and so on. [4] _____ out of the air, sort of recycles energy that [5] _____ , so it's a pretty green energy source at the same time. I think companies have been researching how to harvest energy like this for a long time now and they reckon [6] _____ .

READING

1 Look at the title of the article. Tick (✓) what you would expect to find in this museum.

 a Innovations that nobody wanted ☐
 b Products that didn't work ☐
 c Inventions that inventors could not get backing for ☐

2 Read the article. Answer the questions.

 1 Which answer in Exercise 1 (a, b or c) is the best description of the failed ideas described in the article?
 2 Which of the examples of failed products clearly offered a practical advantage to consumers?
 3 What sentence or phrase sums up why the writer thinks the idea of a museum of failed products is useful?

3 Read the article again. Choose the best answers.

 1 Robert McMath wished to create
  a a collection of bad marketing ideas
  b a collection of products which did not work
  c a complete collection of consumer goods
 2 The writer suggests that most of the products in the museum
  a are no longer on sale
  b are not catalogued in any way
  c were once useful products
 3 The writer suggests that consumers in Asia
  a are easily fooled
  b like new things
  c like funny products

The museum of failed ideas

The NewProductWorks collection, better known by its nickname of 'The Museum of Failed Products', sits in a fairly nondescript building in a business park on the outskirts of Ann Arbor, a medium-sized city in Michigan, USA. The collection began in the New York apartment of marketing professional Robert McMath who, in the 1960s, set about bringing into one place a comprehensive catalogue of every consumable product he could find. The collection soon outgrew his apartment and was bought by global consultants GfK, who moved it to the new premises in Michigan. McMath had no intention of creating a museum of failed products, but since most products do fail, that is what the collection principally became: a reference library of items withdrawn from sale within weeks or months of being launched because no-one wanted them.

The first impression of the museum is that of a giant, badly-organized supermarket with aisle after aisle of food (perishables have been removed) and household items. The difference is that each item is unique and few would now be found in any real supermarket. It's a graveyard of obsolete consumer goods: Clear Pepsi, Reddi-bacon (bacon that cooks in your toaster), Fortune Snookies

(fortune cookies for dogs), A Touch of Yoghurt shampoo. The museum's proprietor, Carol Sherry, is still collecting and is always on the lookout for new products. The Asian market, which has short product life-cycles and demands novelty, provides a good supply of these. One example she gives is a packet of chewing gum developed in Japan which has a small pocket at one end to put your chewed gum in.

Sherry obviously feels some compassion for the developers of many of the products, ordinary working people with mortgages to pay and mouths to feed who were simply trying to do their best. McMath himself, who later wrote a book on the subject, *What were they thinking?* was perhaps less sympathetic. Sherry receives GfK clients from around the country who come to the museum looking for inspiration and a lesson in product design and innovation. Often they are surprised to see previous product failures developed by their own companies.

The moral the museum teaches us – and should teach the breed of upbeat marketing professionals that thought up the products in the first place – is that failure is something we should contemplate more often. Each product on display must have gone through a series of meetings from conception to design to launch in which at least one of the decision-makers involved had serious misgivings about the idea. Yet no-one wanted to appear negative. The problem is that if you do not factor in the potential for failure, it is all the more difficult to deal with when it happens. No-one will want to spend time analyzing why the product was rejected or trying to take lessons from it. They will simply carry on in a relentlessly positive way, imagining that failure is just a temporary setback on the unstoppable journey to success.

4 The writer suggests that GfK uses the museum to

    a help its clients avoid the mistakes their own companies made in the past

    b show its clients that there are many more bad ideas than good ideas

    c show its clients a wide range of different ideas that product designers have had

5 The writer suggests that the reason for a lot of these product failures is

    a people always agreeing with their managers even if at heart they disagree

    b people wanting to be seen as positive and optimistic about new ideas

    c successful people not being accustomed to failure

4 Read the article again. Choose the correct definition (a, b or c) for the words from the article (1–8).

  1 nondescript (paragraph 1)

    a untidy   **b** unremarkable   **c** undiscovered

  2 set about (paragraph 1)

    a had the idea of   **b** started to work on

    c was given the task of

  3 outgrew (paragraph 1)

    a grew larger than   **b** grew to fit   **c** grew outside

  4 perishables (paragraph 2)

    a things which decay   **b** things which are poisonous

    c things which explode

  5 feel compassion for (paragraph 3)

    a feel disbelief at   **b** feel respect for

    c feel sympathy for

  6 moral (paragraph 4)

    a lesson in life   **b** business lesson   **c** difficult lesson

  7 conception (paragraph 4)

    a the forming of an idea   **b** the testing of an idea

    c the discussion of an idea

  8 misgivings (paragraph 4)

    a interests   **b** fears   **c** doubts

VOCABULARY Phrasal verbs: innovation

5 Rewrite the phrases in bold with the correct form of the phrasal verbs in the box. There are three phrasal verbs that you do not need to use.

> bring about   bring up   come up with   ~~get around~~
> get down to   hit on   make up for   pay out
> pull it off   set up take up   try it out

  1 It's just a small problem and I'm sure we can ~~find a solution to~~ *get around* it.

  2 What he lacks in experience, he certainly **compensates for** _____ with his energy and enthusiasm.

  3 To get a real idea of how the app performs, we need to **test it** _____ on an actual mobile device.

  4 The new regulations will **cause** _____ real change in the industry.

5 After a lot of small talk, we finally **started seriously doing** _____ business.

6 Did anyone **raise the issue of** _____ the restructuring of R+D in the meeting?

7 I really didn't think she'd get the deal, but to her credit she **succeeded** _____ .

8 I first **thought of** _____ the idea in about 2010 and the company was **founded** _____ in 2012.

WORDBUILDING *invent, innovate, create, produce*

6 🎧**2 42** Complete the table. Underline the most stressed syllable in each word (1–13). Then listen and check your answers.

verb	adjective	abstract noun	concrete noun	person/ organization
invent	1 _____	2 _____	invention	inventor
innovate	3 _____	4 _____	5 _____	6 _____
create	creative	7 _____	8 _____	9 _____
produce	10 _____	11 _____	12 _____ / production	13 _____

7 Complete the extracts using words from Exercise 6.

  1 The company remained market leader through _____ product development, which continually left its competitors playing catch up.

  2 Smith's clever _____ and _____ all over the court was the key difference between the two players in her 6-3, 6-2 win.

  3 The new system should increase _____ by around 20%, which will mean a further 5,000 cars rolling off the production line each year.

  4 _____ placement, having your brand appear in a film, can cost tens of millions of dollars.

  5 Jony Ive, Apple's _____ genius, studied industrial design at Northumbria University.

  6 Dennis Ritchie was an American computer scientist, who is best known as the _____ of the C programming language.

  7 X-ray crystallography is widely regarded as one of the greatest _____ of the 20th century.

  8 When Van Gogh arrived in Arles in 1888, he was inspired to begin the most _____ period of his career, producing works more rapidly than ever before.

  9 *Forbes Magazine* _____ a stir among universities when it released its 'Best and Worst Master's Degrees for Jobs'.

  10 When the mass _____ of automobiles began in the early 1900s, petroleum began its rise as an energy source.

12.4 To get the best results ...

HANDY TIPS

1 🎧 2 43 Listen to four people giving some advice and tips. Answer the questions.

  1 Which speaker talks about ...
    a a journey? ☐
    b a bread maker? ☐
    c a phone camera? ☐
    d a coffee machine? ☐
  2 Which speaker mentions ...
    a something being difficult and unpleasant? ☐
    b ease of maintenance? ☐
    c changing settings? ☐
    d a timer? ☐

2 🎧 2 43 Complete the extracts from Exercise 1. Listen again and check your answers.

  1 Well, I'd a_____ against getting anything too elaborate, s_____ they generally need a lot of maintenance and cleaning.
  2 Personally, I'd r_____ getting something simple and easy to use.
  3 And s_____ as your kitchen isn't so big, it'd be perfect size-wise.
  4 G_____ that you're going to be setting off in the afternoon, to a_____ getting stuck in traffic, I'd leave the motorway at junction 25 ...
  5 And make sure you take your satnav too, s_____ as not to get lost.
  6 And it's got a function f_____ making jam as well, though I've never used that.
  7 ... you can set it to make the loaf overnight s_____ that it's ready in the morning.
  8 OK, so t_____ get the best results, first don't use the default auto mode.
  9 W_____ all the different settings, a lot of people don't bother changing this for f_____ that they might do something wrong ...
  10 And in o_____ to get as sharp pictures as possible, make sure the resolution is on the highest setting.

3 Find and correct the mistakes in the sentences.

  1 For getting the best results, you want avoid to use the digital zoom.
  _____

  2 I never mess around with the settings in fear that I'll accidentally delete something important.
  _____

  3 I'd advise not travel between 4 and 6, since especially it's a Friday.
  _____

  4 Seen as I'm not from round here, I'm not the best person to ask about places to stay.
  _____

  5 Turn the TV off at the mains so not waste electricity with the TV on stand-by.
  _____

  6 It's a device for measure the temperature inside something you've cooked.
  _____

  7 With you use your mobile all the time, you should turn the screen brightness down in order for saving battery.
  _____

  8 Giving that you can only be there for a couple of days, I'd recommend to stay right in the city centre that you don't waste time travelling around so much.
  _____
  _____
  _____

PRONUNCIATION Word endings

4 🎧 2 44 Underline the word in each group where the word ending (-ure, -age, etc) is pronounced differently. Then listen and check your answers.

  1 measure   picture   nature   mature   fixture
  2 image   passage   massage   shortage   baggage
  3 disgrace   palace   terrace   populace   grimace
  4 gadget   wallet   racket   sachet   nugget
  5 finance   reluctance   compliance   abundance   guidance

WRITING SKILL Reporting verbs

5 Correct the mistakes in the extracts.

1 I must confess to already be a big fan and therefore a bit biased, but the new game is simply out of this world.

_____
_____
_____

2 The speakers promise delivering a full sound with exceptional clarity at the very top and bottom end, which encourages to turn up the volume and hear things you may have never heard before.

_____
_____
_____
_____

3 Users are invited for testing the new version and then, if they wish, receive a free upgrade on completion of a short feedback form.

_____
_____
_____

4 We advise not to upgrade just yet as the new software does seem to have one or two glitches that the company is currently trying to sort out.

_____
_____
_____

5 When installing the software, we suggest to use the default installation settings for an easier setup.

_____
_____

6 I would encourage you getting a completely new system rather than upgrading your current one but, if you insist to upgrade, also try to get a faster processor.

_____
_____
_____

7 We congratulate them producing a first-rate app that will no doubt be on tens of millions of smartphones in no time.

_____
_____
_____

8 The company is offering replace the item or give a full refund. We recommend to take a refund until the problem is completely rectified.

_____
_____
_____

6 Complete the extracts from product reviews using the correct form of the words in the box. Add prepositions and the object where necessary.

> ~~allow/you/play~~ confess/initially/be congratulate/the developers/make discourage/you/guess encourage/you/actively/solve guarantee/transform promise/deliver recommend/change

1 The game *allows you to play* your way, either exploring open-world free roaming or story-driven gameplay.

2 I _____ the settings so that all of your screenshots are saved to their own folder.

3 Compatible with all versions of PowerGo, the makers claim the software is _____ the speed of any system running it and _____ a much enhanced and sharper experience.

4 The BrainTrain app cleverly _____ the answers and _____ the puzzles step by step.

5 I must _____ a little sceptical about the claims. But the app really does deliver. And I must also _____ it available for free.

7 Complete the product review with the correct form of the words in brackets. Add prepositions and the object where necessary.

> TuneFast Radio allows [1] _____ (you/listen) to more than 50,000 radio stations from around the world and is, in our opinion, one of the best streaming-radio apps available. The developers need to be congratulated [2] _____ (produce) an easy-to-use and reliable listening experience. The app has an intuitive interface and clear navigation and enables [3] _____ (you/search) for specific types of programmes or music genres. And TuneFast lives up to its name in that buffering times are very short. We recommend [4] _____ (start) the free version, as we feel this will be adequate for most users. However, and here is our only major grumble, pop-ups are forever inviting [5] _____ (you/upgrade) to the Pro-Version. And while you can't blame [6] _____ (the company/have) these pop-ups, they do appear too frequently. The Pro-Version has a few extra features, most notably it enables [7] _____ (us/record) songs and [8] _____ (save) them on our device. There are also a few performance bugs which sometimes affect track information. As there are many of us who insist [9] _____ (have) the album artwork or the names of the songs we are listening to displayed, I would advise [10] _____ (the developers/fix) this as soon as possible.

121

Writing 6 | A LETTER

IDEAS

You will read a letter written to answer the question below.

> You have read an article in an international magazine on the topic of innovation in developing countries. The magazine has asked readers to tell them about other projects. You decide to write a letter to the magazine. In your letter you should briefly describe an innovation used in developing countries and the effect it has had. You should also analyze the extent to which people living outside the developing countries can fulfil the needs of those within them.

Write your letter in **280–320 words** in an appropriate style.

1 In the question, underline the three topics which need to be included in the letter. What points could be included in each topic?

1 _____
2 _____
3 _____

MODEL

2 Read the article on the right. Which topic is dealt with in each section? Are any of your ideas included?

3 Read the letter again. Answer the questions.

1 Who supplies the solar-powered lights?
2 What are four benefits of using a solar-powered light?
3 Why does the writer think Sunny Money helps people to avoid negative feelings?
4 Why does the writer say that local people should be involved in schemes like Solar Aid?

USEFUL LANGUAGE

4 Find phrases in the model text which mean the same as 1–6.

1 I'd like to suggest …
2 After buying …
3 … it doesn't cost much …
4 This allows them to be used …
5 … so they improve …
6 I believe …

To the editor:

I am writing in response to your request for readers' suggestions of life-changing innovations introduced into developing countries. I would like to put forward the good work being done by the charity Solar Aid. [1] They are working on the provision of solar-powered lights designed to replace kerosene-burning lamps used in many places where electricity is not available.

[2] The benefits of such lights are manifold – not only is the risk of fire reduced, but the lights are also good for both the people using them and the environment. Unlike kerosene lamps, solar-powered lights do not give off noxious gases. Following the initial purchase of one of these lights from Solar Aid's company Sunny Money, costs are minimal as there is no longer a need to purchase fuel. Once charged, they have a long battery life and can be hung anywhere. This enables them to be used long after sunset, for example by children doing their homework, leading to them doing better at school and potentially in the long-term, too.

[3] It is sometimes said that charities imposing their ideas in developing countries can have a detrimental effect, but it is my considered opinion that schemes like that of Solar Aid can be beneficial to communities in these areas, provided they are run in dialogue with local people. In this case, potential users must buy their lamp from Sunny Money, meaning they are investing in it, rather than feeling like the recipients of charity, which could create resentment. Because this can be difficult for some people, Sunny Money offers financing schemes where the cost of buying a lamp is the equivalent of buying kerosene. By working with the community and finding out what they need, these 'outsiders' are able to support 'insiders' in a positive way, a model which should be used as widely as possible.

I hope you will join me in spreading awareness of this worthy endeavour.

Margaret Collins

5 Use one adverb from the box to enhance each sentence from the model text.

already	considerably	constantly	easily
highly	readily		

1 I would like to put forward the good work _____ being done by the charity Solar Aid.

2 They are working on the provision of solar-powered lights designed to replace kerosene-burning lamps used in many places where electricity is not _____ available.

3 Not only is the risk of fire _____ reduced, but the lights are also good for both the people using them and the environment.

4 Costs are minimal as there is no longer a need to _____ purchase fuel.

5 Once charged, they have a long battery life and can _____ be hung anywhere.

6 It is my considered opinion that schemes like that of Solar Aid can be _____ beneficial to communities in these areas.

6 Use the conditional conjunctions in brackets to rewrite sentences 1–5.

1 Deciding if it is necessary to bring in outside innovation can be a thorny issue. (whether or not)

_____

2 If people cannot easily access clean drinking water, they will continue to suffer from a wide range of health problems. (as long as)

_____

3 If charities and aid agencies do not work closely with local people, they run the risk of being seen as intruders. (unless)

_____

4 If the printers are made portable enough and the materials they use accessible enough, 3D-printed prosthetics will change the lives of hundreds of people in developing countries around the world. (provided that)

_____

5 It's important to use resources which are locally available. If not, it will be too expensive. (otherwise)

_____

7 Complete the paragraph by writing one word in each gap.

Bicycle-powered charging stations could ¹_____ a huge impact in many communities. A single station enables one person to charge ²_____ to five devices at once, for example mobile phones or LED lights. In ³_____ to provide ten days worth of light, the cyclist only needs to pedal for 20 minutes. ⁴_____ the energy is provided by pedal power, it can provide access to electricity for communities which are completely off-grid. ⁵_____ who are doing the pedalling also have the chance to charge fees for their services. Nuru Lights, ⁶_____ provider of such bikes, estimates that in a single 20-minute sitting, the cyclist could earn the same as they would previously have done in a whole day.

PLANNING

You will answer the following question.

An economics magazine is planning a feature on how education prepares people for the workplace. You decide to write a letter to the magazine in which you briefly describe how people are trained to do one or two specific jobs in your country and whether this has changed in the past 50 years. You should also assess whether the education and training provided for these jobs is adequate for the future needs of your country.

Write your letter in **280–320 words** in an appropriate style.

8 Plan your letter. Write notes to answer these questions. Don't write full sentences yet.

1 Which job(s) will you write about?

2 How do people train for these jobs?

3 Has this process changed in the past 50 years?

4 Do you believe there is enough education and training for these jobs to help your country in the future?

WRITING

9 Write a letter to reply to the question in Exercise 8. In your letter you should:

• Clearly state the reason you are writing and the jobs being discussed.

• Describe how people train for these jobs.

• Explain any changes to how training is offered which have taken place over the past 50 years.

• Assess whether the training provided is adequate for these jobs, considering the future needs of your country.

Write **280–320 words**.

ANALYSIS

10 Check your letter. Answer the questions.

Content: Does the letter include a reason for writing? Are the training process and any changes to it clearly described for one or two jobs? Is there an assessment of the adequacy of this training? Is the letter 280 to 320 words long?

Communicative achievement: Is it written in a neutral or formal style? Is your opinion about the topic clear to the reader?

Organization: Is the letter logically organized? Does it use clear paragraphs and appropriate linking words?

Language: Does it use correct grammar and vocabulary? Is a good range of structures used?

Answer key

UNIT 1

1.1 Do schools kill creativity?

1

1 Theatre / drama and education
2 In the development of creativity, innovation and human resources in education and in business
3 His TED Talk videos have been seen by a record estimated 250 million people in over 150 countries and his 2006 talk became the most viewed in TED's history.
4 Creativity and innovation, business, arts, education, UK/US cultural relations
5 He was knighted for 'services to the arts'

2

c Leaving the textbook at the classroom door

3

1 Musallam 2 Mulgan 3 Pierson, Musallam
4 Robinson, Mulgan

4

a rousing b poignant c fabled d fun
e succinct

6

I've <u>seen</u> this <u>talk</u> quite a <u>few</u> <u>times</u> and I <u>still</u> get really <u>emotional</u> <u>watching</u> it.

7

I <u>think</u> it has <u>something</u> to do with the <u>kind</u> of <u>overwhelming kindness</u> – <u>love</u> even – that <u>Rita F. Pierson</u> <u>shows</u> her <u>students</u>.

8

1 teacher trainer 2 connections

9

1 vulnerability / background; orator / speaker
2 engage / interest 3 poverty; surroundings / environment 4 every teacher

10

1 a 2 b 3 b 4 b 5 a

1.2 What've you been up to?

1

a 2, 6, 7, 8, 10
b 5, 9
c 1, 3, 4

2

1 made
2 leaped
3 have become
4 have ever created
5 has ever yet come
6 didn't see
7 turned out ('has turned out' is maybe also possible, suggesting that the reflection is grounded in the time of speaking, But the original has 'turned out' suggesting this was realized in the past, possibly shortly after the event)

8 was replaced
9 freed ('has freed' also possible, depending on Jobs' perspective)

3

1 has been 2 've known 3 involved
4 found 5 've been talking 6 have been
7 has been 8 've been told 9 produced
10 had 11 painted 12 worked

4

1 a 's worked b 's been working c was working d worked
2 a 've been finalizing b finalized c Have they finalized d were finalizing
3 a were waiting b waited and waited
   c 've been waiting d 've waited (or 've been waiting)
4 a was going b went c 've been going
   d 've been

5

1 small/tiny 2 vast 3 almost 4 significant
5 tiny/small 6 sizeable 7 Relatively
8 good

6

1 Globally, about one **in** eight males have some form of colour blindness, whereas only about one **in** 200 women is colour blind.
2 About one in **every** 16 Americans plays a musical instrument.
3 In **most** countries, over 99 **per cent** of all students graduating in medicine find jobs or enter further study within six months of graduating.
4 Geography is the worst degree for gaining employment in a number **of** countries, with only around three out **of** every ten graduates in subject-related employment six months after graduating.
5 Research suggests that only one **in** four employees believe they are allowed to fulfil their creative potential at work.
6 According to a study, about four **out** of every ten people consider themselves to be in some way artistic.

7

1 has won a number of awards
2 named him as one of the 100 most influential people
3 he became a Senator for Life
4 has collaborated with a number of other notable architects
5 designed the iconic
6 has been described as having
7 has been chairman of the
8 has also been working
9 was set up as a non-profit organization
10 most notable projects have been completed

1.3 How talent thrives

1

c

2

b

3

1 a 4 b 1 c 2 d 3
2 c (Based on each individual's letters, diaries and interviews and drawing on some secondary sources)
3 a Anthony Trollope b Gertrude Stein
   c Igor Stravinsky
4 a
5 b

4

a breaking down b drawing on c exacting
d procrastination e mundane f increment

5

2 had, inspiration
3 came, idea
4 came, angle
5 take, hobby
6 devoted, work
7 broke, convention
8 build, experience, follow, path

6

1 creation 2 creative 3 creator 4 Creativity
5 creatively 6 creation 7 recreating
8 Creationism / creationists

7

1 demonstrate 2 thinking 3 streak
4 force 5 impression 6 highly
7 stifling 8 foster

1.4 It's not really my thing

1

1 × 2 ✓ 3 × 4 ✓ 5 × 6 ✓ 7 ✓
8 × 9 ✓

2

1 into, not, thing
2 do, not, keen
3 into
4 a, fan, not, into, take, leave
5 a, fan
6 can't, excited, appeal

3

1 playing the piano ✓   singing ×
2 teaching ✓   administrative tasks ×
3 making tea ×   cooking ✓
4 shopping ✓   saving money ×

4

1 that's one thing I'm quite good at
2 I'm not great at singing
3 I think I'm quite a natural at teaching
4 I'm most definitely not a natural when it comes to
5 I can't make a cup of tea to save my life
6 I do have a talent for cooking
7 I'm pretty hopeless at saving it
8 I'm a born spendaholic

5

1 I'm not a fan of rock music.
2 Football's OK, but I can take it or leave it.
3 I can't get excited about modern art. It just doesn't appeal to me.

4 Anna's a natural when it comes to learning languages.
5 I can't cook to save my life.
6 He's a born leader.

6

1 I *do like* watching a good *film*.
2 I *really want* to learn the *piano* one day.
3 The lecture was *quite* good, but I thought it was a bit *slow* in places.
4 Modern art's *really* not my thing, I'm afraid.
5 I quite *like* modern art, actually. Especially *earlier* modern art.
6 Sam *does* tell a good story.
7 I *did* enjoy that *film* last night.
8 I know it's quite *expensive*, but I *really do* think it's worth it.

7

1 intention is
2 decision has been made
3 Clear and open communication
4 has been a significant increase in, the implementation of
5 was/has been a poor response, there were/have been a number of complaints
6 further consultation, the distribution of

8

2 Insufficient sleep
3 There has been a number of changes to/in
4 Advances in technology are alarming.
5 the marketing department's proposal, an unnecessary complication.
6 your suggestion, on my return

9

the development of the two sites was not based on any kind of comprehensive e-commerce strategy. There was not enough thought put into the design and (the) functionality. In addition, there was no proper implementation of credit card transaction processing and order fulfilment was inefficient. Looking forward, we have been in consultation with a specialist e-commerce firm and we are currently in discussion with the board about the availability of additional financial and human resources.

PRESENTATION 1

1

a Tammy   **b** Claudia   **c** Joel   **d** Joel, Claudia   **e** Tammy   **f** Claudia

5

1 b   **2** d   **3** c   **4** a   **5** e

6 (example answers)

1 Hello everyone. Welcome to my presentation. The purpose of this presentation is to talk about a talent I'd like to have.
2 I've always admired people who have an eye for a good photo. I'd really love to get better at using cameras and taking photos. I've been able to practise a little bit, though

I think the best thing would be attending classes.
3 I would need my family to help me with this. I'd need them to understand my goal to develop my photography. They could help me by helping me around the house so I have free time to go to evening classes.
4 I'd be able to take photos for my friends and family. Maybe one day I'd be able to sell my snaps or have them displayed in a picture gallery.
5 That brings us to the end of my talk. Thank you very much for listening to me. If you have any questions, please feel free to ask them.

UNIT 2

2.1 Why I live in mortal dread of public speaking

1

1 F – (Early in her career, she played jazz piano with a number of acts and before going solo, founded a band called Washington.)
2 F – (the lyrics to her songs have been described as a having a beautiful and confessional tone.)
3 F – (Washington has won a number of awards, including Australia's 'Best Female Artist' and 'Breakthrough Artist' following the release of her debut platinum-selling album in 2010. … Since her breakthrough solo album, which reached number three in the Australian charts, she has attracted the attention of a wider audience by appearing on a number of Australian TV music shows.)
4 T
5 T

2

c

3

1 Sting and Tillemann-Dick   **2** The Lady Lifers and Sting   **3** Tillemann-Dick   **4** Gupta

4

a conventional   **b** moving   **c** nasty
d unwavering

6

eyes, stones, load, shoes, do

7

1 the homeless, the marginalized, people in difficult circumstances   **2** the combination of the talk and music adds something more to the experience of listening to Gupta

8

1 medicine; violin   **2** hope   **3** teaching
4 musician; power

9

1 a   **2** c   **3** b   **4** b   **5** b

2.2 Optimist or pessimist?

1

1 P   **2** G   **3** F   **4** F   **5** P   **6** P   **7** F   **8** G/P

2

1 will continue   **2** will have reached
3 is likely to be   **4** will still be growing
5 is going to peak   **6** are holding
7 is slowed   **8** is going to cause
9 don't take   **10** will very likely be facing

3

1 is likely to have, will not/won't be able, may have doubled/may double.
2 continues, will live
3 is/are meeting, will focus/will be focussing
4 will soon be able, will only be, proves, may eventually follow
5 will have started / will start, will be travelling

4

1 to do
2 'll call back
3 's having
4 's
5 starts
6 're going to make
7 'll be having, 'll have finished
8 Are, going to say, 'm going to tell

5

1 In all likelihood, the population will reach eleven million by the year 2100.
2 We're bound to find a cure for cancer sooner or later.
3 A third world war may very well happen one day.
4 It's a foregone conclusion that we'll one day colonize Mars.
5 The US is likely to remain the world's biggest economy for a long time.
6 It's by no means certain that there is life on another planet.

6

1 She's bound to know what to do.
2 It's by no means certain (that) that they'll agree.
3 It may well have been/be my fault.
4 It's highly unlikely to be here/(that) it'll be here.
5 In all likelihood/There's a strong likelihood we'll never hear from them again.

7

1 highly/quite/pretty/very
2 It's, guess
3 may/might/could, out
4 foregone
5 by, certain

8

1 the current birth rate persists
2 will decline significantly
3 may have shrunk by as much as
4 does start to look likely
5 will have one of the worst
6 will have reached retirement
7 will no longer be working and contributing
8 will be increasing

2.3 Expanding your horizons

1

a 2, 3, 4   **b** 5   **c** 1

2

2 serious back pain
3 dyslexia, having to leave school early to work, motor neurone disease
4 financial problems
5 chronic poverty, social discrimination

3

1 natural   2 isn't   3 generally have
4 makes us better able   5 generally learn from   6 relieve the tension   7 minority
8 are overwhelmed

4

1 difficult   2 bigger   3 resist   4 high
5 weight   6 expressed   7 long   8 duty

5

2 and 3

6

1 trying to make ends meet from being a songwriter
2 depression after her mother's death (and being a single mother)
3 in local cafés
4 stick at what you love doing and believe in

7

1 pin   2 dashed   3 giving   4 cold
5 plucked   6 nerves   7 leap   8 limit

8

1 takes   2 favours   3 brave   4 up
5 convictions   6 brave   7 hands   8 have

9

1 braved the elements
2 has / will have the courage of his convictions
3 put up a brave fight
4 It takes guts
5 putting a brave face on it
6 have the guts

2.4 Worst-case scenario

1

1 T   2 F   3 T   4 F   5 T

2

1 aware   2 advise against   3 event of
4 best thing   5 way, 'll   6 advisable to
7 Avoid, chances   8 ensure

3

1 take (my) time to think, Talking to someone is also a good idea.
2 to consider looking for
3 opt for location over facilities
4 For your own peace of mind
5 the best thing is to say, That way you won't

6 'd advise against doing, avoid being, The chances are (that)

4

1 sixth   2 through   3 spring   4 asked
5 clothes   6 length   7 months   8 depth
9 twelfth   10 breathes   11 hundredth
12 filmed   13 health   14 crisps   15 helpful
16 splendid   17 explained   18 instincts
19 facts   20 rejects

5

1 were just going to stay
2 wasn't going to say
3 were originally going to get
4 was going to tell
5 were originally going to hold

6

1 She looked as though she was going to say something
2 The two leaders were going to meet tomorrow
3 Jones was originally going to be discharged yesterday
4 It wasn't supposed to rain
5 Play was due to resume at three
6 It was meant to be a working lunch
7 I was sure he would be waiting for us
8 We were supposed to meet at nine o'clock

7

1 We were going to leave at about six, but we were still there at seven.
2 They were supposed to arrive on Tuesday.
3 I expected (that) they would leave early, but they stayed until the early hours.
4 We weren't going to take a taxi, but it was raining.
5 The flight was due to take off at 5.30, but it was delayed again until seven o'clock.
6 We didn't anticipate/hadn't anticipated (that) it would take so long.

8

1 was supposed to meet
2 were going to have to
3 would take
4 was going to improve
5 wouldn't recognize
6 were originally going to stay
7 were due to move

WRITING 1

1

a description of their work-life balance, the importance of maintaining an appropriate work-life balance, what companies can do to help their employees achieve this
Points to include: student's own ideas

2

Paragraph 1/4 – description of work-life balance; Paragraph 2 – importance of maintaining an appropriate work-life balance; Paragraph 3 – what companies can do to help their employees

3

a 3   **b** 1   **c** 4   **d** 2

4

1 a, b, f   2 c, g, i   3 d, e, h

5

1
Example – **(a)** I came to realize that if I didn't . . .
(b) It suddenly occurred to me that if I didn't . . .
(f) It dawned on me that if I didn't . . .

2
(c) The essence of changing employees' mindsets lies in the way companies encourage them to use their time at work.
(g) A key ingredient of changing employees' mindsets is the way companies encourage them to use their time at work.
(i) The way companies encourage employees to use their time at work is vital to change their mindsets.

3
(d) A possible route to achieve this would be to follow the example of…
(e) One way to approach this is to follow the example of…
(h) A possible course of action for this is to follow the example of…

6

Exhausted, depressed and coming down with a cold

Their stress levels are lower, they take fewer sick days and they are able to complete tasks more efficiently.

I'm happier, healthier and have more of a social life than ever before.

7

by organizing a night out, a weekend away or simply lunch at a local restaurant

by allowing flexi-time, encouraging job shares or letting staff leave early on Fridays

having been awake since six, at my desk since eight, and not likely to get home until seven

they are more productive, more creative and their imaginations are given free rein

living, sleeping and breathing their jobs

10 Sample answer

Seeing the world through new eyes

My fascination with photography began when I opened a beautifully wrapped eighteenth birthday present. At a time when most people, including me, still relied on film cameras, the sight of a brand new digital camera was a real treat. I couldn't wait to try it out.

As time passed, I sought out advice from more experienced photographers through reading magazines and blogs. One of the most useful tips I found was to slow down. By spending a little more time framing each shot, considering the light conditions and positioning the camera exactly, my photos became much more striking. I dedicated time to looking for places to take the perfect photo and I developed a greater appreciation for the small details of life, like dew shining on a spider's web or tiny architectural flourishes on huge buildings.

Encouraging you to take time and notice detail are just two of the manifold benefits that digital cameras have. Unlike with film cameras, there are no limits to the number of photos you can take. That, plus the fact that you don't have to pay for photos to be developed before you can see the results of your efforts, mean that it is possible for everyone to experiment with photography in a way that was never possible before the advent of this technology.

Of course, nowadays everyone has a camera on their phone and there is a constant stream of photos being uploaded to social media. Some people say that this obsession with photography, and the 'selfie' culture that has developed, have removed people's appreciation of a carefully crafted image. While it remains to be seen whether the ease of taking photos nowadays really has made our society more narcissistic, I can't deny that box I opened, all those years ago, changed the way I looked at the world in a profoundly positive way.

UNIT 3

3.1 The 4 ways sound affects us

1

1 Economics, advertising and publishing
2 TPD Publishing, which Treasure started, was very successful (went on to become one of the UK's leading contract magazine publishing companies). He held a number of senior posts in the publishing industry (in various publishing associations and agencies) and in 2002 he received a (Professional Publishers Association) Award for services to the UK magazine publishing industry.
3 His passion for sound and his interest in music led to his interest in 'the noise of modern life'. (As a drummer and musician ... he had for a long time been interested in the noise of modern life, and in particular that produced by the business world and other organizations.)
4 He realized that businesses could improve their performance by becoming more sound-conscious. (As he researched this, he realized that most business sound was having a negative effect on people and he realized there was an opportunity for businesses to improve their results by becoming more sound-conscious.)
5 It has advised on (i) the use of ambient sound to reduce crime in urban areas and (ii) in-store soundscapes that increase both sales and customer satisfaction.

2

c

3

1 Treasure   **2** Lee   **3** Calix (and Treasure and Lee)

4

a gnawing away at   **b** assault   **c** spectrum
d heed   **e** handy

6

4, 2 (4 again)

7

1 – she says that Calix is a composer
2 fascinating   **3** & **4** how she uses music to add to people's perceptions

8

fixed   She is open about the fact we don't really understand the relationship between music and emotions; she doesn't try to be too scientific or to analyze it too deeply.

9

1 tunnel   **2** commuters and leisure
3 installations   **4** emotion   **5** Lisbon
6 singer   **7** (scientific) explanation / words

10

1 c   **2** b   **3** a   **4** a   **5** a

3.2 Judging by appearances

1

1 S   **2** S   **3** S   **4** D   **5** D   **6** D   **7** S   **8** S
9 D   **10** S   **11** S   **12** S (used in the continuous to give a more dynamic sense)
13 S (used in the continuous to give a more dynamic sense)   **14** S   **15** S   **16** S   **17** D
18 S   **19** D   **20** S (used in the continuous to give a more dynamic sense)   **21** S   **22** D

2

1 depends, mean, think, seems, counts
2 're thinking, looks, realize, think, seem, prefer, guess/'m guessing, depend, see
3 is, must've cost, own, rent/'re renting, get

3

1 Do you know, don't look, don't know, know, haven't been working, don't recognize, don't think, work, haven't seen
2 've been meaning, trust, are settling, seems, be going, 'm really enjoying, are you getting on, Have you worked, seems, sounds (also possible is sounding), is going, 'll leave, don't forget, 's, need
3 Do you know, belongs, looks, think, imagine, 'll come back (also possible: be coming back), don't suppose, 'll get

4

1 <u>is</u>, don't get, <u>has</u>
2 <u>matter</u>, say, size
3 <u>don't know</u>, <u>come from</u>, <u>mean</u>, <u>don't always appreciate</u>

5

2 What I don't understand is how on earth this was allowed to happen. / How on earth this was allowed to happen is what I don't understand.

3 I did enjoy that meal.
4 It's not knowing the dangers that worries me.
5 The thing I want to know is where he got all his information from.
6 What surprised me wasn't what he said, but the timing of it.

6

1 struck me is his energy and drive.
2 's the commuting (that) I'm not so keen on.
3 I can't understand is why they are so popular.
4 I really like is that you can get everywhere on foot.
5 enthusiasm for the project is what really impressed me.

7

1 The most important thing in an interview is
2 it's important that
3 The thing that your interviewers will notice next is
4 It's then the next few minutes, the beginning of the actual interview, that
5 And what is particularly vital is
6 This initial impact is what
7 it's often a candidate's performance in the first two minutes of an interview that

3.3 Lights, music, action

2

a passion and excitement; also warnings and 'Stop'
b elegance and power
c health and nature also friendly and 'Go'; also simplicity and modernity
d calm and stability; also simplicity and modernity
e friendliness and fun

3

1 a   **2** c   **3** a   **4** a   **5** a   **6** c

4

1 mourning   **2** stimuli   **3** a (whole) host
4 reverted   **5** shades   **6** eye-catching

5

1 c   **2** f   **3** g   **4** h   **5** i   **6** a   **7** b   **8** d   **9** e

6

1 sensible   **2** sensitive   **3** sensitivity
4 sensory   **5** sensor   **6** sensuous   **7** senseless
8 sensibility   **9** sensitize   **10** sensation

7

1 sensor   **2** sensible   **3** sensitive
4 sensory   **5** sensitivity   **6** sensation
7 sensibility   **8** senseless   **9** desensitized
10 sensuous

3.4 Contrary to popular belief

1

1 F   **2** F   **3** T   **4** F

2

1 conventional, actual

2 Supposedly, reality, seems
3 case, face, apparently, allegedly
4 belief, truth, fact

3

1 You would think that, in actual fact
2 On the face of it.
3 But the truth of the matter, behind the surface lies
4 The popular belief is, The truth, however, is, It seems that
5 the conventional wisdom is, But that's not always the case
6 He gives the outward appearance of, If truth be told

4

1 In terms of light, mixing red and green makes yellow. But with paint it makes a sort of brown colour.
2 They say you can see the Great Wall of China from the moon. But, in fact, you can't.
3 Contrary to popular belief, Thomas Edison didn't invent the light bulb. He did, however, patent and improve an existing design.
4 Bats are not blind. All bat species have eyes and can see and, in fact, some have excellent vision.
5 Humans have more than the five commonly cited senses of sight, smell, taste, touch and hearing. Among other things, humans can sense balance, acceleration, pain and relative temperature.
6 Chameleons do not change colour to match their background. But they do change colour to communicate and as a response to mood, temperature and light conditions.

5

1 In terms of communication and collaboration, an open-plan workspace may have positive results. However, research suggests that it may have an adverse effect when it comes to concentration and productivity.
2 From the point of view of office equipment, heating and electricity costs, an open-plan workspace can benefit a business economically.
3 The chairless office has a number of benefits for the employee, notably when it comes to reported physical well-being.
4 Financially speaking, family-run businesses tend to have long-term rather than short-term goals.
5 From a purely business perspective, the aim is simply to maximize the value of the organization.
6 Statistically, there are more billionaires in London than in any other city in the world, with over 80 claiming the city to be their home.

6

1 From a(n) historical perspective
2 In terms of flexibility
3 Technically (speaking)
4 Environmentally speaking

5 factually (speaking)
6 From a safety perspective

7

1 Historically   2 socially   3 Commercially
4 From a business point of view   5 From a social science perspective   6 in terms of engineering

PRESENTATION 2

1

1 b   2 c   3 a

3 (example answers)

1 This piece of advice will help you become a better cook. It's a tip to help you manage in the kitchen.
2 This advice will be most helpful for people cooking for a medium-sized family.
3 This will help save you time in the kitchen, so you can focus on cooking the best food you can.

5

1 d   2 e   3 b   4 a   5 c

6 (example answers)

1 Hello. My name's (name) and today I'm going to give you a useful piece of advice for when you are studying.
2 Have you ever been overwhelmed by the amount you have to read for an academic assignment? Well don't give up – the solution is actually very simple. You have to be selective in what you read.
3 You do have to really read your assignment carefully. You'll need to work out exactly what the focus is, so that you can decide what you really need to read from the book list. It should help you to read in more detail and save you time because you're not reading material that is not relevant.
4 Going over the main points again, be very selective in what you read and base this on what the assignment is asking you to do. Use this knowledge to plan your reading better.
5 Thank you for listening. If you have any questions, I'll do my best to answer them.

UNIT 4

4.1 Your body language shapes who you are

1

1 From her experiences after her accident, in particular her knowledge of how the brain functions.
2 two (graduated from the University of Colorado in 1998 ... completed an MA in social psychology and earned her PhD in the same subject from Princeton in 2005)
3 'studied circles around everyone'
4 Her professional interests in negotiation, power, influence, empowerment,

stereotyping and discrimination are possibly influenced by her experiences after her road accident, when she possibly faced such challenges herself.
5 The nonverbal communication and body posture aspects of ballet have influenced her interest and specialization in nonverbal communication and how body posture can be empowering ('power posing').

2

c

3

1 Ramsey and Balcetis   2 Dweck and Ramsey   3 Gutman

4

a keep off   b grow   c flex   d walk someone through   e disrupt

6

the suggestio**mb**eing that we **oughtowadop wha**the speaker calls an 'eye on the prize' strategy

7

I **hafda** say, I'm also **kinda** curious about what other similar strategies **coube** developed.

8

1 False – it was to show how motivation can change your perception of your goals when exercising   2 True

9

1 it was further away   2 more quickly
3 to other daily habits, a similar strategy could potentially help people cultivate other healthy habits in their lives   4 because he values exercise and having a healthy lifestyle
5 the appreciation of his progress in weightlifting, the prize of his personal records and incremental improvements

10

1 c   2 a   3 c   4 a   5 c

4.2 How we communicate

1

1 was made, had been limited, weighed, measured, had
2 was working, proposed, would become, marked, accounted, had risen, was communicated/was being communicated
3 had been using, was invented, were, required, was sought, discovered, could be produced, had been developed, could also be produced, wasn't, started

2

1 had been rhythmically beating   2 wasn't
3 was first stretched   4 was   5 were   6 was
7 used   8 would give   9 would also be used

10 were known to have used **11** would carry **12** use **13** would have **14** would recognize **15** had all but ended **16** had become

3

1 had to **2** could've stayed **3** should've said **4** would've been **5** 'd known **6** might well have chosen **7** should've told **8** could've given **9** might not've got **10** might not've been paying

4

1 The Internet might not have been working earlier. / It might be that the Internet wasn't working earlier.
2 I shouldn't have phoned him. I regret it now.
3 I wasn't able to get hold of them. I think I might have the wrong number.
4 My grandparents often used to call me for a long chat at weekends.
5 I would never want to go to bed as a child.
6 Sarah wasn't in the office yesterday so you can't have spoken to her.
7 You could've told me, but I can't remember to be honest.
8 He would constantly be on his phone whether it was WhatsApp or Facebook or whatever.

5

1 So **2** Not until / Only when **3** No sooner **4** Such **5** Only when / Not until **6** Hardly **7** Only by **8** Never before

6

2 Only if the economy suddenly got much stronger would the central bank consider the move.
3 Under no circumstances can you leave the exam room unescorted.
4 Not until he stood at the podium ready to speak did he feel nervous.
5 Not only was I leaving a special place, but also my family and friends.
6 Only after he had fully soaked up the rapturous applause did he finally leave the stage.

7

1 had been trying to decide what to focus on
2 exploring how certain pages linked with other pages
3 which Page later described as the best advice he ever received
4 could have focussed on his research alone
5 had first met when Brin was showing a group of new students around the campus
6 That might well have been the end of it
7 had an index of about 60 million pages and this was growing rapidly
8 not only were Google's search results better than its competitors at the time

4.3 Negotiate better

2

1 C **2** A **3** E **4** F **5** B **6** D

3

1 U – we only know it was the period when postcards had their greatest success among users
2 True
3 False – messages could be sent and replied to within a day (text messages within minutes)
4 True
5 False – it was established in 1902 with the divided back postcard
6 U – they were used for romantic purposes (secret messages), but it doesn't say if this was the preferred way of sending such messages
7 True
8 False – it was the war that interrupted the practice and it was never resumed because of a shortage of postmen and the spread of the telephone

4

2, 3, 4, 5, 6

5

Informal writing style in text messaging and its effects on literacy; governments' struggles to control content on the World Wide Web

6

1 raising **2** shaking **3** folded **4** clenched **5** drumming **6** roll **7** shrugging **8** tapped **9** scowled **10** yawning

7

1 un **2** in **3** il **4** im **5** ir **6** dis **7** non-

8

1 These figures are inaccurate.
2 What you're saying is illogical.
3 It's inadvisable to do that.
4 Your explanation is inadequate.
6 He made a few comments that were distasteful./He made a few distasteful comments.
7 They're often disobedient.
8 It's a nice idea, but impractical.
9 That is improper behaviour.
10 The disease is usually incurable.

4.4 Is that what you meant?

1

a 6 **b** 1 **c** 4 **d** 7 **e** 5 **f** 2 **g** 3

2

1 Bad news **2** not available, suits **3** in person **4** by the way **5** give, ring **6** give, hand **7** at all, mention **8** have, quick word **9** Sorry, hear **10** give, lift **11** put, out **12** drop, off, way **13** get, anything **14** shouldn't have **15** never mind, Another time **16** say, from

3

1 I'm afraid she's **not available** at the moment.
2 I think we should discuss it **in person**.
3 Yep, 6.30 **suits** me.
4 Yes. **Can I get you** something?
5 Yes, can **I have a quick word**?
6 Ah, **you shouldn't have**.
7 Let me **give you a hand** with some of it.
8 I can **give you a lift**. I really don't want to **put you out**.

4

1 A: Bad news, I'm afraid. (↓) I didn't get the job. (-)
  B: Oh, I'm sorry to hear that. (↓)
2 A: Hi Richard.
  B: Ah, Lucas. Can I have a quick word? (↑)
3 A: This is for you. To say thank you.
  B: That's very kind of you, but you really shouldn't have. (-)
4 A: Let me give you a lift. (-)
  B: Are you sure? (↑) I really don't want to put you out. (-)
5 A: See you tomorrow. (↑)
  B: Yeah, bye. Oh, by the way, I'll be a little late in tomorrow. (↓)
6 A: Can I give you a hand with anything? (↑)
  B: That's good of you to offer, but I'm fine thanks. (↓)
7 A: Thanks again for all your help. (-)
  B: Not at all. Don't mention it. (↓)
8 A: That seat's taken, actually. (↓)
  B: Oh sorry. I didn't realize. (-)

5

1 Thank you for <u>taking the time</u> to consider our proposal.
2 Thank you for <u>agreeing to meet</u> with us on Friday, but I really don't want to <u>put you out.</u>
3 I think it's important that you and Susan meet <u>in person</u> as soon as possible.
4 We feel that the proposed relocation is <u>impractical</u> and could in fact be <u>disadvantageous</u>.
5 He has fully admitted that his conduct was <u>improper</u>.
6 I am <u>sorry to hear</u> that the arrangements <u>were</u> not to your satisfaction.
7 I <u>had a quick word</u> with Julian and he has <u>agreed to go</u> ahead with the proposal.
8 Only when we have the full facts <u>can we</u> begin to assess the situation.

6

Dear Alison,

I am writing to request your approval <u>to</u> attend the London Business Conference, which <u>is</u> being held from 15–17 January next year. <u>The</u> conference theme is Risk Management and is aimed <u>at</u> industry stakeholders as <u>a</u> forum <u>to</u> discuss the current state of risk management in private equity. Of <u>particular</u> interest to us, is a focus <u>on</u> co-investments versus fund investments. As well as <u>the</u> main conference talks, there <u>are</u> a number of workshops.

You <u>may recall</u> that Samantha Mitchell <u>attended the</u> conference last year and she found <u>it</u> extremely relevant and useful. I believe she <u>presented</u> some of the key issues to the senior management team, which I think you <u>might have attended</u>. This is something that I am of course prepared to do.

I have included an approximate breakdown of the costs to attend below:

- Conference Registration: £300.00
- Travel, accommodation and meals: £350.00

If you would like to find out more about the conference, their website is Londonbusiness.org.

Thank you in advance for taking the time to consider this and I very much look forward to hearing from you.

Best wishes,

Tom

7

a 3 b 2 c 6 d 8 e 7 f 1 g 5 h 4

8

Dear Sir or Madam,

Below is my reference for Ms Marta Masini

Marta Masini joined Waterwells Books in January last year and since then she has been a reliable, effective and valuable member of the sales team.

Marta is professional and efficient in her approach to her work and has a sound knowledge and understanding of both the book-selling business and the wider retail industry.

She has consistently shown that she is able to work both independently and as part of a team. Her communication skills are excellent and she is very well-liked by her colleagues and always has a good rapport with customers and (with) other clients.

I believe that Marta will be a valuable addition to any organization that she may join. While we regret Marta's decision to move on, I would recommend her without hesitation.

Please get in touch if you should require (any) further information.

Yours faithfully,

Carmen Napoli

WRITING 2

1

a Being culturally appropriate makes a good impression.

b If you make a mistake with cultural norms, it can offend.

c Cultural differences can be difficult to spot.

d They need to be taught to business people to make business run more smoothly.

2

1 c 2 d 3 b 4 a

3

1 'Culture' is the differences in how people act in different social groups.

2 A strong handshake can be too dominant for Filipino customers.

3 You should take small amounts of food throughout the meal, not all of your food at the start.

4 It can influence the negotiations, for example the prices people are willing to pay.

5 They don't expect you to understand everything, but it can increase their respect for you.

4

1 subtle 2 overly 3 explicitly 4 a faux pas
5 nuances 6 norms

5

1 back 2 to 3 To 4 in 5 to 6 for
7 of 8 with 9 of

6

1 d 2 b 3 e 4 a 5 c

7

a 3: frankly unrealistic
b 5: creativity blossoms
c 2: instant gratification
d 4: patently true
e 1: beneficial change

8

People don't engage with the world around them.

Attention is divided and there is a lack of focus.

The Internet gives you access to a lot of information.

It is easy to communicate and work with people in other places.

10 Sample answer

When historians look back on the invention of the smartphone, they may well say that it was revolutionary. The key question, however, is whether this is a beneficial change or not.

Firstly, the fact that people can access the Internet from wherever they are has led to a desire for instant gratification. There is an impatience in society that demands an instant answer to any question and an instant solution to any problem, creating a frankly unrealistic impression of what knowledge is available to us and what we are currently able to use it for. Some people undoubtedly believe that you can find anything on the Internet, even though that is patently not true.

That is not to say that having a powerful computer in our pockets at all times is entirely a bad thing. On the contrary, it is a valuable tool in many situations, from finding directions in an unfamiliar city to telling people you are alive and safe after a natural disaster.

The biggest change that smartphones have brought with them is a new inability for their owners to deal with boredom. No longer are people's minds allowed to wonder and their creativity to blossom. As soon as they start to feel the smallest hint that the situation they are in might not interest

them, they immerse themselves in the world of their phones, rather than focussing on what is in front of them. To the detriment of relationships, they split their attention between this small device and the people they are with.

In conclusion, I believe that, while the smartphone brings many advantages, we must ensure that we do not allow it to take over our lives completely.

UNIT 5

5.1 The magic washing machine

1

1 F – (There is no information about qualifications gained in Mozambique – He studied statistics and medicine at Uppsala University, and then public health at St. John's Medical College, Bangalore, India ... He has also received honorary degrees from universities in Sweden, Norway and the UK and is a member of the Swedish Academy of Sciences.)

2 F – (In 1981, Rosling encountered an outbreak of a paralytic disease called konzo.)

3 F – (... was one of the initiators of Médecins Sans Frontières in Sweden – not the global organization)

4 F – (his main field is global health)

5 T – (Rosling's lectures using Gapminder graphics have gained a global reputation for their creativity and originality and have won numerous awards ... Rosling has received a number of awards and accolades, including 'Speaker of the Year')

2

a

3

1 Kamkwamba and Venkatraman
2 Gosier and Venkatraman 3 Turere and Kamkwamba 4 Gosier

4

1 all-important, solar-powered, trickle-down, electricity-generating, low-cost

6

She talks about how young he is and how his age made her curious to hear him. She describes how he had to deal with solving a major problem.

7

1 by trying out different solutions 2 not giving up

8

1 animals 2 being determined in the face of a challenge 3 win his family's respect
4 both

9

1 c 2 b 3 b 4 a 5 a

5.2 Energy-hungry world

1

2 More appropriate in the passive: Piezoelectricity is the electrical charge produced in certain materials (such as crystals and ceramics) **when physical pressure is applied**.

3 Both active and passive would be appropriate: The United States is the world's second largest energy consumer. It **obtains** the majority of this energy (around 68%) from fossil fuels. / The United States is the world's second largest energy consumer. **The majority of this energy (around 68%) is obtained from fossil fuels**.

4 More appropriate in the passive: The existence of the greenhouse effect was first proposed in 1824. **However, the term 'greenhouse' was not used in this way until the beginning of the 1900s.**

2

2 World energy consumption is the total energy (that is) used by humans. It is usually calculated and measured per year.

3 Wind power is currently being used by more than 80 countries. In 2013, almost 3% of the world's total electricity was generated by wind.

4 Solar energy has been used (by humans) since ancient times and today it is predicted that, by the middle of the century, a third of all global energy could be provided by solar power. CO_2 emissions would consequently be reduced to 'very low levels'.

5 Construction of the new nuclear power plant is expected to be completed by 2025. The government insists that enough energy will be generated to power six million homes.

6 It is generally agreed that energy independence and security is one of today's key political issues and one which needs to be addressed urgently.

3

1 to be reassessed/reassessing
2 not to have been informed
3 not having been consulted
4 being forced, to be introduced/being introduced
5 Having been found, to be sentenced
6 Being beaten, to be sacked

4

2 generated **3** embedded **4** were placed
5 to be tested **6** to be **7** be generated
8 was developed / has been developed

5

2 Professor Helen Stephenson was given the award for her work on climate change. / The award was given to Professor Helen Stephenson for her work on climate change.

3 The court was shown CCTV footage of the incident (by the prosecution lawyer). / CCTV footage of the incident was shown to the court (by the prosecution lawyer).

4 I guess I was sent the email by mistake. / I guess the email was sent to me by mistake.

5 In total, the charity was given over a million dollars. /In total, over a million dollars was given to the charity.

6

1 make an attempt/a decision/an announcement/an assessment/a complaint/an allowance/progress/a compromise

2 reach agreement/a compromise/a decision/a conclusion

3 give consideration (to)/priority (to)/preference (to)/thought (to)/information/an order/an answer

7

2 allowance was made for any delays in the development process.

3 consideration has been given to everything in making this decision.

4 of complaints were made about the service.

5 agreement has been reached on most aspects of the deal.

6 priority needs to be given to renewable energy sources.

7 that a compromise seems to have been reached regarding CO_2 emission quotas.

8 progress was/has been made regarding trade in ozone-depleting substances.

8

1 being released from organic matter
2 can be converted
3 which conversion process has been used
4 results in hydrogen being produced
5 is currently being developed
6 have already been developed

5.3 Lands for all

2

c

3

1 Over 10 million
2 Under 25 million
3 it's becoming stronger
4 Floods, earthquakes, epidemics
5 unemployment, urban poverty, crime, road congestion, inefficient public transport and shortage of food or water
6 do things differently
7 worst case scenarios
8 complaining about government policy / government policies and budgets
9 (injustice of) wealth inequality
10 encourages long-term solutions

4

1 centre **2** meeting **3** smaller **4** once
5 stronger **6** pessimism **7** apparent/clear

5

1 interest **2** bankrupt **3** recession **4** meet
5 recovery **6** Unemployment **7** debts
8 boom **9** operations **10** employees

6

1 landlocked **2** landmark **3** dry land
4 plot of land **5** strip of land **6** live off the land **7** wasteland **8** landslide

7

1 c **2** a **3** b

8

1 landscape **2** landmark **3** landscape
4 landslide **5** landmark

5.4 I can well believe that

1

1 ✓ **2** ✗ **3** ✓ **4** ✗ **5** ✗ **6** ✓ **7** ✗
8 ✓

2

1 believe **2** pinch, case **3** surprise
4 doubt **5** old, truth **6** true
7 misconception **8** believe **9** spot

3

1 I'd take that with a pinch of salt.
2 That's (just) an old wives' tale.
3 I suspect that's true.
4 That's a common misconception.
5 I'd be surprised if that was the case.
6 I can well believe that. It doesn't/wouldn't surprise me at all.
7 I very much doubt that. I think it's nonsense, to be honest.
8 That's what they'd have you believe. I'd have some reservations about that.

4

1 Many students take years to pay off their de**b**ts.
2 Can I have a recei**p**t please?
3 I dou**b**t they'll reach agreement today.
4 He was a co**l**onel in the army.
5 Can I have an ai**s**le seat please?
6 We need a more sub**t**le approach.
7 Can you pass me the s**c**issors?
8 Would you like a bis**c**uit?
9 My sister's an arc**h**itect.
10 He was found **g**uilty of all charges.

5

1 it is predicted that **2** it is estimated that
3 is believed to **4** It is thought to
5 are thought to

6

2 It is thought that ten thousand people took part in the anti-fracking demonstration. Ten thousand people are thought to have taken part in the anti-fracking demonstration.

3 It is expected that the minister will/is to resign within the next 24 hours. The minister is expected to resign within the next 24 hours.

4 It is feared that thousands have been left homeless after the hurricane. Thousands are feared to have been left homeless after the hurricane.

5 It is said that a picture is worth a thousand words.
A picture is said to be worth a thousand words.

6 It is/has been alleged that bribes had been offered.
Bribes are alleged to have been offered.

7

1 it is recommended that, is thought to be
2 is believed to be, It is now feared that
3 it was reported, It is/has been claimed that, is expected to release
4 is said to be, is thought to have escaped

8

It is estimated that global energy consumption will have increased by around 50% by 2050. It is thought that half of that growth will come from China and India. At the moment China and India consume about 21% of world energy, but this is expected to increase to 31% by the middle of the century. It is also calculated that China will use around 60% more energy than the US by 2050. Fossil fuels will still be the dominant energy source and will account for around 70% of world energy use in 2050. Over the same period it is predicted that renewable energy will increase globally by about 3% per year. Despite this, energy-related carbon-dioxide emissions are expected to continue to rise and be 30–40% higher in 2050 than at present.

PRESENTATION 3

1

1 c   **2** b   **3** a

3 (example answers)

1 I decided to take up yoga classes five years ago because I was feeling unfit. I needed to find a way of being healthier.
2 As a result of going to yoga, I feel a lot calmer. I've also noticed that I've become much more flexible and stronger.
3 What is more, another thing I've been able to do is to teach my children a little bit about practising yoga.

5

1 e   **2** a   **3** d   **4** c   **5** b

6 (example answers)

1 Hello, I'm (name). Today I would like to talk about a change in my life I'm planning to make.
2 The change would be learning a new language. I'd really like to learn Arabic as I think this would open up a lot of new cultures and experiences for me. I would love to travel around northern Africa and knowing a bit of Arabic would help me a lot.
3 Learning this language would give me a new outlook on life. I think it's totally different to the other languages I speak – English and Spanish. I know that it isn't exactly the same Arabic that is spoken in

different countries, but it would mean that I could communicate at least a little bit.
4 Not only would it help me when travelling, but I think it could also be of benefit in my job – I'm a language teacher and a lot of my students come from countries where they speak Arabic. Understanding the language might mean I am able to help them learn English better.
5 Finally, I'd like to thank you all for listening. Do you have any questions?

UNIT 6

6.1 Magical houses, made of bamboo

1

1 Her father was a jewellery designer and she grew up surrounded by art and creativity and spent a lot of her time with local village craftsmen, where she learned skills such as carving, painting and batik. She says in setting up Ibuku that she wanted to reconnect with the culture and landscape that she grew up in.
2 *talked herself into* It means she managed to persuade the company to give her a job, even though they perhaps initially didn't want to or didn't have a job available.
3 *bespoke*.
4 He was a designer, albeit of jewellery, and he also designed and built buildings out of bamboo. In fact she was directly inspired by the design and bamboo construction of a building her father and step-mother had recently opened.
5 The innovative aspect of her constructions is that she uses locally-sourced bamboo and other sustainable natural materials, often with bespoke furniture.

2

c

3

1 Green, Joachim and Ban   **2** Joachim (and Green)   **3** Larsson (and Ban)

4

a harsh   **b** abodes   **c** secure   **d** remarkable

6

My firsreaction to this talk was notatall sceptical. I justhought – whata fantastic idea!

7

But **then I** began **to wonder about its impact on** deforestation and about how safe a wooden skyscraper **would be** during an earthquake.

8

1 impact on deforestation; safety in an earthquake
2 it's warm, welcoming and natural; it's environmentally friendly
3 its financial viability; the noises it makes

9

1 T   **2** T   **3** F   **4** U   **5** T

10

1 c   **2** b   **3** c   **4** a   **5** a

6.2 Get someone else to do it

1

1 They're having the floor sanded.
2 They had the boiler serviced.
3 They're having/going to have a sofa delivered.
4 They've had/had an alarm fitted recently.
5 They had the office redecorated.

2

1 to help   **2** tested   **3** to call   **4** to agree
5 working   **6** give   **7** finished   **8** valued

3

1 to get the job done
2 get a professional to do
3 not having an expert do
4 get the heating working
5 get that stuck window unstuck
6 get those long-overdue jobs done
7 have it sorted
8 get a professional to do

4

1 to get one cut
2 to get Jack to change, got him to see
3 have it finished
4 got it caught
5 to get it decorated, to get someone to do

5

go: missing, wrong, blind, red, quiet, crazy, bald, bankrupt, deaf, bad
get: ill, involved, lost, ready, started, pregnant, upset, married, angry, old

6

1 go wrong   **2** go blind   **3** go red   **4** go quiet
5 go crazy   **6** get ill   **7** go bald   **8** get lost
9 go bankrupt   **10** get ready

7

1 getting dark/to get dark
2 get started
3 have gone missing
4 to be getting anywhere/to have got anywhere
5 're going anywhere
6 getting a new TV, is getting a bit old
7 gone rusty
8 get involved

8

1 It is most commonly used to describe the activity
2 having the work done by a professional
3 to describe someone doing something for themselves
4 of having someone else do it for them

5 to get it promoted
6 getting things done yourself
7 the need to get specialists to do

6.3 Better by design

1

1 a public declaration of your aims and policies   **2** political parties

2

1 he trained as an architect and interior designer, but ended up designing functional objects, e.g. record players. These things were linked through a focus on practical design in general.
2 'less, but better' philosophy

3

a 5   **b** 3   **c** 8   **d** 1   **e** 10   **f** 6   **g** 4   **h** 7

4

1 understandable   **2** impenetrable
3 thorough   **4** transient   **5** aesthetic
6 intuitive   **7** unobtrusive   **8** durable

5

1 ✓   **2** ?   **3** ✓   **4** ✓   **5** ✗   **6** ✓   **7** ✓
8 ?   **9** ?   **10** ✓

6

1 shoddily
2 scientifically
3 greatly, highly
4 widely
5 brightly
6 prohibitively, reasonably
7 beautifully, perfectly

7

2 Rams said that good design makes a product (easily) understandable.
3 Ibuku uses natural sustainable materials to create homes and other buildings.
4 Even though it is breakable, carbon fibre is one of the strongest known materials currently used in manufacturing.
5 His art is very hands-on and interactive with a number of exhibits with movable parts.
6 The detail and the intricacy of the painting are unimaginable until you get up close and see it with your own eyes.
7 The book is invaluable and irreplaceable.
8 The band is instantly recognizable as soon as you hear the first few bars of their songs.

8

1 g   **2** f   **3** a   **4** b (note that 'flammable' has the same meaning)   **5** d   **6** e   **7** c   **8** h

9

1 malleable   **2** inflammable   **3** inexplicable
4 illegible   **5** durable   **6** irreparable
7 pliable   **8** edible

6.4 Common sense

1

Extract 1: T   Extract 2: F
Extract 3: U   Extract 4: T

2

1 Do, find, that, depends
2 would, say, suppose, say, why, do, say, that
3 situation, where, would, do, first, instinct, is, would, go, about
4 Imagine, that, what, would, be, that, tricky, question, Let, me, have, think

3

1 In a situation ... what **would** you do?
   I suppose **I'd** talk
2 **Do** you find
   that depends
3 **Imagine** ... what **would** you do?
   That's a tricky question.
4 How would you go about **appealing** to
   Let me have **a** think
5 Would you say **you** are
   My first instinct is **to** say yes
   And why **do** you say that?

4

1 She's got a strong imagin**a**tion and has a lot of very good i**de**as.
2 He's got a lot of inter**na**tional experience.
3 She's got ex**c**ellent communi**ca**tion skills.
4 He's a**ppa**rently got a photog**ra**phic memory.
5 He's got a **back**ground in eco**nom**ics and **po**litics. ('politics' is an exception to the 'penultimate stress in -*ic* words' rule)
6 What experience and qualifi**ca**tions spe**ci**fic to trans**la**tion do you have?
7 We need an e**ffec**tive and cre**a**tive **pu**blic speaker.
8 A lot of what we do re**quires** a strong **in**stinct and intu**i**tion.
9 The **sal**ary will de**pend** on **var**ious factors.
10 I think I'm quite ass**er**tive and enthusi**as**tic.

5

1 I did it before last summer and I managed to get some good sales figures.
2 How do you think the recent changes to EU data protection law will affect the way the company operates?
3 I'd be happy to look into it if you want me to.
4 If you are invited for a second interview, then we will probably need to talk about it.
5 Because you've just graduated in business and because you've got experience and have done the job last year, we thought/ think you might be suitable as our new marketing manager.

6

1 She asked me what I knew about the company.
2 They asked me what I thought the main challenges would be if I got the job.
3 They wanted to know what I thought my colleagues would consider as my best qualities.
4 He said (that) they would be in touch if they needed any further information.
5 They advised me to look at other options before I made a decision. / They advised (me) that I should look at other options before I made a decision.
6 He questioned why I wasn't applying for a more senior position.
7 They told me (that) they thought it would be a week or so before they knew/would know anything.
8 I asked (them) if they knew how many other candidates had been shortlisted.

7

2 asked me/wanted to know what I could offer them that other candidates couldn't. I said/told them (that) I was very experienced, (that) I'd got a lot of insight into the sector and (that) I knew the market.
3 They asked me/wanted to know where I saw myself in five years' time. I said/told them (that) I hoped to be heading up my own marketing team.
4 They asked me/wanted to know what I thought was the number one key to successful marketing, of any product. I said/told them (that) I thought the number one thing was to have a clear strategy, which was implemented consistently.
5 They asked me/wanted to know what I saw as my strengths. I said/told them (that) I'm a good organizer and I plan everything in detail. I'm creative, and as I mentioned, I know the market.
6 They asked me/wanted to know if I could think of any improvements to their products. I said/told them (that) I thought their products were second to none. But (that) I did think the marketing and advertising could be freshened up a little.

WRITING 3

1

the main features of the app
why the features are useful
anything the users should be aware of before they download the app
Points to include: student's own ideas

2

a 2   **b** 4   **c** 1   **d** 3

3

1 The user wants to increase the range of recipes they know.
2 It can be difficult for the user to find the information they want.
3 The app copies the ingredients automatically.

4 Recipe Record allows you to cross off ingredients so you don't forget what you've used.

5 It's simple for some websites, but not all.

6 The user thinks the price is fine because of the range of functions.

4

1 build my repertoire of dishes
2 When it comes to shopping
3 search in vain
4 A note of caution
5 It … was well worth the £6 I paid for it.
6 anyone looking to

5 Suggested answer

Anyone looking to get fit could do worse than download VidFitPlus. You can use it to **build your repertoire of exercises** quickly and easily. No longer will you have to **search in vain** for videos showing you the safest way to stretch your quads or a new yoga breathing technique: they're all in one place within the app. **It's well worth** every minute you spend using VidFitPlus. **When it comes to** the price, it's a bargain at just 99p. **A note of caution** though: it's addictive. Once you start using it, you won't be able to stop! I'd recommend it to all you fitness fans out there.

6

1 What **is the** secret **to** its **success**?
2 Contrary **to what you** might think…
3 It's far **from easy** to do this.
4 **By and** large, the developer manages to….
5 The app **in** question…
6 The app **takes an unusual** approach.

7

1 exceptional, outstanding
2 riveting, gripping
3 dull, tedious
4 entertaining, hilarious
5 baffling, over-complicated
6 extremely, highly
7 undeniably, unquestionably

10 Sample answer

Matt Cutts' TED Talk 'Try something new for 30 days' is short and sweet. Despite being only three minutes long, it has the potential to change your life completely.

You could say I was meant to watch it. On the day in question I was feeling a bit depressed, stuck in a rut at work and uninspired at home. I had the TED app automatically generate an 'inspiration' playlist for me, and this talk was the first one that came up. After listening to the very entertaining Matt Cutts, I'd found the answer to my problems.

In his talk, he describes how he took an unusual approach to changing his lifestyle through a series of 30-day projects. So what is the secret of his success? By breaking down each goal into manageable chunks, he created new habits which fitted

around his life. Another unexpected side effect he described was that life became much more memorable instead of passing by in a tedious haze. Who wouldn't want that?

After watching his talk, I was inspired to have a go at my own 30-day project. I've been learning English for years and had long intended to add a new language to my repertoire. Contrary to what you might expect, after just ten minutes of studying Mandarin a day for a month, I can already have simple conversations and recognize over 200 characters. Matt's 'little and often' approach really works!

As well as providing this kind of motivation and inspiration, TED Talks are wonderful tools for English learners. They cover a wide range of accents, and there are subtitles to help you understand them. Because they range in length from just 50 seconds to eighteen minutes, you can select one that fits the time you have available. So why not make your first 30-day project choosing a TED Talk a day to watch, and start with Matt Cutts' riveting talk to inspire you as he did me?

UNIT 7

7.1 The danger of a single story

1

1 Her parents worked at the university and Adichie attended a secondary school attached to the university and then studied at the university.

2 Professionally, they have mutual respect. Outside this, Adichie grew up in a house once lived in by Chinua Achebe.

3 Medicine and pharmacy (University of Nigeria), communication (Drexel University), communication and political science (Eastern Connecticut State University), MA in creative writing (Johns Hopkins University), MA in African Studies (Yale University)

4 Yes. The book received wide critical acclaim and a number of awards.

5 A fellowship by the Radcliffe Institute for Advanced Study, Harvard University, an array of literary accolades and awards, listed among the 'Leading Women of 2014' by CNN and among the '100 Most Influential People' by *TIME Magazine* in 2015.

2

c A journey to a better place

3

1 Benjamin **2** Abdel-Magied **3** Benjamin and Grant **4** Al-Sakkaf

4

1 challenges (us to look beyond) **2** draws on (stories of shared experience) **3** spotted **4** highlighting

6

Yassmin's talk makes me question how I can still have biases and how I can overcome them.

7

I have worked in the field of second-language learning for over 35 years, exposed to students and educators from many different cultures and perspectives.

8

1 in her work **2** she is still influenced by her biases

9

1 to force us to examine our biases
2 seeing them as less
3 she works with second-language learning students and educators from many different cultures and perspectives
4 that she was bad and immoral
5 that we all have the same needs
6 we are not born with equal opportunity
7 mentor someone from a different background

10

1 b **2** c **3** c **4** c **5** a

7.2 No better, no worse

1

1 You're **far** more likely to stand out if you dress like that.
2 Learning the language is **by** far the best way to get to know a culture.
3 The differences between the two are so slight **as** to be negligible.
4 I always feel **a** whole lot better after a good night's sleep.
5 Invite as many people as you like. **The** more, the merrier.
6 I'm not as open-minded **as** you are, but I'm happy to try most things once.
7 This one's not nearly **as** interesting as that one, don't you think?
8 I think the population is **a** bit bigger, but I'm not sure.

2

2 about 40 times as big/bigger
3 only about a third shorter
4 much greater
5 far bigger/by far the biggest
6 over five times more people than
7 a slightly higher urban population than
8 higher percentage of land used for agriculture than
9 considerably bigger

3

2 The more technology advances, the easier it gets.
3 That was by far the best lecture yet.
4 It was far cheaper/less expensive than we thought it would be.

5 There are not nearly as many people here as (there were) last week.

6 We need to leave and the sooner the better.

4

1 by far **2** a whole lot **3** nearly **4** twice

5

1 would rather, than **2** would prefer, rather than **3** favour, over **4** prefer, to **5** better, having **6** to have, rather than **7** would sooner, than **8** as soon, as

6

1 'd rather sit

2 'd be better off getting (also possible: 're better off getting)

3 'd rather you didn't

4 might be better to speak

5 prefer listening

6 'd prefer if you paid (also possible: prefer you pay/'d prefer you to pay)

7 'd rather you kept

8 'd just as soon watch, go

7

1 women are more or less likely than men

2 is the most gender-equal country

3 almost the same number of women as men

4 are only slightly lower than

5 is considerably lower, with only 26% in work

6 much lower, at just 65% of a man's earnings

7 is much higher at around two in five

7.3 Why more is less

1

b

2

1 and **4**

3

1 b **2** b **3** c **4** b **5** a

4

1 a **2** a **3** c **4** b **5** a

5

1 fence **2** devil **3** cherry **4** brainer **5** bets **6** plunge **7** judgement, evils

6

2 by **3** of **4** matter **5** Freedom **6** left **7** of **8** Hobson's

7

1 by choice **2** spoilt for choice **3** of choice

4 have no choice in the matter **5** left with no choice but to **6** freedom of choice

7 Hobson's choice **8** of your choice

7.4 Having said that ...

1

1 T **2** F **3** T **4** T **5** T **6** F

2

1 by and large, at least

2 On the whole, At the same time

3 As a result, that said / having said that

4 because of this, As a consequence

5 Broadly speaking, at any rate, Having said that

6 I'll grant you that, For that reason

3

1 By_j_and large, the project was a great success.

2 Things improved as far_r_as_exam results are concerned.

3 There was no noticeable difference, among the 11–14 age range at_any rate.

4 As_a result, demand increased significantly.

5 New security measures were introduced as_a consequence.

6 In spite_of the marketing campaign, sales continued to fall.

7 On top_of that, attendance increased by almost 5%.

8 Because_of the delay, extra costs were incurred.

4

1 The graph shows, It compares, The graph also compares

2 What we observe is, It is also worth noting, Looking at, we can see that

3 decreases, falls

4 steadily, sharply, slight, significant

5

2

Attendance declined gradually/gradually declined.

There was a gradual decline in attendance.

3

Sales dropped slightly.

We can see a slight drop in sales.

4

The graph shows that results improved significantly.

The graph shows a significant improvement in results.

5

Temperatures rose steadily.

There was a steady rise in temperature.

6

1 rose **2** observe **3** compares **4** worth **5** Looking, see **6** constant **7** consider, significant **8** shows, declined, steadily

7

1 The graph shows **2** It compares **3** looking at **4** we can see **5** decreases steadily **6** It is worth noting **7** If we look **8** we can observe **9** steady rise

PRESENTATION 4

1

a T

b F – Samira and Angelo had work done on their homes.

c F – Angelo moved home because of his family.

d T

e F – Samira doesn't mention the location of her home.

f T

3

1 c **2** d **3** b **4** a

5

1 c, e **2** a, h **3** d, f **4** b, g

6 (example answers)

1 Hello, I'm (name). Today, I'm going to tell you all about my home.

2 One of the great things about where I live is that it is really quiet and peaceful. We are out in the suburbs of the city, so we don't have to deal with the busy city centre every day. Another advantage of living here is that the cost of renting is not as high as in other parts of the city, so we can save a bit of money for holidays.

3 While it may be a peaceful place to live, sometimes it does feel like there is nothing to do. Even though being in the centre of the city is very noisy, you never have to worry about having nothing to do. I guess that is one of the facts of living in a quieter part of town.

4 Thank you very much for listening to my talk. Let's open the floor for your questions.

UNIT 8

8.1 How I fell in love with a fish

1

1 Helping out on his grandparents' farm as a child.

2 Chez Panisse, Berkeley, California; studied at the French Culinary Institute, New York City; working for chef Michel Rostang, Paris; Bouley, New York City.

3 do something on your own, in this case Barber set up a business on his own

4 a style or an approach that is typical of and identified with an individual or organization, and perhaps unique to the individual or organization

5 Barber is concerned with sustainability of food sources, which he prefers to be locally produced. He also has a concern for the health aspect, as illustrated by his advisory work.

2

a

3

1 Barber **2** Baehr **3** Seaver and Savitz

4

a dilemma **b** adage **c** humane **d** eye-opening **e** take/picture **f** rosy

6

/ˌkɒntrəˈvɜː(r)ʃ(ə)l/ /ɪnˈkluːd/ /ˈpestɪsaɪdz/
/prɪˈzɜː(r)vətɪvz/ /daɪəˈbiːtiːz/ /ˈpruːv/
/ˈθrets/ /əˈmʌŋ/

7

1 and **4**

8

1 confidence **2** advertising **3** farmer, hospital **4** words **5** purchasing **6** organic

9

1 c **2** b **3** b **4** a **5** c

8.2 Mind what you eat

1

1 can't have **2** 've just got to **3** shouldn't have **4** didn't need to **5** should've, could've **6** couldn't, had to **7** can't **8** ought to **9** Might **10** might've

2

1 can **2** don't have to **3** won't need to **4** do need to **5** can **6** should **7** need to **8** mustn't

3

1 should **2** should / ought to **3** might / may **4** should **5** may **6** need to **7** mustn't / shouldn't **8** can / might / may / could **9** can / may **10** need to / should **11** don't need to / needn't **12** can **13** should / need to

4

2 We might/may (well) be going out this weekend.
3 As it turned out, I didn't need to go / I needn't have gone to the meeting after all.
4 She might/may/could have told me, but I really can't remember.
5 You can't have seen him last night. He's in Paris at the moment.
6 They should be/should have been here by now. They might've missed the bus.
7 (Surely) He must have realized what was happening. How could he not (have realized).
8 I have to go to a meeting this evening. But it should be finished by 7.30. So we can/could meet then if you like.

5

1 would **2** might **3** can **4** should **5** needn't **6** wouldn't **7** may, can **8** could, might

6

1 we could actually have eaten
2 all the people who will have done the same
3 all need to think about

4 the vast majority of this food could actually be consumed
5 as you might imagine
6 can't be kept as long as other foods
7 This can be traced primarily to financial and technical

8.3 A contradiction in terms

1

b and **d**

2

1 Some foods are more sustainable than others, but very few foods are truly sustainable
2 You're going to have to compromise; look for what's least damaging to the environment
3 Think about the water and energy used in food production; don't waste food

3

1 some other food (that you thought was OK to eat)
2 eating cactus and insects
3 to buy organic meat
4 cereals that use relatively little water to produce
5 berries as opposed to other sweet foods / sugary treats
6 which fish are OK to eat
7 what food / feed
8 in the case of dairy food
9 at the top of the carbon footprint list
10 the amount of energy and water used in food production

4

1 Vegetable esp. potato peelings; Chewy crisps; olive oil
2 Apple; peelings; Tea; Put in hot water 3–4 mins
3 cheese; vegetables; Beat; vegetables and cheese; 20 minutes
4 veg; meat; Stir fry; wok; oil
5 bones; chicken; Soup or broth; Boil; herbs & seasoning

5

1 ~~amenable~~/laudable/commendable.
2 unavoidable/~~unattainable~~/inevitable.
3 workable/viable/~~agreeable~~
4 plausible/credible/~~negligible~~
5 agreeable/amenable/~~laudable~~
6 feasible/~~commendable~~/doable
7 ~~amenable~~/attainable/achievable.
8 ~~unavoidable~~/irreparable/irreversible.
9 negligible/~~unattainable~~/insignificant

6

2 whip **3** top **4** cut **5** dish **6** drink **7** chop **8** wolfed **9** live **10** gone

7

2 live on **3** whip up **4** drink up **5** dish it up **6** cut down on **7** wolfed down **8** chop up **9** top it up **10** gone off

8

1 Let me top up your glass. / Let me top you up.
2 Drink up and let's go.
3 He virtually lives on ready-meals.
4 He whipped up this amazing meal in no time.
5 I was starving. I wolfed it down.
6 I'm dishing it up in two minutes.
7 You need to heat it up in a pan for a few minutes.
8 I've been cutting down on cheese.

8.4 I'll try anything once ...

1

1 Most open: speaker 2 (I'd say I'm quite adventurous when it comes to food and always open to new experiences. I love tasting new food that I've never had before … I suppose I'm generally happy to try anything)
Least open: speaker 3 (I think I'm really quite conservative when it comes to food … I suppose I'm quite traditional in my tastes. I generally like to take the safe option, something I know … I wouldn't generally eat anything too different)

2

Speaker 1	fish and meat
Speaker 2	extreme things like dog or brain
Speaker 3	food that is not traditionally eaten in his culture

2

1 I'm pretty cautious with what I eat
2 stick with what I know
3 take the safe option
4 I am happy to experiment
5 give something new a go
6 I generally like to play it safe
7 I'm happy to try it out
8 I'd say I'm quite adventurous
9 always open to new experiences
10 I'm generally happy to try anything
11 might draw the line at
12 I'm really quite conservative
13 I'm quite traditional in my tastes

3

1 comes, happy (willing also possible), line
2 when, to, option
3 try, give, a
4 play, stick, cautious

4

1 I don't understand why anyone would want to eat that.
2 Can you ask what's in it?
3 I'll eat most things, within reason.
4 I used to be vegetarian, bud I started eating meat a couple of years ago. (but I = assimilation of /t/ to /d/)
5 Do you know 'Meals for five pounds'? It's a goob book. (elision of d)
6 The whole meal was less than tem pounds. (assimilation of /n/ to /m/)
7 Is this the first time you've eaten here?
8 A table for one, please. It's just me.

5

Having been for many years just a treat for the weekend, a new survey has found that the average Briton now spends over £100 a month on take-away meals. Not having the time or the inclination to cook, or being too tired are the biggest reasons for having a take-away. Picking up the phone or ordering online and having something delivered is quite the norm according to the survey. Men are the biggest fast-food consumers, and get through around 150 take-aways a year, while the figure for women is around 125, with 25- to 34-year-olds being the biggest consumers of take-away food.

Having been overtaken by Chinese and Indian food, the traditional British take-away meal of fish and chips has gone from being the nation's most popular take-away to its third favourite. Closely followed by pizza in fourth place. These four foods make up around 85% of all take-away meals.

6

1 Derived, having included
2 Having lived
3 Opened
4 Weighing, bought/having been bought
5 Having spent
6 grown/being grown

7

2 referred 3 supplying 4 Varying 5 eaten
6 being 7 being 8 cooked

8

2 They had no idea what the food was like, not having eaten there before.
3 Known for its quirky menu, the lively little restaurant attracts visitors from miles around.
4 She decided to give the snails a miss on this occasion, having tried eating them before.
5 Not knowing the area, we had no idea where the best place to eat was.
6 Inspired by the local landscape and the character of its people, the restaurant is usually fully booked for up to six months in advance.

WRITING 4

1

describe the festival

describe two or three events which were particularly interesting

evaluate how the event supports the cultural life of your town

2

1 Overview = Describe the festival
2 Highlights = Events which were particularly interesting
3 Effects = How the event helps cultural life

3

1 Travel writing
2 Most talks sold out. The rest were at least 80% full.
3 More people will borrow his books from libraries.
4 It showed that anyone could be a travel writer, not just people who go to places which are far away.
5 Libraries and museums in the city.

4

1 a wealth of
2 went down very well
3 drew my attention
4 that we might not otherwise have been aware of
5 catering for
6 gain a positive impression of (something)

5

1 I will begin by providing **a general overview** of the festival.
2 **Careful consideration** should be given to whether we can afford to run a similar festival again.
3 **I personally found** her talk to be one of the highlights of the whole event.
4 The organizers were **ably assisted by** a team of volunteers.
5 There were **ample opportunities for** audience members to participate in the discussion.
6 Overall, the festival was **a huge success.**

6

1 c 2 e 3 a 4 f 5 b 6 d

7

1 the aspects covered earlier suggest
2 in light of our findings
3 it would appear then that
4 as mentioned at the outset
5 following on from the previous point
6 it should therefore be questioned whether

10 Sample answer

The objectives of this report are to detail the provision of food services available to tourists visiting Brno and to recommend potential improvements to these services aimed at increasing the number of visitors to the city.

Current situation

As it stands, Brno has a wealth of cafés, restaurants and other places for tourists to eat. There are a handful of restaurants serving foreign cuisine, though the majority serve Czech or Italian food.

For the top end of the market, Spaliček serves traditional Czech cuisine, with a menu in a variety of languages making it easy for tourists to understand. There is also Empire, at premium prices due to its prime location overlooking the main square. Visitors to the city can also go to one of the many mid-priced restaurants and cafés in the city centre. Those on tight budgets can purchase food from a 'hungry window', local stalls serving food like pizza or burek.

Recommendations

While it is true that the range of cuisines represented in the city has increased over recent years, there is still room for improvement. For instance, Mexican or Thai cuisine represent gaps in the market and this additional variety may attract visitors from the surrounding area into the city.

What is also lacking is provision for different dietary requirements. On many menus, vegetarians have a very limited range of options, often consisting only of fried cheese or fried cauliflower. Despite there now being one or two vegetarian restaurants in Brno, the tourist office should encourage an increase in the range of vegetarian options available, as at present traditional restaurants have little to offer them.

Finally, training in food allergies could also be provided, for example, for gluten-free diets. Ensuring waiters understand the implications of cross-contamination will increase people's confidence in the service provided.

Taken together, these changes will open up our city's eating establishments to a wider range of guests.

UNIT 9

9.1 Why videos go viral

1

1 Studying Communication and Film Studies, being a columnist for a university publication, being a performer, writer and director of a comedy sketch show and being involved in duo interpretation have all perhaps provided useful and relevant background experience for his subsequent career.
2 There are constraints to the performance, such as not using props and not touching or making eye-contact.
3 As well as the experiences at university, he has been a film production assistant and producer, a (political satire) writer, producer and editor.
4 It connects users who YouTube feels can benefit from being aware of each other.
5 He has made numerous TV appearances and has been frequently quoted in various publications, including major newspapers.

2

a

3

1 Sadowsky and Ohanian 2 Whitacre
3 Schneider 4 Ohanian

4

a unveils   **b** charged with   **c** labyrinthine
d shoo-in   **e** contests

6

I liked this talk. It starts off modestly and
quietly and then it builds.

7

British

8

3

9

1 (real) magic   **2** classical choral
3 technical knowledge   **4** uncertain /
unconfident (about his material)

10

1 c   **2** a   **3** b   **4** a   **5** b

9.2 Completely lost without it

1

1 incredibly, absolutely
2 incredibly, pretty, quite, fairly
3 very, very, rather
4 somewhat, very
5 totally, very, entirely

2

1 very   **2** practically   **3** a little bit
4 absolutely   **5** highly, pretty   **6** really
7 quite, very   **8** strongly, extremely

3

1 flabbergasted   **2** mortified   **3** fantastic
4 loaded   **5** spotless   **6** deafening   **7** filthy
8 awful   **9** starving   **10** hideous   **11** furious
12 packed   **13** soaked

4

1 filthy   **2** packed   **3** spotless   **4** loaded
5 deafening   **6** flabbergasted   **7** mortified
8 hideous

5

1 b painfully slow
2 d wildly exaggerated
3 c widely accepted
4 a deeply committed
5 h highly controversial
6 e readily admit
7 f fully appreciate
8 g severely disadvantaged
9 j distinctly remember
10 k desperately in need of
11 l sincerely believe
12 i extraordinarily gifted

6

2 wildly exaggerated
3 severely disadvantaged, deeply committed
4 highly controversial
5 readily admit
6 fully appreciate, painfully slow

7 distinctly remember
8 extraordinarily gifted

7

1 a very limited number of sources
2 a reasonably wide range of news topics
3 fairly modest in the number
4 one news source readily admit
5 quite fair and balanced in its delivery
6 considerably narrower
7 primarily concerned
8 a distinctly different perspective

9.3 Same old

2

1 F   **2** F   **3** T   **4** T   **5** U   **6** F – not always

3

1 catchphrases   **2** become extinct
3 synchronized   **4** clumsy   **5** picked on
6 given rise to   **7** disorientated   **8** lucrative

4

1 Dancing inmates of Cebu   **2** grumpy cat,
dancing hamsters   **3** David after dentist, Star
Wars kid   **4** YOLO/You Only Live Once
5 Star Wars kid, Dancing inmates of Cebu
6 Dancing hamsters, Dancing baby   **7** 'Hide
yo' kids, hide yo' wife'   **8** 'Hide yo' kids, hide
yo' wife', David after dentist, Grumpy Cat

5

1 Ice Bucket challenge (compendium)
2 It made a difference by raising money

6

1 encouraging   **2** amazing   **3** shallow
4 meaningful

7

1 blog   **2** podcast   **3** phishing   **4** hotspot
5 crowdfunding   **6** offline   **7** troll   **8** spam

8

1 interconnected   **2** interface
3 interweaves   **4** interdisciplinary
5 intercut   **6** interlocking   **7** interplay
8 interdependent

9.4 Online presence

1

1 Speaker 2 is broadly against, speaker 1 is
broadly for
2 Speaker 1 (…I'm not so sure how we can
actually control things, really. Who do you
censor, and how exactly?)
3 Speaker 2 (The real issue for me is that internet
censorship could open the door for the
powers that be, those doing the censoring, to
follow their own agenda, whatever that may
be. So, who's going to oversee or censor
that? That to me is the main issue.)

2

a 1   **b** 2   **c** 1   **d** 2   **e** 2   **f** 1   **g** 2

3

1 personally   **2** insofar   **3** far   **4** concerned
5 allowing   **6** fact   **7** say   **8** different
9 inasmuch   **10** just   **11** accept

4

1 Personally, I think that
2 I'd say that considering / I'd say
considering that
3 We just have to accept that
4 why should it be any different with, Screen
time is screen time
5 doesn't really come into it
6 Allowing for the fact that
7 insofar as it can
8 As far as your public online presence is
concerned

5

1 Personally, I think it is.
2 As far as I'm concerned, it's a good thing.
3 Our opinion doesn't really come into it.
4 We just have to accept that it's inevitable.
5 In my opinion, it's fair enough.
6 If you ask me, it's not a good idea.
7 Freedom of speech is freedom of speech.
8 Well, it's not a bad thing?

6

Tom Gardener, waiter and duty manager

Professional waiter with duty management
experience in a number of high-end
restaurants and hotels. Team player, but
capable of using own initiative. Hard worker,
but knows the importance of having fun.
Focusses on the detail, but can see the big
picture. Works to high standards and expects
the same. Quick learner and doesn't need
telling twice. Proven track record of getting
things done. Degree in business studies.
Looking to take career to the next level in the
catering or hospitality sector.

7

2 The hotel has got several meeting
rooms.
3 We place a great deal of importance on
staff training.
4 She's a fitness fanatic.
5 She's a best-selling author.
6 He's an ideas person.
7 He put forward an equally compelling
argument.
8 She has an impressive track record.
9 It was an exercise in relationship building.
10 She specializes in medical ethics.

8

2 innovative products
3 a dynamic sales and marketing team
4 marketing strategies
5 marketing budget
6 a proven and unrivalled track record
7 a well-known educational services
marketing agency / a well-known
education marketing agency
8 high-end and exacting clients
9 a good listener

10 long-lasting relationships
11 a collaborative process

PRESENTATION 5

1

a F – (Being vegan could help the environment by reducing carbon emissions.)
b T
c T
d T
e F – (He thinks it's trendy, but it isn't easy.)

3

1 c   **2** d   **3** a   **4** b

5

1 b, h   **2** c, g   **3** d, e   **4** a, f

6   (example answers)

1 Hello. I'm (name) and over the next few minutes I'm going to talk about how we can all live more sustainable lives.
2 An easy change everyone could make is to walk more. When private and public transportation are so readily available, it can be easy to lose sight of how easy it can be to get around on foot. I don't mean that we should walk absolutely everywhere, but for example when you're in the town centre and things are close to each other – why not?
3 If we all walked a little bit more, there would be less demand on public transportation systems, there would be fewer vehicles on the road. Taking the underground and getting on and off trains or squeezing into buses can be an uncomfortable and stressful experience, so why not spend more time travelling above ground? Not only will this help prevent overcrowding, but it will also help people be fitter as they get more exercise.
4 That brings us to the end of the talk. I hope you have enjoyed listening to me today and you have a better idea about living sustainably. Let's open up the discussion – what are your thoughts?

UNIT 10

10.1 A kinder, gentler philosophy of success

1

1 T – (He spent his early childhood in Switzerland and spoke French and German ... he continued his education ... at a boarding school in Oxford, where English became his main language)
2 F – (He began a PhD in French philosophy at Harvard University, but did not complete this)
3 U – (To date, the book has sold two million copies worldwide)
4 F – (offers a variety of classes and workshops on 'developing emotional intelligence' and addressing such issues as 'how to find

fulfilling work, how to develop relationships and how better to understand the world.')
5 T – (... and has contributed to and presented television programmes, ...)

2

c

3

1 Dinsmore and Schwartz (possibly Brooks)
2 Gilbert   **3** Brooks and Dinsmore

4

a miserable   **b** craves   **c** meaningful
d intangible

6

I imagine that most people who watch this talk for the first time have probably never pondered their own two selves.

7

2

8

1 False – she wonders how common it is for people to do this.   **2** True   **3** True   **4** False – she thinks they are relevant to such people, but she does not say she is one of them   **5** True

9

1 b   **2** c   **3** a   **4** a   **5** c

10.2 Self-help

1

1 to talk, to get, dealing
2 to find, find, to get
3 take, to work, to be, talking, speaking
4 to see, to apologize, being, to upset, upsetting

2

1 with advocating   **2** to promote   **3** to achieve
4 of realizing   **5** to thank   **6** to acquire
7 to raise   **8** to sell   **9** on having written
10 in writing   **11** in informing   **12** to publish

3

1 started to become (becoming also 'technically' possible)
2 was possible to take
3 was able/would be able to transform
4 will help you (to) help
5 based on having
6 would be capable of understanding
7 achieving
8 did/has done more than any other book in putting ('to put' also technically possible)

4

2 He was reluctant to open up at first, but he's more expressive now.
3 I'm not convinced he's suited to working in management.
4 Are you serious about looking for another job?
5 Do you think it's worth trying to contact her again?
6 It's useless phoning them. They never answer.

7 I'm interested to know / in knowing what they thought about it.
8 My parents never let me stay up late during the week.

5

1 adamant   **2** amazed/surprised, proud
3 aware   **4** disappointed, had   **5** convinced, surprised/amazed   **6** regret

6

2 I'm determined that I won't/'m not going to get behind with things again.
3 She was upset about not being told any sooner.
4 He's not so keen that we (should) go on the training course.
5 I was pleased to be given the opportunity.
6 I'm not conscious that any decision has been made.
7 I was delighted that I was even considered for the post.
8 We have decided against going ahead with the project.

7

1 I wasn't aware of there being a deadline at all.
2 I'm determined not to get behind with things again.
3 She was upset about not being told any sooner.
4 He's not so keen on us going on the training course.
5 I was pleased to be given the opportunity.
6 I'm not convinced that we should hold the conference in July.
7 I was delighted to be even considered for the post.
8 We have decided against going ahead with the project

8

1 bothered to do any preparation
2 a good idea to know
3 unlikely to be asked directly
4 try to anticipate potential questions
5 it's good to have them
6 worth re-familiarizing yourself

10.3 What generations want

1

1 d   **2** f   **3** a   **4** e   **5** c   **6** b

2

1 and **3** because they argue that each individual should make their own definition of success

3

a 2, 3   **b** 2   **c** 1, 3   **d** 2   **e** 1, 3   **f** 1

4

1 1 and 3   **2** their maturity

5

modify; priorities

6

1 dropping   **2** out   **3** make   **4** it   **5** set
6 heart   **7** realizing   **8** ambition   **9** fall
10 wayside   **11** throw   **12** towel

7

2 e   **3** c   **4** d   **5** a   **6** b   **7** f   **8** i
9 h   **10** g

8

2 stories   **3** overnight, limited   **4** secret
5 key, confident   **6** without   **7** rate   **8** proven

10.4 How did you get on?

1

1 ✓   **2** –   **3** ✗   **4** –   **5** –   **6** ✓

2

1 How did it go with, Did you manage, all
sorted
2 Did you have any luck, could have been
better
3 How did your, go, made, bit, mess
4 How did you get on with, we're getting
there
5 Did you get anywhere with, well, could,
expected
6 How was, Did it go, all went, smoothly

3

1 How did it go with your tutor, it could've
been better
2 Did you have any luck with the insurance,
As well as could be hoped
3 How did you get on with the team-building
day, I'd say it was a success.
4 Did you get anywhere with your boss, we
did make some headway
5 Did you have any trouble convincing them,
It all went very smoothly, It's all sorted
6 How did your presentation go, I made a bit
of a mess of it, Did you manage to adjust

4

1 A: How did your exam go?
B: It could have been better.
2 A: Do you think it will work?
B: Depends if we have any trouble
convincing people.
3 A: How did it go this morning?
B: It all went smoothly, thanks.
4 A: Did it go OK with your boss?
B: It's all sorted now.

5

1 in   **2** to   **3** To   **4** at, of   **5** At, of
6 in, with   **7** in, with   **8** in, to   **9** On, of

6

2 in keeping with   **3** in contrast with
4 in collaboration with   **5** In view of
6 on account of   **7** with reference to
8 Under the circumstances

7

1 This report was commissioned at the
request of our parent company, TechEd

in relation to sales performance and falling
market share.
2 This interim report finds the prospects
of the company to some extent are not
positive. While (the) analysis is still in
progress, we have identified a number of
areas of weakness, particularly in relation to
customer relations and after-sales service.
In view of this, Stephanie Amilhat has been
asked to oversee the customer relations
team for the foreseeable future.
3 I am writing on behalf of the board of
directors with reference to next year's
planned relocation of our production facility
from its current location in Cambridge to
a/the new location in Nottingham. As a
result of new land-use legislation, the
move has been put on hold to enable us to
modify the plans for the new facility.

WRITING 5

1

1 Technology has democratized knowledge.
2 You can contact experts in different fields
directly through social media.
3 Traditional research skills are being lost.
4 People think they know more than they do
because they can search on the Internet.

2

1 a   **2** b   **3** d   **4** c

3

1 Many online courses are cheap or free,
so they are less expensive than university
courses.
2 Social media gives you the chance to be
part of a community.
3 Many documents are still only available in
their original form.
4 Many young people do not know about
what they can find in libraries and archives.
5 We still need to train people in traditional
research skills.

4

1 the advent of the Internet
2 a wealth of
3 perennial problem
4 offset
5 unparalleled access
6 labour under the misconception that

5

1 strongly   **2** widely   **3** undeniably
4 deeply   **5** vehemently   **6** immensely

6

1 It is an indisputable fact that…
2 Nobody would dispute the fact that…
3 It may be the case that…
4 It might also be that…
5 This raises the issue of…
6 An important question to consider is that
of…

7

1 c   **2** a   **3** e   **4** f   **5** d   **6** b

8

1 Some old people have to rely on the
state to support them, rather than their
communities.
2 Some may feel left behind or neglected by
society.
3 Healthcare helps the aging population to
stay fitter for longer.
4 Older people provide valuable support to
society, especially to younger people.

10 Sample answer

In many countries, populations are aging
as birth rates drop. As the balance of
populations changes, what is the role of older
citizens in society today?

It is an incontrovertible fact that older people
still have a lot to offer society. The majority of
volunteering is done by those who are retired,
older people look after their grandchildren
reducing worries about the costs of childcare
for their offspring, and their wealth of
knowledge and experience is also a valuable
commodity for younger generations to draw
on. As science brings new advances in
medicine, we will be able to take advantage of
a longer period of good health to continue to
benefit society.

At the same time, as an ever larger percentage
of the population enter retirement, there are
fewer and fewer working adults to pay for
them, leading to a pressure on the state to
fund pensions and healthcare costs. Another
important question to consider is that of
information from the government, such as
telling about pension schemes, which is
increasingly only available online. Since there
is at present a lower rate of digital literacy
among the elderly, at times it may be difficult
for them to work out where to find or send
the necessary information to gain access to
particular services. This disenfranchises some
older people, since they are no longer able
to exploit all of the services which should be
available to them.

In conclusion, it is my belief that older citizens
still have a vital role to play in the modern
world, and that we must continue to support
them by ensuring they are able to fully
participate in all aspects of society.

UNIT 11

11.1 Build a school in the cloud

1

1 False. His early academic background was
in physics.
2 False. He worked for the company NIIT
from 1990 to 2006.
3 False. The 'Hole in the Wall' experiment
resulted in the idea of MIE.
4 True.

2

a

3

1 Shocken and Mitra   **2** Svitak (and probably Sethi)   **3** Shocken   **4** Shocken and Sethi

4

a curriculum   **b** groundbreaking   **c** tackles   **d** prodigy

6

a 4   **b** 1   **c** 5   **d** 2   **e** 3   Changes between d and e and a and c

7

a

8

2, 3, 5, 6, 7

9

1 c   **2** b   **3** a   **4** a   **5** b   **6** c

11.2   The value of education

1

1 c U   **2** a R   **3** e U   **4** b R   **5** d U   **6** f R

2

1 (do) go   **2** don't have to   **3** had finished
4 may not quite be   **5** may have been
6 hadn't dropped   **7** wasn't/hadn't been
8 would not / wouldn't have benefitted

3

2 have   **3** not carry out   **4** are   **5** to leave
6 would be recorded   **7** may be subject
8 wishes   **9** will have/has   **10** enter

4

2 Should the lecture theatre be unavailable, we'll book a different room.
3 Had you been paying attention, you'd know what to do.
4 Were he (to be) here, I'm sure he'd have a lot to say about the matter.
5 Had it not been for her housemates waking her up, she would have probably slept through the whole exam.
6 If I were to reapply for the course, do you think I'd have a chance?

5

1 If I don't/As long as/Unless I
2 In the event that/Providing that/Assuming that
3 Supposing/Imagine/Unless
4 On condition that/In the event of/In case of
5 Whether or not/But for/If it hadn't been
6 in case of/as long as/providing, Otherwise / If not / Assuming that

6

1 Whether or not   **2** Assuming   **3** otherwise
4 But for   **5** In the event that   **6** unless

7

1 I didn't have
2 wouldn't be in
3 I didn't have that, I wouldn't be teaching
4 the qualification you need
5 you don't have
6 had I not decided to do
7 wouldn't've been able to teach
8 providing you have

11.3   How to remember

2

a Yes (a balanced diet)   **b** No   **c** Yes (aerobic exercise)   **d** Yes   **e** No

3

1 False – it's because we are living longer and more of us are getting mental illnesses
2 True – (even if it's not a very good one)
3 False – the best ones are those which keep you focussed, but in a relaxed way
4 False – he doesn't say if he likes coffee or not
5 True
6 False – he doesn't make any judgement on their future potential

4

(2nd year) master's student;   distracted; laptop, 6–8 hours at a time, two or three a.m., keeping up with friends;   **1** a normal sleep routine   **2** distractions   **3** work time   **4** away from a computer screen

5

1 recall   **2** recite   **3** acquire   **4** hone
5 called   **6** get   **7** assimilate   **8** evoked
9 learning, commit

6

1 d   **2** e   **3** f   **4** a   **5** g   **6** c   **7** b

7

1 memo   **2** memoir(s)   **3** memorabilia
4 memorial   **5** memorize   **6** memorable
7 memento(s)

8

1 If my memory serves me well   **2** in living memory   **3** from memory   **4** brought back a lot of memories, trip down memory lane

11.4   I'll get the hang of it

1

1 teaching English to teenagers
2 half an hour
3 they didn't, they'd got a lesson already prepared
4 (b) quite well
5 awkward language and grammar questions
6 to do a course in teaching English

2

1 e   **2** d   **3** a   **4** b   **5** c   **6** h   **7** j
8 f   **9** g   **10** i

3

1 e   **2** c   **3** d   **4** b   **5** a

4

2 I'll be (a bit) rusty, it'll (all) come back to me
3 it goes in one ear and out (of) the other, pretty straightforward
4 a bit daunting, with my eyes shut, struggle through
5 was (pretty) clueless, out of my depth, on top of things

5

1 He **j** asked me if I wanted to do some English teaching to **w** earn some money.
2 They were **r** a group of teenagers.
3 So **w** anyway, I got to the **j** end of the morning.
4 I wasn't great, by **j** any means.
5 That's how I got into **w** it as a career.
6 It goes in one ear **r** and out the **j** other.
7 I used to be **j** able to do **w** it with my eyes shut.
8 I've no **w** idea what I should be doing.

6

1 After seeing an 8.2 per cent increase in sales for the period leading up to the start of October, the increase dropped to 3.7 per cent for the following six months. With other firms similarly reporting a distinct seasonal difference in sales, it seems a new trend is emerging.
2 Hanson Industries is planning to reduce its debt by passing it on to the holding company and, by doing so will be in a better position to make acquisitions as opportunities arise.
3 Written sources are of prime value to the historian and without devaluing the important contribution made by other kinds of evidence, such as archaeology, by providing an unparalleled depth of insight into human conduct, offer us so much more information about the past.
4 On completing the claim form, please email it directly to us at the address at the bottom of this page. Before sending, please ensure that it has been electronically signed as forms without a signature cannot be accepted.

7

1 On/after   **2** After, by/on ('after' is also possible, but would probably not be used to avoid repetition)   **3** With   **4** by   **5** without
6 Before

8

2 On leaving the building, please ensure that you sign out and return your pass.
3 After completing the required probationary period, annual leave will accrue at an initial rate of half a day per week worked.
4 Without knowing all the facts, it is difficult for us to make a judgement at this time.

5 We help small businesses grow <u>by providing</u> expert assistance with Social Media Search Engine Marketing.
6 <u>By accepting</u> these terms and conditions you also agree to the terms of our Privacy Policy.
7 <u>Without getting/Without wanting to get</u> too technical at this stage, I do have a few concerns regarding the data collection methodology. <u>By using</u> counterbalancing rather than randomization, there could be an element of bias.
8 As you may be aware, over 75% of consumers research a service or product online <u>before making a</u> purchase. And <u>with such a high proportion of potential customers coming</u> from search engines, a user's first impression is critical. In fact, research shows that <u>on visiting</u> a website, a consumer forms an opinion of it within 0.2 seconds.

PRESENTATION 6

1

a Pietro, Hina, Ivana **b** Pietro, Ivana
c Pietro

3

1 Train **2** strategic **3** set **4** Test

5

1 c **2** f **3** b **4** e **5** a **6** d

6 (example answers)

1 Hello. Thank you for being here. Today I'm going to talk about how I learn and memorize things, and I'll suggest how this could help you.
2 Remembering facts and figures is part of daily life, but one thing I've always struggled with is remembering numbers. Of course it's easy to put them into a smartphone or other device, but you don't always have those with you.
3 So, one thing that I do is break down big pieces of information into smaller chunks. For example, memorizing a telephone number by breaking it into sets of three-digit numbers makes the task much easier.
4 This allows me to make the task of remembering numbers a lot more manageable. It's much easier to remember three three-digit numbers than it is to remember nine single numbers. It also frees up my memory so that I can remember more numbers.
5 This may help people who struggle to remember long strings of information. It can work with numbers and letters or words.
6 That's everything I wanted to say. Thank you very much for your attention. Are there any questions from the floor?

UNIT 12

12.1 Creative problem-solving in the face of extreme limits

1

1

He drew on his native India (and other emerging markets such as China) while investigating globalized innovation and how to integrate Western and Eastern perspectives on innovation and leadership.
He became Executive Director of the Centre for India & Global Business at Judge Business School.
His book *Jugaad Innovation* was based on the Indian concept of Jugaad.

2

a He investigated how globalized innovation drives new market structures and organizational models,
b He was Executive Director of the Centre for India & Global Business at Judge Business School, University of Cambridge and currently is a Fellow of Judge Business School
c While at Forrester, he also advised leading organizations worldwide. / He has served as a member of the World Economic Forum's Global Agenda Council on Design Innovation.

3

a coined
b grassroots
c frugal

2

c

3

1 Mashelkar and Prakash **2** Gupta and Roy
3 Roy (and Mashelkar) **4** Prakash and Roy (and Mashelkar)

4

a realm **b** artisans **c** recognition **d** demo

6

1 then **2** As **3** a **4** result

7

professionally interested and curious to know more

8

1 microbes **2** paper **3** real **4** larger
5 potential

9

1 a **2** b **3** b **4** b **5** a

12.2 Patent pending

1

1 likely **2** However **3** also **4** often
5 globally **6** increasingly **7** exactly
8 famously **9** Therefore **10** in turn

2

1 doing things differently, have never been done before
2 highly productive, work passionately towards the company's aim.
3 never happens in a vacuum, highly value, view collaboration positively
4 to fully grasp, face today
5 never take, will usually seek, even if, considerably higher
6 have to continuously reach above and beyond, have done before
7 are never, to think outside the box, do not always know

3

2 According to the research, lying down can significantly boost thinking speeds by up to 10%.
3 This is due to the chemical noradrenalin, which is produced by the brain when we are stressed and which slows mental activity and reduces our attention to detail.
4 When we are standing up, the mind has considerably more to process, and the brain thus produces more noradrenalin.
5 Conversely, when we are lying down, the brain usually has less to process and it therefore produces less noradrenalin.
6 As a result, when lying down, we can generally process information at greater speeds and think more clearly and innovatively.

4

1 Innovation can only occur where you can breathe free.
2 Change is the law of life. And those who look only to the past or present are certain to miss the future.
3 Companies have too many experts who block innovation. True innovation really comes from perpendicular thinking.
4 The biggest risk is not taking any risk … In a world that is changing really quickly, the only strategy that is guaranteed to fail is not taking risks.
5 Radical innovation is difficult to fund. It seems scary. And the really radical things seem even more scary.

5

2 To **3** By **4** In **5** To **6** To
7 On **8** On **9** In **10** With
11 Off, of **12** Out of

6

2 Off the top of my head **3** With respect
4 In her defence **5** To put it bluntly
6 By coincidence **7** To their credit
8 On reflection **9** On the whole
10 Out of interest

7

1 apparently what the device does
2 that are constantly being beamed
3 quite easily be used
4 Basically, it simply takes energy

5 otherwise would be totally wasted
6 they've finally managed to do it

12.3 The inventor's trials

2

1 a
2 Reddi-Bacon, the chewing gum packet
3 The moral the museum teaches us …
is that failure is something we should
contemplate more often

3

1 c **2** a **3** b **4** c **5** b

4

1 b **2** b **3** a **4** a **5** c **6** a **7** a **8** c

5

2 makes up for **3** try it out **4** bring about
5 got down to **6** bring up **7** pulled it off
8 came up with/hit on, set up

6

1 inventive **2** inventiveness **3** innovative
4 innovation **5** innovation **6** innovator
7 creativity **8** creation **9** creator
10 productive **11** productivity **12** product
13 producer

7

1 innovative **2** inventiveness, creativity
3 productivity **4** Product **5** creative
6 creator **7** innovations **8** productive/
creative **9** created **10** production

12.4 To get the best results …

1

1
a speaker 2
b speaker 3
c speaker 4
d speaker 1

2
a speaker 2
b speaker 1
c speaker 4
d speaker 3

2

1 advise, since **2** recommend **3** seeing
4 Given, avoid **5** so **6** for **7** so **8** to
9 With, fear **10** order

3

1 **To get** the best results, you want to **avoid
using** the digital zoom.
2 I never mess around with the settings **for**
fear that I'll accidentally delete something
important.
3 I'd advise **against travelling** between 4
and 6, **especially since** it's a Friday.
4 **Seeing** as I'm not from round here, I'm
not the best person to ask about places to
stay.

5 Turn the TV off at the mains so **as** not **to**
waste electricity with the TV on stand-by.
6 It's a device **for measuring** the
temperature inside something you've
cooked.
7 With you **using** your mobile all the time,
you should turn the screen brightness
down in order **to save** the battery.
8 **Given** that you can only be there for a
couple of days, I'd recommend **staying/
you stay** right in the city centre **so** that
you don't waste time travelling around so
much.

4

1 mature **2** massage **3** disgrace
4 sachet **5** finance

5

1 I must confess to already **being** a big fan
and therefore a bit biased, but the new
game is simply out of this world.
2 The speakers promise **to deliver** a full
sound with exceptional clarity at the very
top and bottom end, which encourages
you to turn up the volume and hear
things you may have never heard before.
3 Users are invited **to test** the new version
and then, if they wish, receive a free
upgrade on completion of a short feedback
form.
4 We advise **you** not to upgrade/**against
upgrading** just yet as the new software
does seem to have one or two glitches
that the company is currently trying to
sort out.
5 When installing the software, we suggest
using the default installation settings for an
easier setup.
6 I would encourage you **to get** a completely
new system rather than upgrading
your current one but, if you insist **on
upgrading**, also try to get a faster
processor.
7 We congratulate them **on** producing a
first-rate app that will no doubt be on tens
of millions of smartphones in no time.
8 The company is offering **to** replace the
item or give a full refund. We recommend
taking a refund until the problem is
completely rectified.

6

2 recommend changing
3 guaranteed to transform, promised/
promises to deliver
4 discourages you from guessing,
encourages you to actively solve
5 confess to initially being, congratulate the
developers on making

7

1 you to listen **2** on producing **3** you to
search **4** starting with **5** you to upgrade
6 the company for having **7** us to record
8 (to) save **9** on having **10** the developers
to fix

WRITING 6

1

1 A description of an innovation used in
developing countries.
2 The effect the innovation has had.
3 An analysis of how much people living
outside developing countries can fulfil the
needs of those within them.

2

1 A description of solar-powered lights.
2 The effect the lights have had.
3 An analysis of how much people living
outside developing countries can fulfil the
needs of those within them.

3

1 The charity Solar Aid
2 It reduces the risk of fire. It is better for
people's health. It is cheaper than a
kerosene lamp because people don't have
to buy fuel. The lights have a long battery
life and can be hung anywhere. They can
be used for a long time after sunset.
3 Because people are buying the lamp
instead of being given it by a charity.
4 Local people can tell 'outsiders' what the
community really needs.

4

1 I would like to put forward…
2 Following the initial purchase of…
3 …costs are minimal…
4 This enables them to be used…
5 …leading to them doing better…
6 It is my considered opinion that…

5

1 already **2** readily **3** considerably
4 constantly **5** easily **6** highly

6

1 Deciding whether or not it is necessary to
bring in outside innovation can be a thorny
issue.
2 As long as people cannot easily access
clean drinking water,…
3 Unless charities and aid agencies work
closely with local people,…
4 Provided that the printers are made
portable enough and the materials they use
accessible enough,…
5 It's important to use resources which are
locally available. Otherwise, it will be too
expensive.

7

1 have **2** up **3** order **4** Since/Because/As
5 Those **6** one/a

10 Sample answer

To the editor:

My purpose in writing is to share with your
magazine how the British education system
prepares those going into trades such as
plumbing and to reflect on whether we are

doing enough to encourage young people to follow this route.

In my considered opinion, education in the UK was for too long aimed primarily at those who are academically minded, meaning that those who found exams difficult had fewer opportunities to gain qualifications relevant to their needs. I am aware that the government attempted to balance this by introducing Modern Apprenticeships in the early 1990s, but more still needs to be done. This scheme enabled under-25s to choose to enter a profession and train on the job, dividing their week between work and study.

As an example, an apprentice might work with a self-employed plumber, observing and assisting with their work for four days a week. On the remaining day, they would attend a local college to cover the more theoretical side and complete the necessary paperwork that would lead them towards a formal qualification, normally an NVQ (National Vocational Qualification).

Since they were first introduced, Modern Apprenticeships have evolved considerably, with apprentices now able to proceed through three levels of NVQ and with the upper age limit being removed so that they are now open to anybody.

Despite this, there is still a huge shortage of skilled plumbers in the UK. To my mind, this is due to the focus in recent decades on trying to encourage young people to follow their hearts instead of choosing qualifications that will secure them a long-term job. Our education system does not place enough emphasis on the trades that keep our economy running, and jobs such as plumbing are not seen as careers to aspire to. Unless we change this, we will find it increasingly difficult to keep our country functioning.

Yours sincerely,

Thomas Johnson

Audioscript

CD1

TRACK 3

My name's Paul Dummett and I'm one of the authors of the *Keynote* series. I've seen this talk quite a few times and I still get really emotional watching it. I think it has something to do with the kind of overwhelming kindness – love even – that Rita F. Pierson shows her students. Her pupils seem vulnerable or they're from disadvantaged backgrounds ... and that sort of tugs at the heartstrings too. I think it also has to do with her power as an orator – a bit like Martin Luther King Jr. or something – she knows how to use words to make an emotional appeal. For example, when she says 'I've had kids so educationally deficient I could have cried'. Or the bit where she talks about all the former pupils coming spontaneously to her mother's funeral.

I'm a teacher and teacher trainer myself and I absolutely know what she says to be true. The best teachers are the ones who seem to befriend their pupils and win them over – being playful with them, but always showing deep down that they like them as people and want them to do well. I don't understand education systems that put a big emphasis on order and discipline. It seems to me that if you're having to demand respect and good behaviour from your students, then you've probably failed to keep them engaged in other ways. I love the example she gives of the boy who got only two questions right out of twenty and she put a smiley face on his paper and told him he was on a roll. Kids have to feel that you're on their side and rooting for them.

One of the most telling things she says is early on in the talk – that we all know why kids underperform at school: it's basically an accident of birth – being born into poverty or the wrong surroundings. I think that's so true. When you're not fed or clothed properly or your family life is a struggle, your chances of doing well at school are really affected.

Unfortunately, Rita F. Pierson died not long after this talk, but she certainly left a legacy – just as she said her mother did – of the power of human friendship and connection. The talk is called 'Every kid needs a champion'. I think it should be renamed 'Every teacher should see this'.

TRACK 6

A: I know you said you don't go to the cinema that often, but what sort of films do you like?

B: Well, yeah, I'm not that into films to be honest. It's not really my thing, I don't know why. I do like watching a good film, yeah, but I'm not very good at sticking with a film that's not doing it for me. It's sort of odd, I hardly ever watch a film, at home or at the cinema, but I do generally enjoy it when I do watch one, if that makes sense. I do like a good psychological thriller, though, something where you really get involved in trying to work out what's what or where you really start to feel for one of the people, one

of the characters. But I'm not so keen on the more lightweight stuff, that there tends to be a lot of.

A: What sports are you into?

B: I'm a huge rugby fan. My favourite sport by a mile. I'm not really into football. It's OK, but I can take it or leave it. I like the big tournaments, like the World Cup, I get into those. And to be honest any big sporting event, I'll tend to watch if I can, tennis, golf, the Olympics. I'm really into live sport, whatever it is.

A: Do you have any favourite artists?

B: Well, I'm a big fan of Van Gogh. I don't really know why and I'm not an expert at all, but I just like him, his colours and just his feeling for things. Whenever I've seen his actual paintings in a gallery, I'm just sort of transfixed by them. There's something quite enchanting or mesmerizing about them. I can't really get excited about much contemporary art, to be honest. It just doesn't appeal to me at all. I much prefer the older painters and old masters. I quite like Turner as well, especially his seascapes.

TRACK 7

1   One thing I'm good at and one thing I'm not good at? OK, let me think. Well, I play the piano so I guess that's one thing I'm quite good at. But I'm not great at singing. In fact, I'm pretty terrible, actually.

2   Well, I think I'm quite a natural at teaching, to be honest. Well, that's what my students tell me and I do find it quite easy and enjoyable. A born teacher, maybe. But I'm most definitely not a natural when it comes to all the admin side of it, like report writing and record keeping and meetings and that sort of thing. I find that a real chore most of the time.

3   Mmm, let me think. Well, I can tell you one thing that I'm no good at, according to my friends that is, and that's making a cup of tea. Apparently, I can't make a cup of tea to save my life. But it always tastes fine to me, so anyway. But at the same time people say I do have a talent for cooking. I've never learned how to cook properly. I just sort of make it up as I go along, or maybe take a recipe and then do my own thing with it. But people are often saying what a good cook I am.

4   Something I'm good at and bad at? Er, well, I'm pretty good at spending money and I'm pretty hopeless at saving it. Is that OK? Will that do? But seriously, I'm a born spendaholic. Life's too short, you only live once. You can't take it with you and all that. What's money for if it's not for spending?

TRACK 10

My name's Mike Harrison and I'm a teacher trainer and materials writer. I've heard the expression that laughter is the best medicine, so I was interested to watch this TED Talk exploring how medicine intersects with

another creative pursuit – music. The person who gives this talk, Robert Gupta, seems to embody this space in between medicine and music – as he was caught between a career as a doctor and as a violinist.

Certainly I know that music has a powerful impact on people and their emotions, but music therapy is still something of a mystery to me. Gupta talks about his medical training and at the same time pursuing his passion of playing the violin.

I think the key point that Gupta makes about music is about its potential to help people in really dire circumstances. Using the example of acting as a violin teacher to a homeless man in Skid Row, Gupta shows us how music can give society's most marginalized some sort of hope that they have not been forgotten.

I love the combination of the talk and the music in this TED Talk – I think it adds something more to the experience of listening to Gupta than if he were just delivering it as a lecture.

Finding out more about how music and sounds affect us is something that does really interest me, in particular how it can stimulate our imagination and creativity. It's something that I've experimented a little with in my own career as a language teacher.

I can't claim to be much of a musician myself – I learned the clarinet in my early teens, but never kept at it – but I really agree with the idea that music has this power to inspire people in many different ways. I think it's sad that most of the time we take music and other sounds for granted, without considering the impact, or potential impact, that it can have on our lives and the lives of people around us, particularly when it can be so effective at articulating our emotions.

I see the sun in your smile
Watching it rise in your eyes
See the dusty road ahead
Stretching out for miles and miles
Sick and tired of skipping the stones
Dodging the holes in the road
I need a helping hand
To help me shoulder this load
Do, do you, well, wouldn't you
Do the same in my shoes?
I wouldn't do, just couldn't do
Another mile without you
Another mile without you

TRACK 13

I've spent most of my life trying to make a career out of being a songwriter. I've had a few successes – a couple of songs that have made it onto albums – but no big hit and it's been really hard sticking at it. I've often had to take other jobs to make ends meet – waiting tables at restaurants, boring clerical jobs and so on. A few years ago I was about to give up, partly 'cos I have a young family now and I just thought it's unfair to expect my partner to shoulder the burden of earning enough to keep us all going. But then by chance I read an article in a magazine while I was waiting to have my hair cut about the author, J.K. Rowling. I'd heard that she hadn't had it easy, but reading the details of her life gave me new impetus. She got the idea for the Harry Potter books when she was coming back from London on the train. But, soon after she started writing it up, her whole life was thrown into turmoil. Her mum died of multiple sclerosis at the age of 45. Feeling kind of lost, she moved to Portugal to teach English, got married to a local and had a daughter. But the marriage failed and she moved back to the UK, where she lived on welfare and looked after her child, writing when she could find the time – mostly in local cafés. During this period she went through terrible bouts of depression, but all the time she kept focussed on bringing that good idea that she'd had to fruition and the rest … well, we all know what happened. And I thought, well, she got it right; she stuck at what she loved doing and what she believed in ... and that's what I should do. And now, actually I'm on the brink of something that could be quite big. I've teamed up with a singer and we're writing songs together and we're getting a lot of interest.

TRACK 14

Plagiarism is when someone copies or paraphrases someone else's work or ideas without full acknowledgement. You need to be aware that the university routinely checks submitted work for evidence of plagiarism and that all essays, assignments and presentations must fully acknowledge other people's work, ideas or data. This is whether they are obtained from published texts, such as books and journals, from unpublished text, such as from lectures, or other students' work or from websites. And on that subject, we strongly advise against using open-source websites such as Wikipedia that have unverifiable content. In the event of plagiarism, you will be given a formal warning and have to rewrite your essay. The worst case scenario is that you risk being kicked off your course and thrown out of the university.

To avoid plagiarism, the best thing is to become familiar with the principles of good academic practice as soon as you start your university studies. That way, you'll more quickly develop an awareness of the requirements and the dos and don'ts of academic writing. Avoiding plagiarism is more than making sure your citations and references are all correct, although it is advisable to thoroughly check them through before you submit your work. Nor is it about changing enough words so your paraphrase will not be noticed. Avoid simply using a few synonyms and changing the word order. The chances are that you will be caught out. Take time and make the effort to make wholesale changes and express the ideas in your own words. It can be a fine line, so if you're not sure, ask your tutor. Following his or her advice will ensure that your work is plagiarism-free.

TRACK 16

My name's Lucy Constable and I'm a Regional Marketing Executive for National Geographic Learning. I couldn't really tell from the title what this talk was going to be about and I had to watch it a couple of times before I got 'the message'. But I didn't mind re-watching, because I found it really fascinating. Mira Calix is a composer and she talks about how she uses music to change people's perceptions of their environment. Actually, I put that badly. It's not her intention to *change* their perceptions, but to *add* to them.

TRACK 17

My name's Lucy Constable and I'm a Regional Marketing Executive for National Geographic Learning. I couldn't really tell from the title what this talk was going to be about and I had to watch it a couple of times before I got 'the message'. But I didn't mind re-watching, because I found it really fascinating. Mira Calix is a composer and she talks about how she uses music to change people's perceptions of their environment. Actually, I put that badly. It's not her intention to *change* their perceptions, but ... to *add* to them.

She worked on a project to transform an old railway tunnel in the city of Bath in England into a commuter walkway and leisure space. It was a really dark and uninviting space, but – along with lighting and design specialists – she made walking through it a great experience. So, as people pass along the tunnel, they trigger light and music installations. She's very open about the fact that we don't really understand exactly how music (and colour and light) affect people's emotions. Instead, she just tries to coax a certain *kind* of emotion out of her audience, leaving the precise interpretation to them.

What I found really thought-provoking was the idea that there are things – sights, sounds, smells – that evoke certain emotions like happiness or sadness, but evoking them doesn't necessarily make us *feel* that way ourselves; it just makes us *think* of those feelings.

When I was in Lisbon about fifteen years ago I went to a bar where a woman was singing *Fado*. *Fado* is a deeply melancholic genre of music – it's about a yearning for things or people lost or things that have disappeared into the past. Her singing didn't make me feel a sense of yearning myself, but I really felt her emotion – in fact, I can still feel it to this day; it was so powerful.

So, ... I think Mira Calix's message is that we mustn't try too hard to analyze or try to be too scientific about music and emotion, because sometimes feelings are beyond words and explanation. That's what I took from it anyhow …

TRACK 20

1 In the work place, the conventional wisdom is that your computer monitor should be about 50–60 cm away. In actual fact, the best distance is as far away as possible while you are still able to read what's on the screen. The 50–60 cm recommendation is probably too near and could be damaging to the eyes over time.

2 Supposedly, we should be drinking eight glasses of water a day. But in reality the amount we need depends on a number of factors, such as what food we eat, and varies from person to person. It seems that this figure was thought up basically as part of an awareness-raising campaign and eight glasses is a nice manageable and easy-to-remember number.

3 It has often been said that Albert Einstein failed mathematics at school. But this, however, is not the case. On the face of it, Einstein was actually very good at maths as a child. He did, however, apparently fail the entrance exam into polytechnic school in 1895. But, at 16, he was two years younger than the other students at the time and he allegedly scored highly in the mathematics and science sections.

4 The popular belief is that Sherlock Holmes used to use the phrase 'Elementary, my dear Watson' when explaining a crime he was solving to his partner Dr Watson. The truth is, however, that the character never actually said those words, not in the original books at least. The words 'my dear Watson' and 'elementary' did both appear a few lines apart in the Sherlock Holmes novel *The Crooked Man*, but they never in fact appeared together as in the famous misquote.

TRACK 24

I'm Nick Yeaton and I'm an Operations Analyst at the Boston office of National Geographic Learning. I watched Emily Balcetis's talk about how perception is ultimately subjective, and that, at times, our 'mind's eye' may actually work against us in life. She explains this by describing an experiment that she conducted with her team examining the connection between fitness, motivation and goals. In the experiment they asked participants to visualize their goal or finish line. The results of the experiment demonstrated that a person's motivation can affect their perception; for example: the finish line in the experiment seemed further away to the unmotivated participants than the motivated ones. The motivated participants also moved at a quicker pace during the experiment, implying that the exercise felt easier to them – the suggestion being that we ought to adopt what the speaker calls an 'eye on the prize' strategy in order to achieve better results in our exercise programmes. More than that the 'eye on the prize' strategy could be transferable to other areas of daily life, meaning that a similar strategy could potentially help people cultivate other healthy habits in their lives, such as stopping smoking or eating more healthily.

Personally, I found this research and these results very compelling, mainly because I am a person who sets great store by fitness and a healthy lifestyle. I found it interesting how the 'eye on the prize' strategy could be used by those who need help adhering to a fitness regimen – who lack the requisite willpower to see such a programme through. I have to say, I'm also kind of curious about what other similar strategies could be developed and deployed to alter a person's perception beneficially in other areas of their lives, such as their work or relationships.

In the past, when my motivation was lacking, I used my own variations of the 'eye on the prize' strategy to continue lifting weights. Appreciating my own progress kept me focussed on my ultimate goals in weightlifting: the 'prize' of personal records each month made the early morning, bleary eyes trips to the weight room possible. Incremental improvements to my levels of strength have been 'prizes' unto themselves, and they have allowed me to remain focussed on my ultimate goals in weightlifting.

TRACK 27

There are various parallels made between Edwardian postcards and modern social-media messaging. One interesting area is the reaction of the establishment at the time to the phenomenon. Some thought that such postcards were insulting in themselves because they showed that the writer could not be bothered to send a proper letter. Also, because the messages were written in informal language, people worried about its effects on literacy, particularly among the younger generation. That is quite a common theme among educators nowadays when they discuss text messaging. *The Times* newspaper and other commentators referred to the postcards as 'vulgar', and 'destructive of style' and 'a threat to standards'. Another concern, perhaps more legitimate, was that the authorities were unable to control the sending of messages which were defamatory or libellous. Effectively, you could say what you liked about someone in a postcard without any comeback or legal implications. This has an obvious parallel in the struggles of governments today to control content on the World Wide Web.

TRACK 28

Conversation 1
A: Bad news. There's a problem with the RBC deal. I think we need to discuss this as soon as possible. How about Friday?
B: I'm not available Friday. Thursday suits me though if that's any good for you. Or we can discuss it over the phone if you like.
A: No, I'd rather we meet in person. But, yeah, Thursday's good. Shall we say my office, two-ish?
B: Oh, by the way, I said I'd tell Julia when we were meeting. Shall I let her know?
A: Sure. Or I can give her a ring if you like.

Conversation 2
A: Can I give you a hand with that? It looks heavy.
B: That's very good of you. Thanks.
A: Not at all. Don't mention it.

Conversation 3
A: Can I have a quick word?
B: Sure. What is it?
A: My mum's gone into hospital. I'm going to have to go up and see her, which'll mean taking a day or two off, if that's OK.
B: Oh, sorry to hear that. And, of course. Just let me know.
A: Yeah, she's been ill for a while now, actually.
B: Oh, I didn't realize. Look, just take a couple of days off. We'll be fine here.

Conversation 4
A: I can give you a lift to the station if you like.
B: Are you sure? I don't want to put you out.
A: No, it's fine. I need to go that way anyway to the bike shop, so I can drop you off on my way.

Conversation 5
A: I'm going to grab a drink. Can I get you anything?
B: Yeah, a coffee thanks.
A: Latte, cappuccino ...?
B: I don't mind, either's fine. Thanks.

Conversation 6
A: This is to say thanks for helping me the other day.
B: Oh, really, you shouldn't have.
A: No, it was a big help. And much appreciated.

Conversation 7
A: I'm meeting Jenny in that new bar on Jackson Street this evening. Fancy joining us?
B: I'd love to, but I'm busy this evening. Shame, I haven't seen Jenny for ages.
A: OK, never mind. Another time.
B: Yeah, for sure. And say hi from me.

TRACK 30

The first thing I noticed about this talk, before I even clicked on the play button, was a picture of the TED speaker and how young he was. I've seen quite a few TED Talks, but I was immediately curious to learn what such a young speaker was going to talk about.

Richard Turere has essentially been given an opportunity to tell an audience how he managed to solve a problem. What I found impressive was that he, at such a young age, was given the responsibility of looking after his father's livestock. He was then faced with a major issue and set about trying to work out a way to resolve it.

TRACK 31

My name's Ruth Goodman and I'm a freelance editor. I've been working on two of the *Keynote* Workbooks.

The first thing I noticed about this talk, before I even clicked on the play button, was a picture of the TED speaker and how young he was. I've seen quite a few TED Talks, but I was immediately curious to learn what such a young speaker was going to talk about.

Richard Turere has essentially been given an opportunity to tell an audience how he managed to solve a problem. What I found impressive was that he, at such a young age, was given the responsibility of looking after his father's livestock. He was then faced with a major issue and set about trying to work out a way to resolve it.

What's nice about his talk is how he takes us through his process of trial and error. He tells us about the failures along the way and what he learned from them. We hear how he analyzes the problem, comes up with some ideas and then works towards a solution.

Whilst I can't really relate to the speaker's experience of being given such a huge responsibility at a young age, what I admire is his determination to learn and not to give up on a challenge. I often want to find a solution to things and always try to find a way through them rather than giving up and becoming down about a difficult situation.

I'd like to know a bit more about Richard Turere's background to get a better understanding of where he got his incredible confidence from. I'd find it really frightening to be in front of such a large audience. How did he get to be so mature? I'd also love to know what made him such a curious child. Was he motivated by not wanting to let his father and the rest of his family down or is he naturally good at working things out? Finally, I think he has an amazing ability to be resourceful. Is that a result of always having only limited resources to fall back on? What did his family teach him that meant he was able to come up with such a great invention?

The talk not only looks at the process of problem-solving, but the speaker inspires people to want to cultivate the same personal qualities of maturity, resourcefulness and curiosity.

TRACK 33

Conversation 1
A: I read something the other day that said that at least a third of an average landfill is made up of packaging material.
B: I can well believe that. I would've thought it was more, to be honest.

Conversation 2
A: Someone the other day was saying that Americans throw away about 50 million plastic bottles every hour.
B: I'd take that with a pinch of salt. That'd be about one in every six people using a plastic bottle at any one time. I'd be surprised if that was the case.

Conversation 3
A: Apparently, over 80% of all household waste can be recycled.
B: That doesn't surprise me at all.

Conversation 4
A: I read the other day that thousands of animal species are becoming extinct every day.
B: I very much doubt that. We were doing something on this at college the other day and no-one really knows. But it's

more likely to be in the low hundreds at the absolute most, and more likely much less, and that's animals and plants.

Conversation 5
A: When I was little we used to say that if there are lots of holly berries on the trees and if trees lose their leaves late in the year, then it's going to be a bad winter.

B: That's just an old wives' tale. I don't think there's any truth in that.

Conversation 6
A: I read the other day that half the world's oxygen is produced by plankton in the oceans.

B: I suspect that's true. Especially when you think over 70% of the earth is water.

Conversation 7
A: We should all drink eight glasses of water a day, right?

B: That's a common misconception, actually. I was talking to my doctor friend about this only the other day. He was saying that each of us needs a different amount, some more and some less, and it depends on things like our size, what we eat, how much we exercise and what our metabolism is like. He thinks it's just a pretty random figure.

A: Well, it was in an ad I saw the other day for some new bottled water.

B: Well, that's what they'd have you believe, isn't it? But, yeah, I think we should all drink probably more than we do, though.

Conversation 8
A: They say the single biggest way we can help the environment is to change our habits when it comes to using energy and electricity. Walking or cycling instead of driving, turning off lights and sockets, putting more clothing on instead of turning the heating up and so on.

B: Yeah, I think they've got that spot on. But unfortunately it's a bit easier said than done, though.

TRACK 37

My name's Karen Richardson and I'm an ELT materials writer and business English trainer. My first reaction to this talk was not at all sceptical. I just thought – what a fantastic idea! But then I began to wonder about its impact on deforestation and about how safe a wooden skyscraper would be during an earthquake. So I was pleased when the speaker addressed and alleviated both these fears in his talk.

Personally, I wouldn't want to live in a wooden skyscraper – but that's not because of the wood – I love wood – it's because I wouldn't want to live in a skyscraper at all. However, if the need for new urban housing is really set to increase at the rate the speaker describes, then, for the sake of the planet, I really hope that new multi-storey homes will be made of wood.

I can completely relate to what he says about people hugging the wooden columns in his

buildings. For me, wood is a warm, natural, welcoming material, and one that I need to have around me. I travel half an hour each week to go to a yoga class which is held in a completely wood-built studio, not because the teacher is better than the ones locally, but because the building itself provides me with a wonderful sense of well-being.

And after working for three years on 'temporary' IKEA plastic desks, I was so pleased to take delivery of new wooden desks made to measure for my office by a local carpenter. I can't begin to describe how much this has improved my work space – mentally and in a tactile way.

There are two questions that I'd like to ask the speaker: one is financial and concerns the length of time it takes even young trees to grow to the size needed to mass-produce the timber panels he talks about – he mentions ten to fifteen years. How would he convince foresters and potential new growers to wait that long before they see a return on their investment? The other question is more of a psychological one: I live in an old house that, although it has been renovated and adapted many times during its life, still cracks and creaks and makes other loud and sudden unsettling noises as the wood expands and contracts – especially during weather and temperature changes. Our loud house only has two floors and an attic. I wonder what these noises would sound like if they were multiplied by twenty storeys.

TRACK 40
A: Would you say Henry Hoover's innovative?

B: Well, yes – there's nothing else like it, is there?

A: That's not the point. It's supposed to achieve a harmony between form and function that didn't exist before.

B: Well, I'd say it did. Also, it's completely obvious what it is.

A: OK and is it aesthetic?

B: Definitely ... and fun.

A: What about understandable and unobtrusive?

B: Yes, its functions are all really obvious, but actually by painting a face on it, they've kind of made it jump out at you haven't they?

A: Yes – I'm not sure I agree with Rams that a product shouldn't be showy.

B: So does that mean it isn't honest?

A: No, I don't think so. It's not like they're pretending it's anything else; they've just given it some character

B: Are they long-lasting?

A: Too early to tell – I've only had mine a year.

B: But the design has been around for ages.

A: Yes, it has, so in that sense yes.

B: Is the design thorough down to the last detail?

A: Can't really comment on that – I wasn't the designer.

B: No ... I see that. What about environmentally friendly?

A: Umm ... I don't think it's any more efficient that other vacuum cleaners, is it?

B: Not as far as I know.

A: And lastly is the design pure and simple?

B: Definitely. There are no frills or gadgets in a Henry Hoover.

TRACK 41

Conversation 1
A: Do you find that working at home makes it easier or harder to be self-disciplined? I imagine there are a lot of potential distractions.

B: Well, that depends, I guess. When the work's flowing, it's easy to stay focussed. But sometimes, when things aren't progressing so well, for whatever reason, then yeah, it's a bit easier to get distracted or to go off and do something else. But, in a word, I think I'm pretty self-disciplined.

Conversation 2
A: In what environment do you work best, would you say?

B: Mmm, I suppose I'd say, like, a small office or workspace environment, say with two or three people.

A: And why do you say that?

B: Well, I've worked in open plan, and I don't find it so conducive. In my experience, they tend to be a bit unnaturally quiet, no-one wanting to disturb anyone else. But in a small office it's easy to get your head down but, as long as you all get on, can be quite interactive as well.

Conversation 3
A: In a situation where you, for some reason, think someone else in the company is making, or has made, a bad decision or is not performing as you think they should, what would you do?

B: My first instinct is to say that I'd keep quiet and see how things develop. It might not be my place to get involved. But if it directly affects me in some negative way, then I think I'd probably have to talk to someone about it. Someone above us.

A: And how would you go about doing this?

B: Well, I suppose it depends on the situation. But I guess I'd ask for a meeting and explain my concerns.

Conversation 4
A: And one final question. Imagine that you're on a deserted island and can take with you just one book, what would it be?

B: Mm, that's a tricky question. Let me have a think. Er, can I take a blank book, with empty pages, like an exercise book?

A: Er, yes. Why not.

B: OK, then a book with blank pages, so I could write in it. Assuming I could also have a pen, that is.

CD2

TRACK 3

My name's Laura Le Dréan and I'm an executive editor at National Geographic Learning. I believe Yassmin Abdel-Magied's message is that we need to challenge our subconscious biases and look for ways of overcoming them. She forces us to examine our biases by cleverly changing her outfit while talking. And she asks us to look past our initial preconceptions of people who do not share our experience or looks and to embrace diversity. I love this message – it resonates loud and clear with me. The unconscious bias is something I have grappled with for a long time. We all have these inner biases and, no matter how much we realize intellectually that they are unfounded and wrong, we still see people who are not like us as 'different'. And 'different' often implies 'less' of some attribute.

Yassmin's talk makes me question how I can still have biases and how I can overcome them. I have worked in the field of second-language learning for over 35 years, exposed to students and educators from many different cultures and perspectives, so I have no excuse. I have had the privilege of a good education and a rich, multi-cultural life. I should not have biases and yet I still sometimes have the gut reaction of 'my way' being the right way versus 'their way'.

Just last week, I was sitting next to a Saudi woman on a plane. She was wearing an abaya and hijab and all I could see were her hands and eyes. I was wearing an abaya, but my head was not covered. Rather than saying hello as I sat down, I took out my iPad and thought, 'She probably thinks I am immoral and bad'. Then during the flight, we hit turbulence and my neighbour was clearly nervous and upset. I reached out and took her hand and tried to reassure her that we were safe. She was very grateful and thanked me. In that short episode, she had become a person with the same needs as me.

I was particularly struck by one simple sentence in Yassmin's talk: People are not born with equal opportunity. I travel all around the world and when I see people really living hand to mouth, without access to education or basic health, I feel a huge weight, a sadness. I feel the injustice of poverty and want.

I love Yassmin's simple and practical suggestion to mentor someone who comes from a different background as a solution to these unconscious biases, because it can be enlightening for both the person mentored and the mentor themselves. It's brilliant and something I can do tomorrow.

TRACK 7

A: On the whole, most people on social media sites like Facebook, Instagram and Twitter, well going by my friends at least, post pretty interesting stuff, and in moderation. It's a great way to know what people are up to and to keep in touch. On the other hand, there are some people who seem to think that we are interested in all sorts of little details about their life, things that are obviously important to them, but I think there's a lack of awareness of how mundane, self-indulgent or me-oriented it can sometimes seem – you know, this is what I'm doing at the moment or look what a great social life I have. Admittedly, we all, including me, probably post stuff that tends to reflect on us and our interests and project a certain image of us, and maybe irritate some people, but I try to be mindful of this and personally only post things, usually a photo or a light news item that I know at least some of my friends will appreciate, once every few weeks or even months. Anyway, because of that, I've started to unfollow people when they're endlessly posting this kind of stuff. However, having said that, judging by the number of likes and comments people get, there are certainly a lot of people who do like this kind of thing and it might be me who's missing the point.

B: By and large, we tend to see the press and the media in our own country as being pretty impartial and factually accurate and have faith in what we're being told. As a consequence, I think we tend generally not to question what we see or hear in the news, most of the time at any rate. Having said that, of course the different publications and news organizations within a country will present things differently with their own bias and so on, which is quite understandable, but I think most people are aware of that, as far as the press in their own countries is concerned. However, I know from being in other countries, that the take on particularly international stories, can be really very different from country to country and region to region, which I suppose isn't surprising. But on top of that, versions of events can sometimes be directly contradictory and can even go as far as criticizing the press in other countries and accusing them of distorting things or, let's say, even not being truthful. I've been in other countries when major global news stories have broken, or in the aftermath, and have at times been really surprised and, to be honest, quite shocked by the different viewpoints and what are seen as the facts. As a result, I've had discussions with people who, for instance, have insisted that certain photos that I just didn't question for a moment are fakes and that these things never happened. Anyway, that said, it's pretty interesting and I guess pretty central to how the world is seen. And a range of views and interpretations is probably inevitable and probably a good thing in some ways. But there is a fine line between interpretation and opinion and distortion and propaganda, which can be quite damaging. I'd like to think, though, that the press here in my country is fair and accurate. But that's no doubt what most people think.

TRACK 9

… I was blown away by both his confidence and obvious passion for the controversial topic of nutrition. Birke starts by summarizing the key problems, which include false advertising, GMOs, pesticides, and preservatives. This is a very real problem – we only have to look at statistics showing the dramatic increases in diabetes, cancer, heart problems, and other diseases to prove the serious health threats among our generation.

TRACK 10

My name's Paul Grainger and I'm the National Geographic Learning Product Manager for Asia. One of my favourite TED Talks is Birke Baehr's 'What's wrong with our food system'.

This is the first time I've watched a TED Talk delivered by a kid of eleven years, and I was blown away by both his confidence and obvious passion for the controversial topic of nutrition. Birke starts by summarizing what he sees as the key problems, which include false advertising, GMOs, pesticides, and preservatives. These things have very real public health consequences – we only have to look at statistics showing the dramatic increases in diabetes, cancer, heart problems, and other diseases, to prove the serious health threats among our generation. My personal experience, over the last few years, fully supports the notion that 'You are what you eat', but the sad thing is that many people are turning a blind eye to this as they refuse to even slightly change their eating habits. I love Birke's quote '…it seems to me that we can either pay the farmer, or we can pay the hospital.' So true.

In the second half of his short talk, Birke offers some practical solutions to help us make more informed food choices. It's amazing how this child of eleven years has not only figured out how to work around the system, by opening his eyes and mind, but also acts on his words. I was inspired enough to read through the comments on the discussion page and saw a post from his mother saying that it was Birke who was the one in their family that insisted they change their eating, consuming and purchasing habits based on his own research. He led. They followed. I think this speaks volumes about him.

Finally, anyone wise enough to want to become an organic farmer instead of an NFL football player in order to have a greater impact on the world is OK in my book. This kid rocks!

TRACK 13

Using scraps and items that would normally just be thrown away is an excellent way to cut down on food waste and to come up with novel recipes at the same time. I was inspired by my grandmother who was brought up in harder times and never let anything go to waste. If I'm honest, I used to find some of the things she made a bit off-putting, but now I see the sense in it, I've revised my opinion completely.

The first thing is making chewy crisps out of vegetable peelings. I like to do this particularly with potato peelings; put them in a baking tray, sprinkle some olive oil on them, then shake them around a bit, add salt and pepper and bake them in a hot oven for 25 minutes. They make a great snack.

You can also use apple peelings – and the cores of apples too – to make delicious tea. Just sit them in hot water for three or four minutes then strain off the water into a cup.

One of the biggest sources of waste is leftover stuff in the fridge – bits of cheese, tired-looking vegetables, etc. What I do with these is to put them all in a large baking tray, beat four or five eggs and add them to the vegetables and cheese, then bake in the oven for twenty minutes and hey presto – you've got a tasty frittata (a bit like a Spanish omelette without the potato).

Leftover veg and meat can also be used to make a stir fry – just chop into small pieces and cook in a wok with a small amount of oil.

Lastly, never throw away old meat bones or chicken carcasses. If you boil them up in water and add a few herbs and a bit of seasoning, they make a very healthy soup. Russians swear by their daily helping of chicken broth!

TRACK 14

Speaker 1

Well, I'm vegetarian, so I have to be careful when I'm somewhere I don't know so well. You know, to make sure I don't eat any meat or fish. So, I guess on the whole I'm pretty cautious with what I eat and I generally like to stick with what I know and take the safe option. I *am* happy to experiment and give something new a go, but I do need to know 100% that's it's OK for me. On a number of occasions, in different countries, I've been told something is vegetarian and it turns out it's got fish in it or ham. I think the concept of being vegetarian is quite different in different cultures. So, I generally like to play it safe. But if I'm confident that something is OK, then I'm happy to try it out.

Speaker 2

I'd say I'm quite adventurous when it comes to food and always open to new experiences. I love tasting new food that I've never had before. That's one of the great things about travel, one of the things I really look forward to; new food and new tastes. I suppose I'm generally happy to try anything, though I might draw the line at some of the more extreme things, like some of the things they eat in some parts of the world like dog or brain. I've been to a few countries and I've seen, what to me at least, are some pretty

grim things in markets. But, as I said, it's considered quite normal there.

Speaker 3

I think I'm really quite conservative when it comes to food. I think people of my generation are. We grew up with much less variety than we have today and I suppose that's reflected in our tastes. I suppose I'm quite traditional in my tastes. I generally like to take the safe option, something I know, like meat and two veg. That's a proper meal to me. I'm not so keen on rice and pasta and fancy things like that. We just didn't have it when I was younger. No, when it comes to food, I wouldn't generally eat anything too different. It'd be a waste if I didn't like it.

TRACK 18

My name's Karen Spiller, and I've put together the writing and editorial teams and worked with them to develop the *Keynote* course. I liked this talk. It starts off modestly and quietly and then it builds – a bit like Eric Whitacre's own career – until it reaches a point of real magic. I've seen a few talks about viral videos and YouTube sensations and I have to say, while the content of the videos themselves can be amusing, often they're fairly inane and trivial; a bit like celebrity culture, the age of the internet meme throws up some pretty irrelevant objects for our attention. But this is anything but inane. I don't want to give too much away, suffice to say it features a collaborative online singing project that has amazing results. Eric Whitacre, perhaps like a lot of people, wanted to be a pop star as a kid, but he ended up joining a college choir and getting hooked on classical choral music. From there he had the idea of getting people to sing online for him, but actually he had no great technical knowledge or ability to bring all this together, but then one of the online community just popped up and offered to help put it all together. And that's the bit of the story – and the aspect of the Internet – that I find most powerful …. Well, there are two aspects really: that many people have a much more accessible outlet for their creativity than they had in the past and also the spirit of community – the Internet's this place where people love to co-operate and co-create. I think that's great. I have a comedian friend who wanted to perform at the Edinburgh Festival, but felt uncertain about his material … When he put a post about his predicament on Facebook, not only did people come forward with support and suggestions, someone actually started a funding campaign to finance his stay in Edinburgh. And he went, and his routine went down really well, and ultimately it wasn't about the money – it was just about making connections with people – and I think that's what Whitacre's message is as well.

TRACK 21

A: Hey, listen to this. 'The compendium of Ice Bucket challenge videos officially reached the 1 billion views milestone yesterday, making it, according to sources at YouTube, one of the biggest

internet video memes of all time.' Well, I find that rather encouraging.

B: What – those videos where celebrities get a bucket of icy cold water tipped over them?

A: Yes ….

B: Sorry, in what way is that encouraging?

A: Don't you know about it? It's a challenge that people get sponsored to do to raise money for charity – I can't remember what the Americans call the condition – but it's what we call MND, motor neurone disease. It's amazing – they've raised hundreds of millions of dollars for research into a cure.

B: Oh, I didn't know that.

A: Yes, that's why I said 'encouraging' … There are some memes that try to make a difference. I know most are a bit shallow – they just comment on a fashion or a funny thing someone said. But some try to make people aware of things that aren't right: like the 'That's none of my business' series of memes that tried to show – in a humorous way, of course – that it was wrong to put details of people's personal lives up on the Internet.

B: Oh, I know the ones you mean – with Kermit the Frog?

A: Yeah, that's right. But actually there are very few like the Ice Bucket one that actually *do* something about a problem. I mean it's all very well to go on about being 'aware' that something's wrong – you know, that MND is a bad condition to have – but ultimately, It's got to be meaningful.

TRACK 22

Speaker 1:

Well, personally, I think that there should ideally be freedom of expression and people should, by and large, be able to post whatever they like and have whatever online presence they want. However, going beyond the everyday uses of the Internet, there is a very serious element to this and I don't think there should be absolute freedom, insofar as there should be limits to what is acceptable. What I mean is, if there is no censorship at all, there can be a lot of people promoting quite extreme ideas, which can have a very negative influencing effect and can be quite inciting. Considering that this can have some very serious consequences, I really can see the need for censorship, or monitoring and blocking certain individuals or organizations, at least. Also, as far as the individual is concerned, some people can be victims of abusive content and things like flaming, you know, insulting people online, and cyber-bullying. But allowing for the fact that no-one actually controls the Internet as such, I'm not so sure how we can actually control things, really. I mean who do you censor, and how exactly? But, in a word, I'd say that censorship would probably be a good thing.

Speaker 2:

Well, put simply, as far as I'm concerned, censoring the Internet would be a violation of people's freedom of speech. And this would actually be illegal in my country, the USA, where the First Amendment prohibits any laws that infringe freedom of speech. So, why should it be any different with the Internet? However, the real issue for me is that internet censorship could open the door for the powers that be, those doing the censoring, to follow their own agenda, whatever that may be. So, who's going to oversee or censor that? That to me is the main issue. I know in some countries, internet content is controlled, inasmuch as the government allows or disallows access to certain websites, but I think in some cases it's quite easy to get round that if you have the inclination. So, basically, I think we need to trust individuals to self-monitor and take control themselves of how they use the Internet. I think the vast majority of people are aware of the dangers and potential negative influences and will be sensible in their approach. I think we just have to accept that that's the reality and that it isn't really going to change.

TRACK 25

I'm Leila Hishmeh and I'm the media editor for National Geographic Learning. I imagine that most people who watch this talk for the first time have probably never pondered their own two selves. Watching it made me question how common it is for people to choose their 'eulogy' self for fear of not fulfilling their egotistical side, or the self that is more concerned with money, material things, power, and control. I think in this way the talk provokes an important dialogue … and consideration of what is an individual's definition of success and how that may evolve over time.

I am most curious about exploring the issue of the average person's ability to balance their two selves. I think, in practice, this is a tall order for the majority of people. Balancing your two lives is a dynamic and often baffling task. I am also interested to better understand David Brooks's take on how charitable and selfless acts (volunteerism, for example) can help strengthen one's understanding of the importance of 'the other side' of one's life.

I think many people will find the topic very relatable: for example, those with more than one job, working parents, driven and hard-working people with a variety of interests. I would also be very curious to analyze reactions to this topic according to people's different ages and level of work experience. I actually think the talk may be more important or pertinent for a younger generation who are in the process of trying to determine their career or life paths.

TRACK 29

A: How were your students' 'What's success?' essays? Did you get any good answers?
B: Yeah, quite a few, actually. You know – I'm always amazed at how mature some of the answers are. I'm sure I wouldn't have written anything quite so thoughtful at the age of seventeen – maybe I would, but I doubt it …
A: Why … what sort of thing did they say?
B: Well, actually there was one in particular struck me like that – Anna Janska
A: Oh, yes, I know … with the brother in year 8. …
B: Yeah, that's her … she pointed out that to be truly successful in life you have to keep reassessing your view of what success means, because a true definition of success not only varies from person to person, it also develops and changes throughout your life. For someone of seventeen, I think that's a pretty incredible realization. I mean I'm 42 and I'm just coming to terms with that idea now …
A: Yes, I think we all get to that point, don't we … when our ambitions need to be modified …
B: No, I didn't mean it exactly like that. I meant our priorities – when what you once considered to be important becomes less important, like for example, when you think your career is everything and then you have children and the whole world changes …There was another essay that picked up on that theme, talking about their mum who had been a successful athlete …

TRACK 31

Conversation 1
A: How did it go with Silvia? Did you manage to get things sorted?
B: Yeah, it's all sorted now. It was just one big misunderstanding.

Conversation 2
A: Did you have any luck getting that extension for your assignment?
B: Well, it could've been better. I got an extra couple of days, until the end of the week, but I really need a bit more than that.

Conversation 3
A: How did your exam go?
B: Mmm, not great, to be honest. I made a bit of a mess of it, actually.

Conversation 4
A: How did you get on with booking those flights?
B: Well, we're getting there. I think I've narrowed it down, but none of them are that good. They've all got quite a long stopover. I'll show you them later. Tell me what you think.

Conversation 5
A: Did you get anywhere with that refund?
B: As well as could be expected, I guess. They agreed to refund the flight but not the hotel or anything else. They say they're not liable. It's in the small print apparently.

Conversation 6
A: How was the meeting? Did it go OK?
B: It all went very smoothly, thanks. They liked the idea, so we're going to meet again in a couple of weeks to flesh out some of the detail.

TRACK 33

Before watching *The child-driven education* I'd never come across the TED speaker Sugata Mitra – heard his theories of education before – but I have to say that he was, his talk immediately grabbed my attention.

TRACK 34

My name is Harry Cullinane and I work for the Italian book publisher and distributor, ELI. Before watching *The child-driven education* I'd never come across the TED speaker Sugata Mitra – heard his theories of education before – but I have to say that he was, his talk immediately grabbed my attention. The ideas he put forward, it was at the same time entertaining, compelling and most of all, extremely credible.

What did he talk about? His own experiences of providing children with the bare necessities for learning. So, a teacher, a classroom with some textbooks and a board to write on, you might say. And of course, you would be wrong, as Sugata provided the children with nothing more than a computer with a link to the web. And the results were outstanding. More importantly, the results were outstanding no matter the circumstances of the child, be it the speaker's 'Hole in the Wall' approach used in some of the slums of the larger Indian cities or sitting in a modern classroom in the UK. In my mind, there is no doubt as to the efficacy of his approach as we see another example of how he carried out the same experiments in Turin, Italy, where the ten-year-olds had no command of English, with similar positive results.

The point he is making is clear to all. That how we approach educating our children has to be …. that we have to redefine it. By taking the approach even further with his SOLE concept (Self Organized Learning Environment) the results were even more self-evident. Teachers take note, because the implications could be far-reaching!

It is all the more intriguing because Sugata has demonstrated time and again that children learning by this approach are then more than capable of passing standard tests and examinations. I am excited to see how Sugata's project will play out, his vision of making schooling available to all children who currently have no access to a school through the use of cloud networks. Fascinating!

TRACK 36

P = presenter, J = Jordan, G = Gareth
P: OK, we have our next caller, Jordan, an anthropology master's student from Manchester, on the line. Hello, Jordan.
J: Hi, there.
P: So, do you have advice to give or are you looking for advice?
J: No, I'm … well, I'm in a situation where I was functioning pretty well, being efficient and on it, but I've kind of lost it. These days I'm not concentrating

properly and, even in social situations, I feel distracted: for example, often I can't remember people's names or how to tell a joke ….

P: OK, so how did this change come about, exactly? Can you tell us a bit more about your situation?

J: Yeah, … I'm a second year graduate student. My first year went really well, but, as the work has built up … um … basically I've been working so hard in the last few months, sitting at my laptop for six, seven, eight hours at a time to finish assignments – not to mention trying to manage all the rest of my life – and then getting to bed at two or three in the morning, I think it's had a really negative effect on my memory and concentration and, like I say, so much else, like how I interact with people. And I don't really know if it's permanent damage that I've done to my brain or if there's something I can do about it …

G: Can I come in here?

P: Of course.

G: I think what's happening is that you're letting the pressure of your assignments interfere with everything else you do – your sleep habits, certainly, and, I suspect, also your eating and social time too. Am I right?

J: Well, I'm not seeing many friends, but I try to keep up with them on Facebook and WhatsApp …

G: Yes, that may be part of the problem. So, here's what I recommend: first of all get back into a more normal sleep routine – like 10 till 6 or 12 till 8 or whatever seems to suit you, but just make sure it's regular. Secondly, get rid of distractions – switch off Facebook and WhatsApp while you're working, plus any other websites you have a habit of using. You could even try switching off Facebook for a few days at a time. The world won't stop turning! Then just prioritize your work and keep at it, slow and steady. Make sure that some of that work time is 'think time' away from a computer screen – it could be on a walk or just sitting with a notebook on the sofa. I guarantee that if you follow these simple steps, within a few weeks you'll find your memory and concentration – and, more importantly, your general state of mind will improve enormously.

TRACK 37

Well, my first teaching job, I absolutely was thrown in at the deep end. I was at university doing a post grad course and it was the Easter holidays. I was still in bed and there was a knock on the door. Well, I got out of bed and it was a friend of mine, who asked me if I wanted to do some English teaching to earn some money during the university holiday. I saw it as a good chance to earn some money, so I said 'sure, when?'. 'In half an hour,' he said. He told me they'd got a lesson already prepared for me, which turned out to basically be a few games – they were a group of teenagers – and convinced me I could do it with my eyes shut. I think they had been let down at the last minute. So, anyway, after throwing some clothes on, literally 30 minutes later I was in a class. I had no idea what I was doing, totally out of my depth. Anyway, even though it was pretty daunting, I struggled through and got to the end of the morning. But I'm a pretty quick learner and as I was doing a post graduate education degree, I soon got the hang of it over the next few days and started to feel on top of it. I wasn't great, by any means, but I was doing OK. As they had already prepared lots of the lessons, it all seemed pretty straightforward, apart from the awkward language and grammar questions, which I was pretty clueless about at the time. Anyway, that sort of inspired me and, after my uni course, I did a course in teaching English and that's how I got into it as a career.

TRACK 40

My name's Jon Hird and I'm one of the authors of this Workbook. Biology is a subject that really fascinates me and I am always keen to hear or read about new developments in the field. The speaker starts off by explaining the importance of microscopy in identifying microbes and reminds us of such diseases as malaria, sleeping sickness, TB and giardia that affect millions and potentially even billions of people each year. He then goes on to say that most microscopes that can accurately identify such microbes are too bulky or complicated to be used out in the field. As a result, many people are waiting too long for a diagnosis. The speaker then describes how some research students of his came up with the idea of a 'foldscope', which is a functioning microscope with a built-in projector that is pressed and folded out of paper and which has micro-optics embedded in the paper and which is made of just 50 cents' worth of material. Actually, he doesn't specify precisely if this is the final cost of producing the item, and I have to say I would think this unlikely, but, as someone who started out in life as a biologist and spent many hours at university looking down microscopes, I find this very interesting and am eager to see the device in action.

After part-demonstrating the construction, the speaker then dims the lights and shows a couple of projected magnified images. The second image remains after the foldscope is moved away, and it is therefore difficult to tell if this was an actual real-time image that was captured or if the image was a pre-taken photo. Also, the images showed structures and organisms that are larger than microbes.

One, for example, showed the antennae of a mosquito. I would have liked to see and hear more about the detail and definition of what the microscope can see at microbe level and seeing this demonstrated would, in my opinion, have given the presentation much more impact – it would have swayed me more anyway. But, all in all, if this really can identify pathogens at the microbe level, then it would be a fantastic invention that potentially could make a huge difference and possibly save many lives. I also liked the idea that the device has lots of potential for educational and school use.

TRACK 43

Speaker 1

Well, I'd advise against getting anything too elaborate, since they generally need a lot of maintenance and cleaning. A friend of mine has a really fancy one, but he regrets buying it as he says it's a real hassle to clean. Personally, I'd recommend getting something simple and easy to use. The one we have is great. You just put a little capsule in it, press one button and that's it. And there are about 20 different types that you can get, all different strengths and flavours. And the best thing is that there's no cleaning or maintenance. It's really straightforward. Couldn't be easier. And seeing as your kitchen isn't so big, it'd be perfect size-wise. It's not much bigger than a toaster.

Speaker 2

Given that you're going to be setting off in the afternoon, to avoid getting stuck in traffic, I'd leave the motorway at junction 25 and rejoin it at 27, or even at 28. It's a bit of a detour, but that stretch is always a nightmare at that time, especially on a Friday. And make sure you take your satnav too, so as not to get lost. It's pretty straightforward, but just in case.

Speaker 3

Well, the one I've got is great. Very easy to use. You basically just weigh out the ingredients: flour, yeast, butter, salt and sugar and some water and put them all in together and press go. You can make all different kinds. It makes a really nice pizza dough, actually. And it's got a function for making jam as well, though I've never used that. And it's got a delay timer, so you can set it to make the loaf overnight so that it's ready in the morning. I think you can set it for up to fifteen hours ahead.

Speaker 4

OK, so to get the best results, first don't use the default auto mode. With all the different settings, a lot of people don't bother changing this for fear that they might do something wrong, but it's really easy. When it's not in auto you can manually change the focus, the exposure and the ISO, which is its sensitivity to light. And in order to get as sharp pictures as possible, make sure the resolution is on the highest setting. By doing all this you can really improve the quality of your photos and get a bit creative too.